Spanish irregular verb conjugation chart.

oír — *to hear*

Participles	Present	Imperfect	Preterite	Future	Conditional	Pres. Subj.	Imperf. Subj. (-se)	Imperf. Subj. (-ra)	Imperative
oído	oyes	oías	oíste	oirás	oirías	oigas	oyeses	oyeras	oye
	oye	oía	oyó	oirá	oiría	oiga	oyese	oyera	oíd
	oímos	oíamos	oímos	oiremos	oiríamos	oigamos	oyésemos	oyéramos	
	oís	oíais	oísteis	oiréis	oiríais	oigáis	oyeseis	oyerais	
	oyen	oían	oyeron	oirán	oirían	oigan	oyesen	oyeran	

poder — *to be able, can*

Participles	Present	Imperfect	Preterite	Future	Conditional	Pres. Subj.	Imperf. Subj. (-se)	Imperf. Subj. (-ra)	Imperative
pudiendo	puedo	podía	pude	podré	podría	pueda	pudiese	pudiera	
podido	puedes	podías	pudiste	podrás	podrías	puedas	pudieses		
	puede	podía	pudo	podrá	podría	pueda	pudiese		
	podemos	podíamos	pudimos	podremos	podríamos	podamos	pudiésemos		
	podéis	podíais	pudisteis	podréis	podríais	podáis	pudieseis		
	pueden	podían	pudieron	podrán	podrían	puedan	pudiesen		

poner — *to put*

Participles	Present	Imperfect	Preterite	Future	Conditional	Pres. Subj.	Imperf. Subj. (-se)	Imperf. Subj. (-ra)	Imperative
poniendo	pongo	ponía	puse	pondré	pondría	ponga	pusiese		pon
puesto	pones	ponías	pusiste	pondrás	pondrías	pongas	pusieses		poned
	pone	ponía	puso	pondrá	pondría	ponga	pusiese		
	ponemos	poníamos	pusimos	pondremos	pondríamos	pongamos	pusiésemos		
	ponéis	poníais	pusisteis	pondréis	pondríais	pongáis	pusieseis		
	ponen	ponían	pusieron	pondrán	pondrían	pongan	pusiesen		

querer — *to wish*

Participles	Present	Imperfect	Preterite	Future	Conditional	Pres. Subj.	Imperf. Subj. (-se)	Imperf. Subj. (-ra)	Imperative
queriendo	quiero	quería	quise	querré	querría	quiera	quisiese		quiere
querido	quieres	querías	quisiste	querrás	querrías	quieras	quisieses		quered
	quiere	quería	quiso	querrá	querría	quiera	quisiese		
	queremos	queríamos	quisimos	querremos	querríamos	queramos	quisiésem		
	queréis	queríais	quisisteis	querréis	querríais	queráis	quisieseis		
	quieren	querían	quisieron	querrán	querrían	quieran	quisiesen		

saber — *to know, know how*

Participles	Present	Imperfect	Preterite	Future	Conditional	Pres. Subj.	Imperf. Subj. (-se)	Imperf. Subj. (-ra)	Imperative
sabiendo	sé	sabía	supe	sabré	sabría	sepa	supiese		sabe
sabido	sabes	sabías	supiste	sabrás	sabrías	sepas	supieses		sabe
	sabe	sabía	supo	sabrá	sabría	sepa	supiese		
	sabemos	sabíamos	supimos	sabremos	sabríamos	sepamos	supiésemos		
	sabéis	sabíais	supisteis	sabréis	sabríais	sepáis	supieseis		
	saben	sabían	supieron	sabrán	sabrían	sepan	supiesen		

salir — *to go out, to leave*

Participles	Present	Imperfect	Preterite	Future	Conditional	Pres. Subj.	Imperf. Subj. (-se)	Imperf. Subj. (-ra)	Imperative
saliendo	salgo	salía	salí	saldré	saldría	salga	saliese	saliera	sal
salido	sales	salías	saliste	saldrás	saldrías	salgas	salieses	salieras	salid
	sale	salía	salió	saldrá	saldría	salga	saliese	saliera	
	salimos	salíamos	salimos	saldremos	saldríamos	salgamos	saliésemos	saliéramos	
	salís	salíais	salisteis	saldréis	saldríais	salgáis	salieseis	salierais	
	salen	salían	salieron	saldrán	saldrían	salgan	saliesen	salieran	

Essentials of SPANISH
through Practice

SECOND EDITION

THE SCRIBNER SPANISH SERIES
General Editor, JUAN R.-CASTELLANO

Essentials of SPANISH
through Practice

SECOND EDITION

Herbert A. Van Scoy
ARIZONA STATE UNIVERSITY

Margaret M. Davis
UNIVERSITY OF ALABAMA

CHARLES SCRIBNER'S SONS   New York

PREFACE

In the Second Edition of *Essentials of Spanish Through Practice* the authors have maintained the principal features of the original text, but have added material designed to elicit more oral response and to increase the amount of drill on constructions and idioms. *Laboratory tape scripts*, prepared by the authors, are available for this edition which cover the reading material and the exercises on the grammatical material.

As in the original edition, emphasis has been placed upon the basic grammatical constructions, vocabulary, and idioms considered essential for beginning students of Spanish. Grammatical explanations are brief and simple. Verb drill and practice are given prominence in the belief that proper understanding of verbs is the phase of language learning in which the average student rises or falls.

The material contained in the individual lessons has been rearranged to conform to the order which many instructors preferred: vocabulary; model sentences in Spanish and English, followed by a group of similar sentences in English to be translated to Spanish; a short reading section, followed by questions over the reading and a set of general or personalized questions; grammatical explanations; a series of exercises on the grammatical material, concluding with a written exercise.

Emphasis has been placed on proper Spanish pronunciation. In addition to the section on pronunciation at the beginning of the book, short pronunciation drills appear at the beginning of the first ten lessons. The model sentences offer a constant opportunity for insistence upon proper pronunciation and intonation.

Each model sentence in Spanish illustrates an important construction or idiom. It is recommended that students memorize these sentences after the instructor has first conducted a pronunciation drill on them. These model sentences may be recited in Spanish individually or in unison for practice in pronunciation and language patterns. The English or the Spanish version may be given by the teacher to be reproduced in the corresponding language. Students may be paired off to give the English and Spanish sentences to each other to insure full class participation. Working from the model sentences the student will give orally or write a number of sentences in Spanish which follow the model sentences closely, varying only in vocabulary or person involved.

A few of the reading sections have been altered to provide a change of locale from Cuba to Mexico. These reading sections may be used for assignment of memory work, dictation, or translation. The questions following these sections have been increased in number to provide opportunity for more oral expression.

The exercises following the grammatical material have also been increased in number and type with the intention of giving more structural drill and more oral work. Many of the exercises, however, may be assigned as written work if the instructor so desires.

Continued review of vocabulary, idioms, and constructions has been maintained as the lessons progress. Specific review periods and review examinations can best be determined by the instructor as he analyzes the progress and difficulties of his students.

The Appendix contains a table of regular verbs, a discussion of commands and imperatives, a list of verbs which require spelling changes, the cardinal numbers and a summary of the uses of the subjunctive. Irregular and stemchanging verbs are given in a chart on the inside covers of the book.

The text may be completed in one semester, but good results may be obtained by extending the grammar study over two semesters, devoting a part of the time to the collateral use of an elementary reader. If this procedure is followed, a suggested goal for the first semester would be fifteen lessons.

The authors wish to express their appreciation to their colleagues for their assistance, encouragement, and constructive criticism. Special acknowledgement is made to Dr. Juan R.-Castellano and the editorial staff of Charles Scribner's Sons for their advice and counsel during the preparation of this Second Edition.

H. A. V. S.
M. M. D.

CONTENTS

vii

CONTENTS

CONTENTS

CONTENTS

Essentials of SPANISH
through Practice

SECOND EDITION

PRONUNCIATION

THE SPANISH ALPHABET

LETTER	NAME	LETTER	NAME	LETTER	NAME
a	*a*	j	*jota*	r	*ere*
b	*be*	k	*ka*	rr	*erre*
c	*ce*	l	*ele*	s	*ese*
ch	*che*	ll	*elle*	t	*te*
d	*de*	m	*eme*	u	*u*
e	*e*	n	*ene*	v	*ve*
f	*efe*	ñ	*eñe*	w	*doble ve, doble u*
g	*ge*	o	*o*	x	*equis*
h	*hache*	p	*pe*	y	*i griega*
i	*i*	q	*cu*	z	*zeta*

The combinations **ch, ll, ñ** and **rr** are considered as single letters. In a dictionary or a vocabulary, words beginning with **ch, ll** and **ñ** follow those beginning with **c, l** and **n**. The letters **k** and **w** are found in foreign words only.

Vowels

Each vowel in Spanish must be pronounced clearly, uniformly and briefly, regardless of whether the vowel is stressed or not. There is no drawling or glide sound following the vowel as in English. In studying the English equivalents of the following Spanish vowels, remember that they are only approximate. Imitate your teacher in order to attain correct pronunciation.

The Spanish vowels **a, i, u** and **y** have only one pronunciation. The vowels **e** and **o** have two pronunciations depending upon whether the syllable

3

ends in a vowel or a consonant. Syllables ending in a consonant will be referred to as *checked* syllables.

a	as in f*a*ther	casa, fama, mala
e (*ends syllable*)	as *e* in th*e*y (*no glide*)	mesa, beso, tema
e (*checked*)	as in m*e*t	papel, comer, usted
i	as in mach*i*ne	vida, misa, sin
o (*ends syllable*)	as in n*o*te (*no glide*)	nota, tono, como
o (*checked*)	as in f*o*r	amor, órgano, soldado
u	as *oo* in m*oo*n	luna, cura, pluma
y (*alone or at the end of a word*)	as *i* in mach*i*ne	y, hay, muy, soy

Consonants

The consonants **f, l, m** and **p** are pronounced approximately as in English.

b and **v** are pronounced exactly alike. At the beginning of words or following **m** or **n** the sound is like that of English *b*, but pronounced with less force: **bueno, vino, ambos, vamos.**

In other cases these letters have a sound differing from English *v* in that it is pronounced between the lips, and not between the upper teeth and the lower lips: **Cuba, lavo, uva, ave.**

c has two sounds. Before a consonant or before **a, o** and **u** it is pronounced like English *k*: **clase, cada, como, cuna.**

c before **e** and **i** is pronounced as the *s* in *sent*: **cerca, cinco, dice, cine.**

(This is the Spanish-American pronunciation. In Castilian Spanish this **c** is pronounced like **th** as in *thin*.)

ch is always pronounced as *ch* in *church*: **chico, muchacho, coche.**

d has two sounds. At the beginning of a word, and after **l** and **n** it has a hard pronunciation, less forceful than the English *d*: **donde, doble, falda, conde.**

In other cases **d** is pronounced as *th* in *this*: **cada, usted, madre, verdad, tarde.**

g has two sounds. Before a consonant or before **a, o** and **u** it is pronounced as in English *go*: **gato, grande, gota, gusta.**

This sound of **g** is written **gu** before **e** and **i.** The **u** is not pronounced. It merely indicates that the **g** is to be pronounced as in *go*: **guerra, seguir.**

4

g before **e** and **i** has the sound of a harsh or aspirated *h*. This sound is best learned by closely imitating your teacher: **gente, gitano, general, gime.**

If **gue** or **gui** is to be pronounced as a diphthong, a diaeresis is placed over the **u, ü: vergüenza, güiro.**

h is always silent: **hombre, hablan, hora, hilo.**

j is pronounced exactly as **g** before **e** and **i**, that is, a strongly aspirated *h* sound: **joven, hijo, justicia, bajar.**

k is found only in foreign words: **kanguro, kilómetro, kimono.**

ll is a single letter, pronounced somewhat as *lli* in *million*. In most of Spanish-America it is pronounced as *y* in yes: **caballo, bello, llamar, lleno.**

n is pronounced as in English in most cases: **nada, gana, carne.**

n is pronounced approximately as an **m** before **b, v,** or **p: un vaso (um vaso), en pie (em pie), un buen día (um buen día).**

ñ is a separate letter of the alphabet, pronounced like *ny* in *canyon*: **año, niño, español.**

q is used only in the combinations **que** or **qui** and is pronounced as English *k*: **queso, quinto, querer.**

r (rr) A single **r** at the beginning of a word or preceded by **n, l** or **s** is strongly trilled, three or four flips of the tongue against the gums of the upper front teeth. This sound is also written **rr** when not at the beginning of a word: **rico, perro, honra, arriba, alrededor, Israel.**

r otherwise is pronounced with one single tap of the tongue against the gums of the upper teeth: **para, pero, padre.**

s has two sounds. In most cases it is pronounced as *s* in *sent*: **sin, señora, sal.**

Before the voiced consonants, **b, d, g, l, m, n** and **v**, the sound is that of English *z*: **isla, desde, mismo, asno, es verdad.**

t is pronounced with the tip of the tongue against the upper teeth: **tinta, todo, cuatro.**

w occurs only in foreign words.

x has two sounds. Between two vowels **x** has the sound of English *gs*: **examen, exacto, éxito.**

Before a consonant **x** is pronounced as the *s* in *sat*: **extraño, extremo, explicar.**

y as a consonant is pronounced as *y* in *yes*: **yo, ayudo, vaya.**

z is pronounced like the Spanish **c** before **e** and **i**, as the *s* in *sent*: **zapato, capaz, vez.**

(In Castilian Spanish the **z** is pronounced as *th* in *thin*.)

5

Diphthongs

STRONG VOWELS	WEAK VOWELS
a, e, o	**i (y), u**

A diphthong is any combination of a strong vowel and a weak vowel, or of two weak vowels. The vowels of a diphthong are pronounced as if each stood alone, but they are run together by rapid pronunciation. The strong vowel receives the stress in a combination of a strong and weak vowel. In a combination of two weak vowels, the second of the two weak vowels is stressed. Two strong vowels do not form a diphthong.

ai (ay)	aire, hay, baile	io	serio, comió
au	causa, gaucho, aula	iu	ciudad, viuda
ei (ey)	reina, ley, seis	oi (oy)	oigo, soy, hoy
eu	deuda, Europa, feudal	ua	cuatro, suave, cuadro
ia	gloria, diablo	ue	bueno, suelo, fuego
ie	bien, siete, hierro	ui (uy)	cuido, ruido, muy
		uo	cuota, antiguo, averiguo

Triphthongs

A triphthong is a combination of a strong vowel between two weak ones, to be pronounced as one syllable. The combinations are:

iai	estudiáis	uai (uay)	acentuáis, Paraguay
iei	estudiéis	uei (uey)	acentuéis, buey

Note that a written accent on a weak vowel of a diphthong or triphthong breaks down the diphthong into two strong vowels, and the triphthong into a vowel plus a diphthong.

tenía te ní -a	viviríais vi vi rí -ais

Division of Words into Syllables

(*a*) In dividing words into syllables, single consonants are placed with the following vowel: **ca-sa, bo-ni-ta.**

Remember that **ch, ll** and **rr** are considered as single consonants and cannot be divided: **mu-cha-cho, ca-lla, pe-rro.**

(*b*) A diphthong is considered as a single vowel sound and cannot be divided: **se-rio, fue-ra, ciu-dad.**

(*c*) When two consonants occur together they are usually divided: **ac-to, cin-co, gus-tar.**

(*d*) A consonant + **r**, and a consonant + **l**, are inseparable combinations and cannot be divided. The combination goes with the following vowel: (The exceptions to this rule occur so rarely that the beginning student need not be concerned with them.) **pa-dre, ta-bla, ha-blar, ma-dre.**

Accentuation (Stress)

Spanish words are usually stressed on the last or next to the last syllable.

Words which end in a consonant, except **n** or **s**, are accented on the last syllable: **ge-ne-*ral*, ha-*blar*, mi-*tad*.**

Words which end in a vowel, or **n** or **s**, are accented on the next to the last syllable: **ca-*mi*-no, a-*ma*-ban, *ha*-blas.**

Exceptions to the above rules are indicated by a written accent: *mé*-di-co, a-de-*más*, a-pren-*dí*.

Punctuation

Marks of punctuation are generally the same as in English. Differences are:

(*a*) The use of an inverted interrogation or exclamation point at the beginning of a question or exclamation.

¿Dónde vive Juan?	*Where does John live?*
¡Viva México!	*Long live Mexico!*

(*b*) A dash (—) is generally used instead of quotation marks. It appears only at the beginning of each speech, unless a narrative word follows.

—Sí, señor García.	*" Yes, Mr. Garcia."*
—Aquí está su libro—dijo Juan.	*"Here is your book," said John.*

Capitalization

Capital letters are used much less frequently in Spanish than in English. Small letters are used for the days of the week, months, adjectives and nouns of nationality, and the pronoun *I*.

lunes	*Monday*	español	*Spaniard, Spanish*
mayo	*May*	yo	*I*

EXERCISE

Divide the following words into syllables, underline the stressed syllable and pronounce.

señorita	buenos	español	habla
zapato	siete	verdad	entrarán
profesor	cuatro	tarde	libros
general	idea	máquina	interesante
caballo	creen	contestar	historia
vamos	leo	enseñan	biblioteca
tener	puerta	estudiar	contento
muchacho	automóvil	entonces	diccionario
gitano	familia	lección	nosotros
mañana	gracias	asiento	nuestro

PRONUNCIATION EXERCISES

a	casa	lana	saca
	habla	mala	cara
	hasta	bala	gala
i	vida	describí	fino
	libro	viví	mira
	pide	allí	lista

VOCABULARY

adiós *good-bye*
el alumno *the pupil (m.), student*
la alumna *the pupil (f.), student*
Anita *Anne*
bien *well*
Blanco *White*
bueno, -a *good*
Carlos *Charles*
la clase *the class*
¿cómo? *how?*
¿cuántos? *how many?*
de *of, from*
el día *the day*
en *in, on*

es *he, she is, you (sing.) are*
el español *Spanish (language)*
está *he, she is, you (sing.) are*
están *they are, you (pl.) are*
la familia *the family*
gracias *thank you*
habla *he, she speaks*
hablan *they speak*
hasta *until*
hay *there is, there are*
la madre *the mother*
mañana *tomorrow*
la mañana *the morning*
mi, mis *my*

9

muy *very*

no *no, not*

el padre *the father*

los padres *the parents*

pero *but*

el profesor *the teacher (m.)*

la profesora *the teacher (f.)*

¿quién? *who?*

el señor *Mr., sir, gentleman*

la señorita *Miss, madam, lady*

sí *yes*

su, sus *your, his, her*

la tarde *the afternoon*

todos *all*

usted, ustedes *you*

buenos días   *good morning*

buenas tardes   *good afternoon*

hasta mañana   *see you tomorrow*

por la mañana   *in the morning*

por la tarde   *in the afternoon*

NUMBERS (1–10)

1	uno, una	3	tres	5	cinco	7	siete	9	nueve
2	dos	4	cuatro	6	seis	8	ocho	10	diez

MODEL SENTENCES

1. Buenos días, señor García. ¿Cómo está usted?
2. Muy bien, gracias. ¿Cómo están sus padres?
3. Mis padres están muy bien.
4. La señorita Blanco habla bien el español.
5. Carlos no habla español.

1. *Good morning, Mr. García. How are you?*
2. *Very well, thank you. How are your parents?*
3. *My parents are very well.*
4. *Miss White speaks Spanish well.*
5. *Charles does not speak Spanish.*

EXPRESS IN SPANISH

1. Good morning, Miss White. How are you? Good morning, Charles. How are you? Good afternoon, Anne. How are you?
2. Very well, thank you. How is your father? How are the pupils?
3. My father is very well. The pupils are very well. My mother is not well.
4. Miss White speaks Spanish well. Five pupils speak Spanish well.
5. Anne does not speak Spanish. My mother does not speak Spanish.

En las clases de español

El profesor de español es el señor García. El señor García habla
bien el español. Los alumnos no hablan español. La señorita Blanco es
profesora de español. ¿Cuántos alumnos hay en la clase de la señorita
Blanco? Hay seis alumnos y cuatro alumnas en la clase.

Por la mañana:

—Buenos días, Anita.   —Buenos días, señor García.
—¿Cómo está usted?   —Muy bien, gracias.
—¿Cómo está su familia?   —Todos están bien, gracias.
—¿Está bien su padre, Carlos?   —Sí, señor, mi padre está bien,
                                          pero mi madre no está bien.

Por la tarde:

—Buenas tardes, señorita Blanco.   —Buenas tardes. ¿Cómo están ustedes?
—Muy bien gracias, señorita.   —Adiós, hasta mañana.
—Hasta mañana, señorita.

el hermano – brother
la hermana – sister

QUESTIONS

A. Answer in complete sentences in Spanish:

1. ¿Quién es el profesor de español?
2. ¿Habla español el señor García?
3. ¿Hablan español los alumnos?
4. ¿Quién es la profesora de español?
5. ¿Cuántos alumnos hay en la clase de la señorita Blanco?
6. ¿Cómo está la familia de Anita?
7. ¿Está bien el padre de Carlos?
8. ¿Cómo está la madre de Carlos?

B. Personalized questions. Answer in complete sentences in Spanish:

1. ¿Cómo está usted?
2. ¿Cómo está su madre?
3. ¿Quién es su profesor de español?
4. ¿Habla español su padre?
5. ¿Cuántos hay en su familia?
6. ¿Cómo está su familia?
7. ¿Hablan español los alumnos?
8. ¿Cuántos alumnos hay en su clase de español?

GRAMMAR

1. Gender of Nouns

All nouns in Spanish are either masculine or feminine. Most nouns ending in **-o** are masculine, and most of those ending in **-a** are feminine. The definite article indicates the gender and should be memorized with nouns which do not follow this rule.

2. The Forms of the Definite Article (*the*):

	MASCULINE	FEMININE
Singular	**el**	**la**
Plural	**los**	**las**

3. Plural of Nouns

The plural of nouns is regularly formed by adding **-s** to nouns ending in a vowel and **-es** to nouns ending in a consonant. The definite article agrees in number and gender with the noun it modifies.

el alumno	*the student*	los alumnos	*the students*
la señorita	*the young lady*	las señoritas	*the young ladies*
la madre	*the mother*	las madres	*the mothers*
el profesor	*the teacher*	los profesores	*the teachers*

Note that the masculine plural of nouns indicating persons may include both sexes.

los padres	*the fathers* or *the parents*
los alumnos	*the students*, referring to boys only or to boys and girls

4. Special Uses of the Definite Article

(*a*) The definite article is used with titles such as *professor, Mr., Mrs., Miss*, etc., except in direct address.

El profesor García habla español.	*Professor García speaks Spanish.*
El señor García está bien.	*Mr. García is well.*
BUT:	
Buenos días, señorita Blanco.	*Good morning, Miss White.*

(*b*) The definite article is used with the name of a language or course of study, except after the prepositions **de** and **en** and *directly* after some commonly used verbs, such as **hablar,** *to speak,* and **estudiar,** *to study.*

El español es interesante.   *Spanish is interesting.*
La historia es difícil.   *History is difficult.*
El alumno habla bien el español.   *The student speaks Spanish well.*
la clase de español   *the Spanish class*
en español   *in Spanish*
Carlos habla español.   *Charles speaks Spanish.*

5. A Negative Sentence

A negative sentence is formed by placing **no** before the verb.

El alumno no habla español.   *The student does not speak Spanish.*
Anita no está bien.   *Anne is not well.*

EXERCISES

A. Repeat the following words in the singular, then in the plural form, giving the definite article:

EXAMPLE: padre   el padre, los padres

1. padre	5. día	9. profesora
2. alumno	6. familia	10. señorita
3. tarde	7. mañana	11. clase
4. señor	8. profesor	12. madre

B. Read in Spanish and give again in the negative:
1. El señor García es el profesor de español.
2. Hay nueve alumnos en la clase.
3. Mi padre está bien.
4. Hay clases por la tarde.
5. Mis padres hablan español.

C. Read in Spanish, supplying the definite article when it is necessary:
1. _____ señor García habla bien _____ español.
2. El alumno habla en _____ español.
3. Buenos días, _____ señorita Blanco.
4. Hay seis alumnos en la clase de _____ español.
5. _____ profesor García habla _____ español.

D. Give the correct answers in Spanish:

EXAMPLE: uno y dos
Uno y dos son tres.

1. uno y dos
2. dos y dos
3. tres y tres
4. cinco y uno
5. cuatro y cuatro
6. nueve y uno
7. siete y dos
8. cinco y cinco

E. Write in Spanish:

1. Mr. García is the Spanish teacher.
2. There are nine boys and eight girls in the Spanish class.
3. How is your family?
4. My father is well.
5. My parents speak Spanish.
6. The students do not speak Spanish.
7. Good-bye, Miss White.
8. See you tomorrow, Charles.
9. My parents are very well.
10. Miss White is my teacher.

PRONUNCIATION EXERCISES

e (*ending syllable*)	mesa	debe	bebe
	beso	mete	café
	tarde	parece	pena

e (*checked syllable*)	papel	perla	aprender
	tercer	entro	tonel
	comer	verde	hacer

VOCABULARY

contestar (a)   *to answer*
enseñar   *to teach*
entrar (en)   *to enter*
estudiar   *to study*
hablar   *to speak*
preguntar   *to ask* (a question)

a   *to, at*
la casa   *house, home*
con   *with*
dice   *he, she says*
diez y ocho   *eighteen*
difícil   *difficult*

España   *Spain*
fácil   *easy*
el inglés   *English*
la lección (*pl.* lecciones)   *lesson*
el libro   *book*
lo (*obj. pron.*)   *it*
la mesa   *table*
México   *Mexico*
mucho   *much, a great deal*
nuestro, -a   *our*
para   *for*
un poco   *a little*
porque   *because*

que *that*

¿qué? *what?*

la sala (large) *room*

si *if*

también *also*

un, una *a*

la verdad *truth*

y *and*

en casa	*at home*
es verdad	*it is true*
sala de clase	*classroom*
todos los días	*every day*

MODEL SENTENCES

1. Yo estudio mucho el español.
2. El español es difícil.
3. Anita y yo hablamos inglés.
4. El profesor enseña la lección al alumno.
5. Hay diez y ocho alumnos en la clase del profesor.

1. *I study Spanish a great deal.*
2. *Spanish is difficult.*
3. *Anne and I speak English.*
4. *The professor teaches the lesson to the student.*
5. *There are eighteen pupils in the professor's class.*

EXPRESS IN SPANISH

1. Anne studies English a great deal. She speaks English a great deal. Charles speaks Spanish a little.
2. English is not difficult. English is easy. Spanish is not easy.
3. My father and I speak Spanish. Charles and I enter. Anne and I study.
4. Miss White and Mr. García teach the lessons to the students. I speak English to (*con*) my father. Charles speaks English to (*con*) the professor.
5. There are eighteen students in Mr. García's class. There are ten students in Miss White's class.

¿ Qué hablan ustedes?

El señor García enseña nuestra clase de español. Él es de España. La familia del señor García es de España también, y todos hablan español.

LESSON TWO

Hay diez y ocho alumnos en la clase del señor García. Hay una
5 mesa para el profesor. Los libros del profesor están en la mesa. Él entra
en la clase y dice:

—Buenos días, alumnos.

—Buenos días, señor García—contestamos al profesor.

—¿Hablan ustedes el español?—él pregunta.

10 —No, señor, nosotros no hablamos español, hablamos inglés.

Anita dice: —Los padres de Carlos hablan español, señor, y
Carlos lo habla un poco, porque él habla con sus padres y estudia los
libros de su padre en casa.

—¿Es verdad, Carlos?

15 —Sí, señor, es verdad—contesta Carlos. —Mi padre es de México
y habla muy bien el español. Todos los días hablamos español en casa.
Mi padre dice que el español es fácil.

—Sí, el español no es difícil, si ustedes lo estudian y lo hablan
todos los días.

QUESTIONS

A. Answer in complete sentences in Spanish:

1. ¿Qué enseña el señor García?
2. ¿Qué habla la familia del señor García?
3. ¿Cuántos alumnos hay en la clase?
4. ¿Qué hay para el profesor?
5. ¿Qué pregunta el profesor?
6. ¿Qué contestan los alumnos?
7. ¿Qué hablan los padres de Carlos?
8. ¿Es difícil el español?

B. Personalized questions. Answer in complete sentences in Spanish:

1. ¿Habla usted el inglés?
2. ¿Estudia usted el español?
3. ¿Enseña usted la clase?
4. ¿Contesta usted al profesor?
5. ¿Entra usted en la clase?
6. ¿Habla usted mucho?
7. ¿Hablan ustedes mucho con el profesor?
8. ¿Estudian ustedes todos los días?

GRAMMAR

6. First Conjugation. Infinitive and present indicative of verbs ending in **-ar.**

In Spanish the present indicative of regular verbs ending in **-ar** is formed by adding certain endings to the stem of the verb. The stem is determined by dropping the infinitive **-ar** ending. (For example, the stem of **hablar** is **habl-.**) The endings which are added to the stem indicate person and number. The following are the endings in the first conjugation.

SINGULAR		PLURAL	
1st person (*I*)	**-o**	1st person (*we*)	**-amos**
2nd person (*you,* familiar)	**-as**	2nd person (*you,* familiar)	**-áis**
2nd person (*you,* polite)	**-a**	2nd person (*you,* polite)	**-an**
3rd person (*he, she, it*)	**-a**	3rd person (*they*)	**-an**

Present Indicative of **hablar,** *to speak*

SINGULAR

yo	hablo	*I speak, am speaking, do speak*
tú (*familiar*)	hablas	*you speak, are speaking, do speak*
usted (*polite*)	habla	*you speak, are speaking, do speak*
él	habla	*he speaks, is speaking, does speak*
ella	habla	*she speaks, is speaking, does speak*

PLURAL

nosotros, -as	hablamos	*we speak, are speaking, do speak*
vosotros, -as (*fam.*)	habláis	*you speak, are speaking, do speak*
ustedes (*polite*)	hablan	*you speak, are speaking, do speak*
ellos	hablan	*they* (m.) *speak, are speaking, do speak*
ellas	hablan	*they* (f.) *speak, are speaking, do speak*

It should be noted that a single Spanish verb may be translated in several different ways. For example:

DECLARATIVE	Yo hablo.	*I speak, I am speaking, I do speak.*
NEGATIVE	Yo no hablo.	*I do not speak, I am not speaking.*
INTERROGATIVE	¿Hablo yo?	*Do I speak? Am I speaking?*

7. Subject Pronouns

Since the verb endings indicate the subject in the first person singular and plural and in the familiar forms of the second person, these pronouns are often omitted in Spanish. The subject pronouns most often needed to make the meaning clear are **usted, él, ella, ustedes, ellos** and **ellas.** Subject pronouns do not need to be repeated in the same sentence.

It as a subject is rarely expressed. Subject pronouns are used to call attention to a change in subject, or in the case of a combined subject.

Ella y yo estudiamos.	*She and I study.*
Yo hablo español y él habla inglés.	*I speak Spanish and he speaks English.*

The familiar forms **tú** and **vosotros** are used between members of the same family, relatives and intimate friends. The formal or polite **usted** and **ustedes,** which are used with the same form as the third person of the verb, are to be used by students in oral and written exercises unless otherwise indicated. These forms may be abbreviated to **Vd.** and **Vds.**

8. Questions

In questions the subject pronoun usually follows the verb. When the subject of a question is a noun the usual word order is: *verb + noun object* or *predicate adjective + subject.* If the question is introduced by an interrogative word this word precedes the verb and has a written accent.

¿Estudia usted el español?	*Do you study Spanish?*
¿Enseña inglés el profesor?	*Does the professor teach English?*
¿Es fácil la lección?	*Is the lesson easy?*
¿Cómo está la familia?	*How is the family?*
¿Qué habla ella?	*What does she speak?*

9. The Preposition *de*

In Spanish **de** is used (*a*) to express possession, since there is no apostrophe in Spanish; and (*b*) with a noun to form an adjective phrase.

(*a*) los libros de Anita	*Anne's books*
la familia del señor García	*Mr. García's family*
(*b*) la clase de español	*the Spanish class*
el profesor de inglés	*the English teacher*

19

10. Contractions

(*a*) The preposition **a** (*to, at*) when used with the definite article **el** contracts to **al (a + el = al)**.

al profesor	*to the professor*
al señor García	*to Mr. García*

(*b*) The preposition **de** (*of, from*) when used with **el** contracts to **del** (**de + el = del**).

del profesor	*of (from) the professor*
del alumno	*of (from) the student*

There is no contraction with the other articles: **a la, a los, a las, de la, de los, de las.**

EXERCISES

A. Change these statements to questions:

EXAMPLE: Ellos preguntan.
¿Preguntan ellos?

1. Ellos preguntan.
2. Los alumnos contestan.
3. El profesor enseña español.
4. La lección es fácil.
5. El libro es difícil.
6. Los alumnos estudian.

B. Substitute pronoun or proper name for italicized subject, making proper verb changes:

1. *Carlos* estudia español.
   Anita y María, nosotros, ella, usted
2. *María* entra en la casa.
   yo, él, nosotros, ustedes
3. *El señor García* enseña español.
   mis padres, la señorita Blanco, nosotros, los profesores
4. *Los alumnos* contestan al profesor.
   nosotros, Anita y María, usted, Carlos
5. *La señorita Blanco* no habla bien el inglés.
   el profesor, el señor García, los alumnos, nosotros

6. *Carlos* entra en la sala de clase.
   Anita y yo, el alumno, las señoritas, ustedes

7. *Los alumnos* no estudian mucho.
   nosotros, ustedes, ella, yo

8. *La señorita García* enseña inglés al alumno.
   los profesores, ella, María y yo, usted

C. Answer the following questions in the negative. (**No** may mean *no* or *not*.)

EXAMPLE: ¿Habla español la señorita Blanco?
No, la señorita Blanco no habla español.

1. ¿Habla español la señorita Blanco?
2. ¿Es fácil la lección de español?
3. ¿Hay una mesa para Carlos?
4. ¿Entran los alumnos en la clase?
5. ¿Contestamos al profesor?
6. ¿Hablan español los padres de Carlos?
7. ¿Estudia María los libros del profesor?
8. ¿Contesta el profesor a los alumnos?

D. Answer the following questions affirmatively, substituting a subject pronoun for the italicized subject.

EXAMPLE: ¿Estudia mucho *María*?
Sí, *ella* estudia mucho.

1. ¿Estudia mucho *María*?
2. ¿Entra *Anita* en la sala de clase?
3. ¿Habla español *el padre de Carlos*?
4. ¿Es de España *la madre de María*?
5. ¿Contestamos *Carlos y yo* al profesor?
6. ¿Enseña la lección *el profesor García*?
7. ¿Estudia *Carlos* los libros del profesor?
8. ¿Contesta *el profesor* a los alumnos?

E. Give in Spanish:

1. Anne's books
2. the professor's table
3. the girl's father
4. the student's books
5. Mr. García's class
6. to the professor
7. to the parents
8. to Miss White

21

F. Write in Spanish:

(*a*)
1. We teach.
2. I enter.
3. I do not teach.
4. Charles enters.
5. Does Anne study?
6. Are you studying?
7. Are they speaking?
8. Does he teach?
9. Do you answer?
10. What does Charles ask?

(*b*)
1. We study every day.
2. We speak Spanish at home.
3. Charles answers the professor.
4. Anne says: "I do not speak very well."
5. Mr. García's family is from Spain.
6. Charles' father is from Mexico.
7. My books are on the table.
8. There are eighteen students in our English class.
9. Is it true, Anne? Yes, sir, it is true.
10. She speaks English and he speaks Spanish.

PRONUNCIATION EXERCISES

o (*ending syllable*)	como	loco	todo
	bobo	bonito	solo
	tomo	oso	modo
o (*checked syllable*)	señor	amor	flor
	sol	corto	mayor
	soldado	temor	español
u	pluma	usted	universidad
	mucho	fuma	saludo
	luna	pura	ocupado

VOCABULARY

aprender *to learn*
comer *to eat*
escribir *to write*
leer *to read*
preparar *to prepare*
vivir *to live*

alto, -a *tall*
la amiga *friend (f.)*
el amigo *friend (m.)*

aquí *here*
bajo, -a *low, short*
blanco, -a *white*
bonito, -a *pretty*
cerca de *near*
dicen *they say*
¿dónde? *where?*
el dormitorio *dormitory*
el ejercicio *exercise*
español, española *Spanish*

el (la) estudiante *student*
grande *large, big*
la historia *history*
inteligente *intelligent*
interesante *interesting*
joven *young*
el (la) joven *young man, young woman*
los jóvenes *young people*
Juan *John*
la lengua *language*
malo, -a *bad, poor*
María *Mary*
mismo, -a *same*

moreno, -a *dark, brunette*
la muchacha *girl*
el muchacho *boy*
muchos, -as *many*
la noche *night*
Pancho *Frank*
pequeño, -a *small*
el restaurante *restaurant*
rubio, -a *fair, blond(e)*
son *they are*
todo, -a *all*
la vez (*pl.* veces) *time*
el vocabulario *vocabulary*

muchas veces — *often*
por la noche (*tarde*) — *at night* (in the afternoon)
todas las tardes (*noches*) — *every afternoon* (night)
¿verdad? ¿no es verdad? — *aren't they? isn't he?*

MODEL SENTENCES

1. Pancho y Carlos son buenos amigos.
2. Pancho es un joven alto y moreno.
3. Carlos vive en una casa blanca.
4. María y yo escribimos los ejercicios.
5. ¿Es interesante la historia?

1. *Frank and Charles are good friends.*
2. *Frank is a tall, dark young man.*
3. *Charles lives in a white house.*
4. *Mary and I write the exercises.*
5. *Is history interesting?*

EXPRESS IN SPANISH

1. Mary and Anne are good friends. Mr. García and Miss White are good friends.
2. Charles is short and dark. Mr. Martínez is very dark. The girls are pretty and blonde. Mary is not dark.
3. Franks lives in a large dormitory. Many students live in the dormitory. I live in a small house.
4. Mr. García and I eat in a restaurant. My friend and I live in a large house. My father and I speak English.
5. Is Spanish interesting? Are the lessons interesting? Is the dormitory white? Is the house large?

LESSON THREE

Dos amigos

Pancho es un amigo de Carlos. Ellos son buenos amigos. ¿Dónde viven? Pancho vive en un dormitorio grande y Carlos vive con sus padres en una casa blanca. La casa de Carlos no es grande; es pequeña y bonita.

5   Pancho es un joven alto y moreno. Carlos es moreno también. No es alto, es bajo. Los dos jóvenes son inteligentes. Todas las tardes estudian español en casa de Carlos. El señor Juan Martínez, el padre de Carlos, lee la lección con los muchachos. Ellos escriben los ejercicios. Son buenos estudiantes, ¿verdad?

10   —¿Quién es la amiga de Anita?

    —Es María, una muchacha bonita y rubia. Ella y Anita aprenden español con el mismo profesor. Dicen que es una lengua muy interesante. Todas las noches aprenden el vocabulario y escriben los ejercicios. Ellas también son buenas estudiantes, ¿no es verdad?

15   —¿Qué estudia usted?

    —Yo estudio inglés, historia y español. No son muy difíciles. La historia es fácil.

    —¿Cómo prepara usted las lecciones?

    —Muchas veces leo los libros de historia y escribo la lección de
20 inglés por la noche. Aprendo la lección de español por la tarde. No estudio todas las tardes porque hablo mucho con mis amigos. Como con Pancho en un restaurante muy bueno cerca de aquí. Carlos come en casa con su familia.

QUESTIONS

A. Answer in complete sentences in Spanish:

1. ¿Quién es Pancho?
2. ¿Dónde vive él?
3. ¿Dónde vive Carlos?
4. ¿Es grande la casa de Carlos?
5. ¿Quién es el señor Martínez?
6. ¿Dónde estudian español Pancho y Carlos?
7. ¿Qué escriben María y Anita?
8. ¿Es bonita María?

B. Personalized questions. Answer in Spanish:

1. ¿Dónde vive usted?
2. ¿Dónde come por la tarde?
3. ¿Es grande o pequeña su casa?
4. ¿Escribe usted muchos ejercicios?
5. ¿Estudia usted todas las noches?
6. ¿Aprende mucho en la clase?
7. ¿Es interesante la historia?
8. ¿Cuántas muchachas rubias hay en la clase de español?

GRAMMAR

11. Second and Third Conjugations. Infinitive and present indicative of verbs ending in **-er** and **-ir.**

Verbs of the second conjugation (**-er**) and verbs of the third conjugation (**-ir**) form the present indicative by adding the following endings to the stem of the verb: (Note that they differ only in the first and second plural.)

	SECOND CONJUGATION		THIRD CONJUGATION	
	Singular	*Plural*	*Singular*	*Plural*
1st person	**-o**	**-emos**	**-o**	**-imos**
2nd person (*familiar*)	**-es**	**-éis**	**-es**	**-ís**
2nd person (*polite*)	**-e**	**-en**	**-e**	**-en**
3rd person	**-e**	**-en**	**-e**	**-en**

Present Indicative of **aprender,** *to learn*

(*yo*)	aprendo	*I learn, am learning, do learn*
(*tú*)	aprendes	*you learn, are learning, do learn*
(*usted*)	aprende	*you learn, are learning, do learn*
(*él*)	aprende	*he learns, is learning, does learn*
(*ella*)	aprende	*she learns, is learning, does learn*
(*nosotros, -as*)	aprendemos	*we learn, are learning, do learn*
(*vosotros, -as*)	aprendéis	*you learn, are learning, do learn*
(*ustedes*)	aprenden	*you learn, are learning, do learn*
(*ellos*)	aprenden	*they learn, are learning, do learn*
(*ellas*)	aprenden	*they learn, are learning, do learn*

Present Indicative of **vivir,** *to live*

(*yo*)	vivo	*I live, am living, do live*
(*tú*)	vives	*you live, are living, do live*
(*usted*)	vive	*you live, are living, do live*
(*él*)	vive	*he lives, is living, does live*
(*ella*)	vive	*she lives, is living, does live*
(*nosotros, -as*)	vivimos	*we live, are living, do live*
(*vosotros, -as*)	vivís	*you live, are living, do live*
(*ustedes*)	viven	*you live, are living, do live*
(*ellos*)	viven	*they live, are living, do live*
(*ellas*)	viven	*they live, are living, do live*

12. The Forms of the Indefinite Article (*a, an*)

MASCULINE	FEMININE
un	**una**

The indefinite article agrees with the noun which it modifies.

un ejercicio	*an exercise*
una casa	*a house*
unos libros	*some books*
unas plumas	*some pens*

13. Adjectives

(*a*) *Forms*

Singular			*Plural*	
MASCULINE	FEMININE		MASCULINE	FEMININE
blanco	blanca	*white*	blancos	blancas
fácil	fácil	*easy*	fáciles	fáciles
interesante	interesante	*interesting*	interesantes	interesantes
español	española	*Spanish*	españoles	españolas

Adjectives ending in **-o** in the masculine singular change **-o** to **-a** to form the feminine. Those ending in **-e** or in a consonant usually do not change to form the feminine. However, adjectives of nationality which end in a consonant in the masculine singular add **-a** to form the feminine. Adjectives form their plural like nouns, by adding **-s** to a vowel or **-es** to a consonant.

(*b*) *Agreement.* Adjectives agree in number and gender with the nouns and pronouns which they modify.

un profesor alto	*a tall professor*
una muchacha rubia	*a blonde girl*
libros interesantes	*interesting books*
una amiga española	*a Spanish friend* (f.)
amigos españoles	*Spanish friends* (m.)

(*c*) *Position*

(1) Articles, numerals and other limiting words such as: *many, some, this, your,* etc., usually precede the noun which they modify.

doce muchachos	*twelve boys*
muchos libros	*many books*

(2) An adjective which describes a noun and distinguishes it from others of the same class will usually follow the noun.

una casa blanca	*a white house*
un joven inteligente	*an intelligent young man*

(3) The descriptive adjectives **bueno,** *good,* and **malo,** *bad,* often precede the noun. (Before a masculine singular noun the **-o** is dropped.)

buenas tardes	*good afternoon*
un buen amigo	*a good friend*
un mal estudiante	*a bad (poor) student*

(4) In questions the predicate adjective precedes the noun subject, which is usually last in the sentence.

¿Es inteligente el joven?	*Is the young man intelligent?*
¿Son bonitas las muchachas?	*Are the girls pretty?*

EXERCISES

A. Substitute pronoun or proper name for italicized subject, making proper verb changes:

1. *Pancho* lee la lección.
   yo, nosotros, María, ustedes
2. ¿Come mucho *usted*?
   Carlos, María y Anita, usted y Pancho, su padre

3. *El muchacho* no escribe bien.
   usted, yo, usted y yo, ustedes
4. *Juan* prepara su lección de español.
   ellos, nosotros, usted, yo
5. *María* vive en una casa grande.
   ella y yo, Carlos y Pancho, Anita, Juan
6. *El joven* lee un libro interesante.
   nosotros, María y Anita, usted, Carlos
7. Muchas veces *Pancho* escribe a María.
   yo, nosotros, ustedes, ella
8. *Anita* come en un restaurante.
   Anita y yo, Carlos, Pancho y el profesor

B. Make questions of the following statements, paying attention to position of adjective:

EXAMPLE: Pancho es alto.
¿Es alto Pancho?

1. Pancho es alto.
2. Los ejercicios son difíciles.
3. La lección es interesante.
4. Pancho es moreno.
5. Los dos jóvenes son inteligentes.
6. María es morena.
7. La señorita es española.
8. Las lecciones son fáciles.

C. Read in singular, then repeat in plural form:

EXAMPLE: joven inteligente
jóvenes inteligentes

1. joven inteligente
2. buen amigo
3. lección difícil
4. ejercicio fácil
5. muchacha inteligente
6. casa pequeña
7. muchacha baja
8. libro interesante

D. Give in the plural:

EXAMPLE: El libro del muchacho no es grande.
Los libros de los muchachos no son grandes.

1. El libro del muchacho no es grande.
2. La muchacha vive en el dormitorio.
3. Yo como con un amigo.
4. El buen alumno prepara la lección.
5. El joven español no estudia.
6. La mesa del profesor es pequeña.
7. ¿Está bien su padre?
8. ¿Escribe usted a su madre?

E. Answer in the negative:

EXAMPLE: ¿Vive usted en el dormitorio?
No, yo no vivo en el dormitorio.

1. ¿Vive usted en el dormitorio?
2. ¿Estudia usted mucho?
3. ¿Estudia mucho su amigo?
4. ¿Come usted en casa?

5. ¿Enseña usted la historia?
6. ¿Es morena María?
7. ¿Es alto y rubio Carlos?
8. ¿Son difíciles las lecciones?

F. Write in Spanish:

(*a*) 1. I learn.
2. Mary and I read.
3. Anne and I write.
4. Frank and Charles eat.

5. Where do you live?
6. What do they study?
7. What does Anne read?
8. My parents and I live here.

(*b*) 1. Pancho is tall, isn't he?
2. Do you write the exercises every day?
3. The boys are intelligent, aren't they?
4. They learn a great deal because they study every night.
5. My house is large and white.
6. Is history difficult?
7. We study at home in the afternoon.
8. The Spanish lessons are not easy.

PRONUNCIATION EXERCISES

c (*k*)	café	como	Cuba	qu (*k*)	queso	quince
	cada	cosa	cura		quedar	quien
	carta	comer	curso		querer	quinto

c (*s*) or	cena	cinco		z (*s*) or	zeta	ázimo
(*th*)	cerca	cine		(*th*)	Zeus	zigzag
	centro	cinta			Zelandia	zinc

VOCABULARY

ir *to go*
llegar (a) *to arrive (at)*
ser *to be*
tener *to have*
tomar *to take*

alguno, -a *some*
antes de *before*
el asiento *seat*
el café *coffee*
la cafetería *cafeteria*
el cuaderno *notebook*
¿cuándo? *when?*
el cuarto *room; quarter*

Cuba *Cuba*
después *afterwards*
después de *after*
la hora *hour, time*
el lápiz (*pl.* lápices) *pencil*
medio, -a *half*
menos *minus, less*
otro, -a *another (pl. other)*
la pluma *pen*
la pregunta *question*
la puerta *door*
simpático, -a *charming, attractive*
su *their*
tarde *late*

31

¿a dónde va?	*where is he going?*
algunas veces	*sometimes*
antes de las ocho	*before eight o'clock*
¿de dónde es?	*where is he from?*
de la mañana	*in the morning,* A.M.
de la tarde	*in the afternoon,* P.M.
en punto	*exactly* (time)
otras veces	*at other times*

NUMBERS (11–90)

11	once	18	diez y ocho	30	treinta
12	doce	19	diez y nueve	40	cuarenta
13	trece	20	veinte	50	cincuenta
14	catorce	21	veinte y uno, una	60	sesenta
15	quince	23	veinte y tres	70	setenta
16	diez y seis	25	veinte y cinco	80	ochenta
17	diez y siete	27	veinte y siete	90	noventa

MODEL SENTENCES

1. ¿Qué hora es? Son las diez menos veinte de la mañana.
2. Yo voy al dormitorio a las once y diez. No tenemos clases por la tarde.
3. Carlos tiene su clase de historia a la una de la tarde.
4. Nuestro profesor es de México. Él es alto y moreno.
5. El libro es de María. Ella es una estudiante inteligente.

1. *What time is it? It is twenty minutes to ten* A.M.
2. *I am going to the dormitory at ten minutes past eleven. We don't have classes in the afternoon.*
3. *Charles has his history class at one in the afternoon.*
4. *Our professor is from Mexico. He is tall and dark.*
5. *The book is Mary's. She is an intelligent student.*

EXPRESS IN SPANISH

1. What time is it? It is ten minutes to eight A.M. It is a quarter to twelve.
2. We are going to the dormitory at two-twenty. He doesn't have classes in the afternoon.

3. I have my English class at one P.M. They have their history class at two P.M.
4. My father is from Spain. He is short and blond. We are from Cuba. We are tall and dark.
5. The pen is Frank's. He is an intelligent student. The books are Mr. García's. He is a Spaniard.

La hora

—Buenos días, Carlos, ¿qué hora es?—pregunta Pancho.

—Son las ocho menos diez, y tenemos nuestra clase de inglés a las ocho—contesta Carlos. —Tengo historia a las diez de la mañana y la clase de español a las dos de la tarde.

5   Los dos jóvenes llegan a la clase a las ocho en punto. Algunos alumnos llegan antes de las ocho, otros llegan después. El profesor Smith entra en la sala de clase a las ocho y diez. Anita y su amiga María llegan tarde, a las ocho y cuarto, y toman asiento cerca de la puerta. Los alumnos tienen libros, cuadernos, lápices y plumas.
10 Algunas veces ellos contestan a las preguntas del profesor, otras veces escriben en los cuadernos.

Después de la clase los cuatro jóvenes van a la cafetería. Todos toman café y hablan de sus clases. Anita y María leen su lección de español.

15 —¿Es difícil su lección de español?—pregunta Carlos.

—Sí, es difícil, pero la profesora es buena.

—¿De dónde es la profesora?

—Ella es de Cuba, y es muy simpática.

Las muchachas van al cuarto de Anita. Aprenden el vocabulario
20 de la lección de español. Van a la clase a las dos. No llegan tarde. Después de la clase estudian sus otras lecciones. María come en su casa a las siete, y Anita come en la cafetería a las seis y media.

QUESTIONS

A. Answer in complete sentences in Spanish:

1. ¿A qué hora tienen Carlos y Pancho su clase de inglés?
2. ¿A qué hora llegan ellos a la clase?
3. ¿A qué hora entra el señor Smith?

4. ¿A qué hora llegan Anita y María?
5. ¿Qué tienen los alumnos?
6. ¿Qué hacen ellos algunas veces?
7. ¿A dónde van los cuatro jóvenes después de la clase?
8. ¿De dónde es la profesora?
9. ¿Qué aprenden las muchachas en el cuarto de Anita?
10. ¿A qué hora van a la clase de español?

B. Personalized questions. Answer in Spanish:

1. ¿Qué hora es?
2. ¿A qué hora tenemos nuestra clase de español?
3. ¿A qué hora tiene usted clases por la tarde?
4. ¿Estudia usted en la cafetería?
5. ¿Cuántos libros tiene?
6. ¿A qué hora va a su casa?
7. ¿Cuántas horas estudia por la noche?
8. ¿Cuántos alumnos hay en nuestra clase?
9. ¿Cuántas alumnas?

GRAMMAR

14. The Present Indicative of the Irregular Verbs *tener*, *ser*, and *ir*

Present Indicative of **tener,** *to have (possess)*

(*yo*)	tengo	*I have*	(*nosotros, -as*)	tenemos	*we have*
(*tú*)	tienes	*you have*	(*vosotros, -as*)	tenéis	*you have*
(*usted*)	tiene	*you have*	(*ustedes*)	tienen	*you have*
(*él*)	tiene	*he has*	(*ellos*)	tienen	*they have*
(*ella*)	tiene	*she has*	(*ellas*)	tienen	*they have*

Present Indicative of **ser,** *to be*

(*yo*)	soy	*I am*	(*nosotros, -as*)	somos	*we are*
(*tú*)	eres	*you are*	(*vosotros, -as*)	sois	*you are*
(*usted*)	es	*you are*	(*ustedes*)	son	*you are*
(*él*)	es	*he is*	(*ellos*)	son	*they are*
(*ella*)	es	*she is*	(*ellas*)	son	*they are*

Present Indicative of **ir**, *to go*

(*yo*)	voy	*I go, am going*	(*nosotros, -as*)	vamos	*we go, are going*
(*tú*)	vas	*you go, are going*	(*vosotros, -as*)	vais	*you go, are going*
(*usted*)	va	*you go, are going*	(*ustedes*)	van	*you go, are going*
(*él*)	va	*he goes, is going*	(*ellos*)	van	*they go, are going*
(*ella*)	va	*she goes, is going*	(*ellas*)	van	*they go, are going*

15. Uses of the Verb *ser*. *Ser* is used:

(*a*) *When followed by a predicate noun*

Pancho es alumno.	*Frank is a student.*
Su padre es profesor.	*His father is a teacher.*
Es una lección fácil.	*It is an easy lesson.*
El señor Gómez es español.	*Mr. Gómez is a Spaniard.*

Note in the above examples that with an unmodified predicative noun indicating occupation, nationality or the like, the indefinite article is omitted after **ser.**

(*b*) *To indicate possession*

El libro es de Carlos.	*The book is Charles'.*
Las plumas son de Anita.	*The pens are Anne's.*

(*c*) *To show origin*

Pancho es de Cuba.	*Frank is from Cuba.*
Ellos son de España.	*They are from Spain.*

(*d*) *When followed by a predicate adjective which denotes a basic, essential characteristic or quality*

María es simpática.	*Mary is attractive.*
Carlos es bajo y moreno.	*Charles is short and dark.*
Las casas son pequeñas.	*The houses are small.*

(*e*) *To tell time* (See 16 below.)

16. Telling Time

In giving the time (**hora**), **la** or **las** stands for **hora** or **horas.** The singular verb **es** is used to express one o'clock.

¿Qué hora es?	*What time is it?*
Es la una.	*It is one o'clock.*

35

The plural verb **son** is used for all other hours.

Son las dos.   *It is two o'clock.*

Son las once y media.   *It is eleven-thirty.*

Minutes after the hour are expressed by the word **y** (*and*) plus the number of minutes or the fraction of an hour. Minutes before the hour are preceded by **menos** (*less*).

Son las tres y diez.   *It is ten minutes after three.*

Son las siete menos quince. *It is a quarter to seven.*

In the morning, in the afternoon, in the evening and *at night* are translated by **de la mañana, de la tarde** and **de la noche,** when a definite time is mentioned.

a las ocho de la mañana   *at eight o'clock in the morning*

Son las nueve de la noche.   *It is nine o'clock at night.*

If no specific time is mentioned the expressions **por la mañana, por la tarde** and **por la noche** are used.

Él no toma café por la tarde.

He doesn't drink coffee in the afternoon.

EXERCISES

A.

(*a*) Count from 10 to 90 by tens.

(*b*) Give the following numbers in Spanish:

13, 15, 16, 20, 22, 29, 31, 37, 43, 48,

54, 56, 62, 69, 73, 77, 85, 88, 91, 99.

B. Complete sentences using nouns or expressions following the verbs:

EXAMPLE: Yo tengo (doce libros, quince plumas)

Yo tengo doce libros.

Yo tengo quince plumas.

1. Yo tengo (doce libros, quince plumas)
2. Ella es (simpática, profesora, alta, morena, bonita)
3. Ellos son (profesores, alumnos, españoles, ingleses)
4. María tiene (muchos lápices, muchas amigas, muchos libros, muchas lecciones)

36

5. No tenemos   (lecciones difíciles, un buen profesor, una amiga española, una
                 casa grande)
6. Carlos y Pancho tienen   (un cuarto grande, una casa pequeña,
                         una lección difícil, un amigo español)
7. Él va   (a casa, a la clase, a España, al restaurante, al dormitorio)
8. Vamos   (a las ocho y media, a las diez en punto, a la una, por la mañana)

C. Read in Spanish, giving the proper form of **ser, tener,** or **ir**:

    1. Carlos y yo _____ al dormitorio.
    2. Ella no _____ clases por la tarde.
    3. Anita y María _____ buenas alumnas.
    4. El señor García _____ de España.
    5. ¿A qué hora _____ ustedes la clase de inglés?
    6. Carlos y Pancho _____ al restaurante.
    7. Los lápices _____ de Anita.
    8. ¿A dónde _____ usted y Carlos después de la clase?
    9. Nosotros _____ una lección difícil.
  10. _____ la una y diez de la tarde.

D. Answer the following questions, using the hour in parentheses:

    EXAMPLE: ¿A qué hora va usted a la escuela?   (8:00 A.M.)
                 Voy a la escuela a las ocho de la mañana.

    1. ¿A qué hora va usted a la escuela?   (8:00 A.M.)
    2. ¿A qué hora va María a su casa?   (11:30 A.M.)
    3. ¿A qué hora van ustedes a su cuarto?   (in the afternoon)
    4. ¿A qué hora va usted a la cafetería?   (12:15 P.M.)
    5. ¿A qué hora llega su padre a la casa?   (5:45 P.M.)
    6. ¿A qué hora tiene usted la clase de español?   (10:00 A.M.)
    7. ¿A qué hora van Carlos y usted al dormitorio?   (7:30 P.M.)
    8. ¿A qué hora tiene Pancho su clase de historia?   (3:00 P.M.)

E. Write in Spanish:

  (*a*) 1. I am a student.
      2. Mr. Smith is the English teacher.
      3. We are not from Mexico.
      4. The pencil is Mary's.
      5. The books are large.
      6. Is English difficult?
      7. Is Anne attractive?

(*b*) 1. There are no classes at night.
2. We have a class in the afternoon.
3. I am going before five in the afternoon.
4. Mary eats at home at six-thirty.
5. Other students eat in the cafeteria.
6. Mr. García and his family are from Spain.
7. I am not from Spain.
8. Sometimes I arrive late at (**a la**) class.

PRONUNCIATION EXERCISES

g (*hard*)	gala	gota	gusta	guerra	guitarra
	gana	goma	gula	guerrero	guindo
	gato	golfo	gusano	pague	guía
g, i (*harsh h*)	general	gitano	jamás	jefe	José
	gesto	giro	jamón	Jesús	joven
	gente	gigante	Japón	jirafa	julio

VOCABULARY

acompañar *to accompany*
decir *to say*
estar *to be*
hacer *to make, to do*
salir (de) *to leave, go out*
terminar *to finish*
ver *to see*

algo *something*
allí *there*
el artículo *article*
la biblioteca *library*
bueno, -a (*adj.*) *well, good*
bueno (*adv.*) *well*   bien
cansado, -a *tired*
la comida *meal, dinner*

contento, -a *satisfied, happy*
el diccionario *dictionary*
enfermo, -a *ill, sick*
en frente de *in front of*
entonces *then*
guapo, -a *good-looking, handsome*
juntos, -as *together*
la lectura *reading*
lejos *far away*
ocupado, -a *busy*
Pedro *Peter*
¿por qué? *why?*
que *which, who*
¿a quién? *whom?*
varios, -as *several*
ya *already*

39

a casa	*home* (after a verb of motion)
al salir de la biblioteca	*on leaving the library*
cansado de estudiar	*tired of studying*
de pronto	*suddenly*
en vez de entrar	*instead of entering*
sala de lectura	*reading room*
tener que + *inf.*	*to have to* + verb

MODEL SENTENCES

1. Nosotros somos alumnos. Estamos en la universidad.
2. Yo estoy cansado pero no estoy enfermo.
3. Anita va a estudiar. María va a preparar la comida.
4. Pedro ve a María. Anita ve a varios amigos.
5. Mis libros están en la mesa. Sus libros están en casa.

1. *We are students. We are at the university.*
2. *I am tired but I am not sick.*
3. *Anne is going to study. Mary is going to prepare the meal.*
4. *Peter sees Mary. Anne sees several friends.*
5. *My books are on the table. Your (his, her, their) books are at home.*

EXPRESS IN SPANISH

1. We are teachers. We are in the library. They are students. They are in the dormitory.
2. They are tired but they are not sick. Mary is sick. Charles is tired.
3. Peter is going to read. The girls are going to study. We are going to write.
4. Mary sees Charles. They see several friends. Peter accompanies Mary.
5. Your books are at home. My friends are in the library. Our books are on the table.

En la biblioteca

Anita y María salen de la clase juntas.

—Yo voy a la biblioteca, María—dice Anita.

—¿Por qué? ¿Qué va usted a hacer allí?—pregunta su amiga.

—Ya son las tres y estamos cansadas de estudiar. Yo voy a casa porque
5 mi madre está enferma y tengo que preparar la comida.

—Bueno, María, tengo que leer un artículo en un libro que está
en la biblioteca. Voy a terminar antes de salir de la biblioteca.

Entonces ellas ven a un joven que está en frente de la biblioteca.
Es Pedro, el amigo de María. Es un joven alto, guapo y rubio.

10   De pronto Pedro ve a las dos muchachas, y en vez de entrar en
la biblioteca, él acompaña a María a su casa, que no está lejos.

Anita ve a varios amigos en la sala de lectura de la biblioteca.
Algunos estudiantes leen, otros escriben en sus cuadernos. Dos señoritas
están ocupadas con el diccionario. Todos hacen algo.

15   Después de media hora Anita está muy cansada. Ella no termina
el artículo y al salir de la biblioteca no está muy contenta.

QUESTIONS

A. Answer in complete sentences in Spanish:

1. ¿Quiénes (*pl. of* ¿quién?) salen juntas?
2. ¿Qué dice Anita?
3. ¿Por qué va María a su casa?
4. ¿Qué tiene que hacer Anita?
5. ¿A quién ven las muchachas?

6. ¿Cómo es Pedro?
7. ¿Qué hace Pedro?
8. ¿Está lejos o cerca la casa de María?
9. ¿A quiénes ve Anita en la sala de lectura?
10. ¿Por qué no está muy contenta Anita?

B. Personalized questions. Answer in complete sentences in Spanish:

1. ¿Dónde está usted?
2. ¿Qué hora es?
3. ¿A quiénes ve usted aquí?
4. ¿Quién es el profesor?
5. ¿Cómo es él?

6. ¿A qué hora va usted a la biblioteca?
7. ¿Ve a su amigo (amiga) en la biblioteca?
8. ¿Cómo es él (ella)?
9. ¿Estudia usted mucho el diccionario?
10. ¿Está usted muy cansado de estudiar?

GRAMMAR

17. The Present Indicative of the Irregular Verbs *estar*, *decir*, *hacer*, *salir* and *ver*

estar, *to be*

estoy	*I am*	estamos	*we are*
estás	*you are*	estáis	*you are*
está	*you are*	están	*you are*
está	*he is*	están	*they are*
está	*she is*	están	*they are*

decir, *to say*

digo	*I say*	decimos	*we say*
dices	*you say*	decís	*you say*
dice	*you say*	dicen	*you say*
dice	*he says*	dicen	*they say*
dice	*she says*	dicen	*they say*

4I

hacer, *to do, to make*		**salir,** *to leave*		**ver,** *to see*	
hago	hacemos	salgo	salimos	veo	vemos
haces	hacéis	sales	salís	ves	veis
hace	hacen	sale	salen	ve	ven

18. Uses of *estar*

(*a*) **Estar** is always used to express location.

María está en la biblioteca.	*Mary is in the library.*
La casa no está lejos.	*The house is not far away.*

(*b*) **Estar** is used with adjectives that denote a state or condition. (Remember that **ser** is always used with predicate nouns.)

Anita está cansada.	*Anne is tired.*
Ellos están enfermos.	*They are sick.*

(*c*) An adjective following the English verb *to be* must be analyzed to determine if it denotes an essential characteristic or quality (**ser**), or if it denotes a state or condition (**estar**).

Ella es simpática.	*She is charming.* (quality)
Ella está contenta.	*She is satisfied.* (condition)

The difference between **ser** and **estar** can also be illustrated by their use with the same adjective or interrogative word.

Él es bueno.	*He is good.* (A good person)
Él está bueno.	*He is well.* (In good health)
¿Cómo es Pedro?	*How is Peter?* (What is he like?)
¿Cómo está Pedro?	*How is Peter?* (How is his health?)

19. Possessive Adjectives

The possessive adjectives have been used previously, with the exception of the familiar forms **tu** and **vuestro,** which will not be employed in this text unless specially indicated.

SINGULAR	PLURAL	
mi	mis	*my*
tu	tus	*your*
su	sus	*your, his, her, its*
nuestro, -a	nuestros, -as	*our*
vuestro, -a	vuestros, -as	*your*
su	sus	*your, their*

Note that these possessive adjectives differ from the corresponding English possessives in that they agree with the *thing possessed*, as to number and gender, not with the *possessor*.

mi libro, mis libros	*my book, my books*
su casa	*your (his, her, their) house*
nuestra escuela	*our school*

20. Special Uses of the Preposition *a*

(*a*) After verbs of motion such as **ir,** *to go,* and **venir,** *to come,* etc., the preposition **a** is required before a following infinitive.

Voy a terminar el ejercicio.	*I am going to finish the exercise.*
Vienen a comer a las siete.	*They are coming to eat at seven.*

(*b*) Personal **a.** The preposition **a** precedes the object of a verb when it refers to a definite person.

Ellas ven al joven.	*They see the young man.*
Anita no acompaña a María.	*Anne does not go with Mary.*

21. Infinitive after Prepositions

The infinitive is used in Spanish after a preposition.

antes de terminar	*before finishing*
después de escribir	*after writing*

EXERCISES

A. Read in Spanish, using proper form of **ser** or **estar:**

EXAMPLE: Los alumnos son de México.

1. _____ de México.	6. _____ en la biblioteca.
2. _____ inteligentes.	7. _____ cansados.
3. _____ ocupados.	8. _____ de España.
4. _____ simpáticos.	9. _____ contentos.
5. _____ jóvenes.	10. _____ guapos.

43

B. Read the following sentences in Spanish, then repeat, changing the noun and possessive adjective to the plural:

EXAMPLE: Yo tengo mi libro.
Yo tengo mis libros.

1. Yo tengo mi libro.
2. Nosotros tenemos nuestro libro.
3. Ellos tienen su libro.
4. Yo voy a mi clase.
5. Nosotros vamos a nuestra clase.
6. Veo a mi amigo.
7. Él ve a su amiga.
8. Ustedes ven a su profesor.

C. Substitute the pronoun or proper name for italicized subject, making proper verb changes:

1. *Mis amigos* están en la biblioteca.
   yo, Pedro, nosotros, María y Carlos

2. *Carlos* va a estudiar.
   ella, Pedro y yo, María y él, Pancho

3. *Anita* siempre dice la verdad.
   nosotros, yo, ellos, usted

4. *Pancho* ve a sus amigos.
   ustedes, Carlos, María y Anita, ella

5. *Todos* tienen que hacer algo.
   yo, usted, nosotros, ellos

6. *Pedro* acompaña a María a su casa.
   Carlos y Anita, nosotros, ellos, él

7. *Yo* voy a terminar el ejercicio.
   Pancho, María y yo, ustedes, Anita y Carlos

8. *Pedro* dice que va a casa.
   Anita y María, nosotros, ella, ustedes

D. Supply the proper Spanish possessive adjective, then read the sentence:

1. Ella tiene (her) diccionario.
2. ¿Va usted a (your) casa?
3. (Our) clase es muy interesante.
4. Escriben (their) ejercicios.
5. Tenemos (our) lápices.
6. (My) padres están en (their) cuarto.
7. (Our) biblioteca es muy grande.
8. Ustedes tienen que estudiar (your) lecciones.
9. (My) madre está enferma.
10. Él no tiene (his) libros.

44

E. Supply the proper form of **ser** or **estar:**

1. Anita y María _____ cansadas.
2. Mi amigo _____ inteligente.
3. El señor García _____ ocupado.
4. Las muchachas _____ bonitas.
5. Pedro _____ muy simpático.
6. ¿ _____ usted contento?
7. Los diccionarios _____ grandes.
8. Ella no _____ enferma.
9. Las lecciones _____ fáciles.
10. Los alumnos _____ ocupados.

F. Write in Spanish:

1. We have to leave the library.
2. Do you have to read an article?
3. On entering he sees several friends.
4. Before leaving she writes in her notebook.
5. Instead of studying they talk.
6. It is already four o'clock.
7. I am tired of studying.
8. The other girls are very busy.
9. Several young men are in front of the library.
10. Mary and Peter leave the house together.

PRONUNCIATION EXERCISES

d (*hard*)	día	**d** (*as th*)	adiós	medio
	donde		padre	ocupado
	dice		madre	cansado
	dan		todo	comida

VOCABULARY

ayudar (a)   *to help*
dar   *to give*
levantar   *to lift, raise*
levantarse   *to get up*
llamar   *to call*
llamarse   *to be named*
poner   *to put, place*
saber   *to know* (a fact)
trabajar   *to work*

el agua (*f.*)   *water*
el año   *year*
el apetito   *appetite*
el banco   *bank*
el calor   *heat*
la cama   *bed*

el desayuno   *breakfast*
el frío   *cold*
el hambre (*f.*)   *hunger*
helado, -a   *iced*
la hermana   *sister*
el hermano   *brother*
la hija   *daughter*
el hijo   *son*
los hijos   *children*
Isabel   *Elizabeth*
Julio   *Julius*
la leche   *milk*
el miembro   *member*
el momento   *moment*
el plato   *plate, dish*
la sed   *thirst*

la señora   *Mrs., lady*
siempre   *always*
me siento   *I sit down*
se sienta   *he sits down*
se sientan   *they sit down*

siguiente   *next, following*
la sopa   *soup*
el té   *tea*
unos, unas   *a few, some*
el vaso   *glass*

antes del desayuno	*before breakfast*
en la cama	*in bed*
la señora de Pérez	*Mrs. Pérez*
se llama Julio	*his name is Julius*
tiene mucha hambre	*he is very hungry*
tiene ocho años	*he is eight years old*

MODEL SENTENCES

1. ¿Cómo se llama usted?
2. Yo me llamo María Pérez.
3. Pedro se levanta a las seis.
4. Van a levantarse tarde.
5. Yo no tengo mucho frío. Tengo mucha hambre y mucha sed.

1. *What is your name?*
2. *My name is Mary Pérez.*
3. *Peter gets up at six o'clock.*
4. *They are going to get up late.*
5. *I am not very cold. I am very hungry and very thirsty.*

EXPRESS IN SPANISH

1. What is the girl's name? What is her name? What is the boy's name? What is his name?
2 My name is _____. My mother's name is _____. The girl's name is _____.
3. Charles gets up at nine o'clock. They get up at eight o'clock. We get up at six-thirty.
4. He is going to get up before a quarter past seven. Mary is not going to get up late.
5. He is very cold. He is not very hot. Are you hungry? We are very thirsty.

La familia de María

Hay cinco en la familia de María: su padre, su madre, una hermana, un hermano, y ella. Su padre, el señor Julio Pérez, trabaja en un banco. Su madre, la señora de Pérez, trabaja en casa.

47

Cuando María llega a casa ve a su madre en la cama. María tiene
5 que preparar la comida porque su madre está enferma. Su madre se
levanta unos momentos para tomar un vaso de leche y un plato de sopa.
Isabel, la hermana de María, y su hermano, que se llama Julio y tiene
ocho años, ponen la comida en la mesa. Van a comer a las seis en punto
porque tienen mucha hambre.

10 El señor Pérez está muy contento al ver la buena comida, porque
él también tiene hambre. Todos se sientan a la mesa y comen con
apetito. El señor Pérez y sus hijas toman té helado porque tienen calor.
Julio, que siempre tiene sed, toma leche y dos vasos de agua.

A la mañana siguiente María se levanta a las seis. Tiene que
15 estudiar antes de ir a sus clases. Ella no sabe bien la lección de español
y va a estudiar una hora antes del desayuno. Los otros miembros de la
familia se levantan a las siete. A las siete y media se sientan a la mesa a
tomar el desayuno.

QUESTIONS

A. Answer in complete sentences in Spanish:

1. ¿Cuántos hay en la familia de María?
2. ¿Quiénes son?
3. ¿Cómo se llama el padre de María?
4. ¿Dónde trabaja su padre?
5. ¿Cómo se llaman sus hermanos?
6. ¿A qué hora van a comer?
7. ¿Qué toman el señor Pérez y sus hijas?
8. ¿Por qué toma Julio dos vasos de agua?
9. ¿Por qué se levanta María a las seis de la mañana?
10. ¿A qué hora se levantan los otros miembros de la familia?

B. Personalized questions. Answer in complete sentences in Spanish:

1. ¿Cómo se llama usted?
2. ¿Dónde vive usted?
3. ¿Cuántos hay en su familia?
4. ¿Quiénes son?
5. ¿Cómo se llaman?
6. ¿Cuántos años tiene usted? y ¿su padre?
7. ¿Cómo es su padre? y ¿su madre?

8. ¿Cómo están sus padres?
9. ¿Hablan inglés y español los miembros de su familia?
10. ¿Quién pone la comida en la mesa en su casa?

C. Dígale a un amigo: (Tell a friend)

1. que su madre trabaja en casa.
2. que hay cinco en su familia.
3. que usted no tiene hambre.
4. que no tiene mucha sed.
5. que no sabe la lección de español.

GRAMMAR

22. The Present Indicative of the Irregular Verbs *saber, poner* and *dar*

saber, *to know (a fact),* *to know how*		**poner,** *to put,* *to place*		**dar,** *to give*	
sé	sabemos	pongo	ponemos	doy	damos
sabes	sabéis	pones	ponéis	das	dais
sabe	saben	pone	ponen	da	dan

23. Reflexive Verbs

A reflexive verb is one whose action refers back directly or indirectly upon the subject. In English this idea is expressed through use of the reflexive pronouns *myself, yourself, himself,* etc. The reflexive pronouns are:

me	*myself*	nos	*ourselves*
te	*yourself*	os	*yourselves*
se	*yourself, himself, herself, itself*	se	*yourselves, themselves*

These reflexive pronouns agree with the subject. They precede the verb forms unless the verb is in the infinitive, in which case the pronoun follows and is attached to the infinitive. (The reflexive pronoun also follows the present participle and affirmative commands, which will be given later.)

Present Indicative of **levantarse,** *to get up*

(*yo*)	me levanto	*I get up*	(*nosotros*)	nos levantamos	*we get up*
(*tú*)	te levantas	*you get up*	(*vosotros*)	os levantáis	*you get up*
(*usted*)	se levanta	*you get up*	(*ustedes*)	se levantan	*you get up*
(*él*)	se levanta	*he gets up*	(*ellos*)	se levantan	*they get up*
(*ella*)	se levanta	*she gets up*	(*ellas*)	se levantan	*they get up*

49

Many verbs are reflexive in Spanish whereas in English the reflexive idea is absent.

Yo me siento.	*I sit down (I seat myself).*
Él se llama Carlos.	*His name is (he calls himself) Charles.*
Nos levantamos.	*We get up (we get ourselves up).*
Yo voy a levantarme.	*I am going to get (myself) up.*

When the action of the verb does not reflect on the subject but has some other object the reflexive pronoun is not used:

Voy a sentar a Pancho aquí.	*I am going to seat Frank here.*
Isabel levanta el vaso.	*Elizabeth lifts the glass.*
Julio llama a María.	*Julius calls Mary.*

24. Idioms with *tener*

The verb **tener,** usually meaning *to have* (*to possess*), is used in Spanish in many common expressions referring to the physical or emotional states of a person. In English the verb *to be* is used in such expressions. **Tener** is used with a noun and therefore **mucho** is used as a modifier to mean *very* (instead of **muy**). Some common idioms with **tener** are:

tener calor	*to be hot*	tener hambre (*f.*)	*to be hungry*
tener frío	*to be cold*	tener... años	*to be . . . years old*
tener sed (*f.*)	*to be thirsty*	¿cuántos años tiene?	*how old is he?*

Tengo mucho calor.	*I am very hot.*
Tenemos mucha sed.	*We are very thirsty.*
¿Tiene usted mucho frío?	*Are you very cold?*
Mi hermano tiene diez años.	*My brother is ten years old.*

EXERCISES

A. Substitute pronoun or proper name for the italicized subject, making proper changes in the verb and reflexive pronoun:

1. *Isabel* se levanta tarde.
   él, yo, ellos, usted

2. *Carlos* va a levantarse a las siete.
   ella, nosotros, yo, ustedes

3. ¿Cómo se llama *él*?
   usted, ellos, ella, ustedes

4. *Los muchachos* se levantan a las seis.
   Carlos, nosotros, ella, Julio y yo

5. *Pedro* tiene mucho calor.
   ellas, Pancho, ustedes, nosotros

6. *Julio* siempre tiene mucha sed.
   yo, usted, ellos, Carlos y yo

7. ¿Tiene *María* mucho frío?
   él, ustedes, nosotros, yo

8. *Yo* tengo mucha hambre antes del desayuno.
   Julio y María, Isabel, Carlos y yo, usted

B. Answer the following questions in the negative:

EXAMPLE: ¿Tiene usted frío?
No, no tengo frío.

1. ¿Tiene usted frío?
2. ¿Sabe usted bien la lección?
3. ¿Tienen ustedes mucha sed?
4. ¿Se levantan tarde Julio y Pancho?
5. ¿Pone la mesa Isabel?
6. ¿Tiene Julio veinte años?
7. ¿Se sienta Carlos a la mesa?
8. ¿Tiene usted mucha hambre?
9. ¿Se levantan ustedes tarde?
10. ¿Va a levantarse usted a las cinco?

C. Give in Spanish:

1. We are not very hot.
2. They are cold.
3. Who is thirsty?
4. Julio is very hungry.
5. Mary is twenty years old.
6. Mrs. Pérez calls Elizabeth.
7. Elizabeth helps Mary.
8. What is your sister's name?
9. The boys' names are Charles and Peter.
10. We know very little.

D. Write in Spanish:

1. There are five in Mary's family.
2. Her father is Mr. Julio Pérez.
3. Mary sees her mother in bed.
4. She has to prepare dinner because her mother is sick.
5. Mr. Pérez is very happy on seeing the good meal.
6. They all sit down at the table.
7. Julio does not drink two glasses of milk.
8. His father and his sisters drink iced tea.
9. What is their mother's name?
10. I do not answer because I do not know.

51

la manzana o el plátano
la lima - LEMON (small) - Lime
el limón - big Lemon
la manzana - apple
la pera - pear
la fruita   la canasta
la ciruela - plum o la cesta - basket
las fresas - strawberries
las cerezas - cherries

PRONUNCIATION EXERCISES

ll	ñ	r	r	rr
ella	niño	ir	pero	perro
silla	año	ver	caro	carro
llamar	señor	ser	para	parra
llevar	mañana	decir	tres	rico

VOCABULARY

asistir (a) *to attend*
buscar *to look for*
desayunarse *to eat* (*have*) *breakfast*
encontrar *to find*
jugar a *to play* (a game)
llevar *to take, carry*
poder *to be able*
querer *to wish, want, love*

agradable *pleasant*
ahora *now*
el autobús *bus*
el béisbol *baseball*
el campo *country* (not town)
el cereal *cereal*
el cine *movies*

la escuela *school*
el fútbol *football*
había *there was, there were*
el huevo *egg*
el juego *game*
el jugo *juice*
libre *free, unoccupied*
más *more*
la naranja *orange*
el niño, la niña *boy, girl, child*
severo, -a *strict, hard*
el tocino *bacon*
el tomate *tomato*
las tostadas *toast*
la universidad *university*
la vida *life*

52

a la escuela	*to school*
después del desayuno	*after breakfast*
en la escuela	*at* (in) *school*
horas libres	*free time*
jugar al béisbol	*to play baseball*
lejos de	*far from*

MODEL SENTENCES

1. Cuando yo era niño yo vivía en el campo.
2. Yo tenía muchos amigos y los (les) veía todos los días.
3. El señor García jugaba al béisbol cuando era joven.
4. Mi hermano quería ir al cine, pero no podía hacerlo.
5. Nos levantábamos a las seis.

1. *When I was a child I lived in the country.*
2. *I had many friends and I would (used to) see them every day.*
3. *Mr. García played baseball when he was young.*
4. *My brother wanted to go to the movies, but he couldn't do it.*
5. *We used to get up at six o'clock.*

EXPRESS IN SPANISH

1. When my father was a child he lived in Mexico. When my mother was a child she lived near the school.
2. My brother had many books and he would take them to school every day. When we had a difficult lesson we studied it.
3. We used to play football when we were young. They used to play baseball when they were in school.
4. My mother wanted to find the books but she couldn't do it. We wanted to play football but we couldn't do it.
5. They used to get up at nine o'clock. I used to get up at seven-thirty.

Cuando Pancho era niño

Cuando Pancho era niño vivía en el campo con su familia. Él y su hermano asistían a una escuela muy lejos de su casa. Ellos iban a la escuela todos los días en un autobús. Salían de su casa antes de las ocho.

La madre de Pancho llamaba a los niños antes de las seis. Algunas
5 veces los llamaba dos o tres veces, porque no querían levantarse pronto.

53

Ella siempre preparaba un buen desayuno: jugo de naranja o de tomate, cereal, tostadas, huevos, tocino y leche. Se desayunaban a las siete.

Después del desayuno los niños buscaban los libros. Si ellos no podían encontrarlos su madre los buscaba. Los niños siempre los
10 llevaban con ellos pero no los estudiaban todas las noches. Las lecciones no eran difíciles y Pancho podía prepararlas en la escuela. Muchas noches él iba al cine con un amigo. Para Pancho la vida en la escuela era muy agradable. Los profesores no eran muy severos, las lecciones eran fáciles, y él no tenía que estudiar mucho. En sus horas libres los
15 estudiantes jugaban al fútbol, al béisbol, o a otros juegos.

Ahora Pancho asiste a la universidad. Tiene que estudiar por las tardes y no puede jugar al béisbol. Cuando él era niño la vida era más agradable.

QUESTIONS

A. Answer in complete sentences in Spanish:

    1. ¿Dónde vivía Pancho cuando era niño?
    2. ¿A qué hora salían Pancho y su hermano de la casa?
    3. ¿A qué hora los llamaba su madre?
    4. ¿Qué tomaban ellos para su desayuno?
    5. ¿A qué hora se desayunaban?
    6. ¿Qué llevaban los muchachos a la escuela?
    7. ¿Eran difíciles las lecciones?
    8. ¿Qué hacía Pancho muchas noches?
    9. ¿Qué hacían en sus horas libres?
    10. ¿Por qué no puede Pancho jugar al béisbol ahora?

B. Personalized questions. Answer in complete sentences in Spanish:

    1. ¿Dónde vivía usted cuando era niño?
    2. ¿Cómo iba usted a la escuela?
    3. ¿Qué preparaba su madre para el desayuno?
    4. ¿Estudiaba usted en casa por la noche?
    5. ¿Cuándo iba usted al cine?
    6. ¿A qué jugaba en sus horas libres?
    7. ¿Quería usted levantarse temprano todos los días?
    8. ¿A qué hora salía de su casa para ir a la escuela?
    9. ¿Estaba su casa lejos de la escuela?
    10. ¿Tenía que estudiar por la tarde?

C. Dígale a un amigo:

    1. que usted siempre se desayunaba a las siete.

    2. que algunas veces iba al cine.

    3. que tenía que estudiar por las noches.

    4. que sus lecciones no eran difíciles.

    5. que veía a María todos los días.

GRAMMAR

25. The Present Indicative of the Irregular Verbs *poder* and *querer*

poder, *to be able, can*		**querer,** *to want, to wish, to love*	
puedo	podemos	quiero	queremos
puedes	podéis	quieres	queréis
puede	pueden	quiere	quieren

26. The Imperfect Indicative of Regular Verbs

The imperfect indicative of all verbs of the first conjugation is formed by adding **-aba, -abas, -aba, -ábamos, -abais, -aban** to the stem of the verb. In the second and third conjugations the endings added to the stem of the verb are **-ía, -ías, -ía, -íamos, -íais, -ían.** Note that in the first conjugation only the first person plural has an accent, while in the second and third conjugations all forms are accented on the **i** of the ending.

Imperfect of **hablar, aprender,** and **vivir**

hablaba {	*I talked* *I was talking* *I used to talk*	aprendía {	*I learned* *I was learning* *I used to learn*	vivía {	*I lived* *I was living* *I used to live*
hablabas		aprendías		vivías	
hablaba		aprendía		vivía	
hablábamos		aprendíamos		vivíamos	
hablabais		aprendíais		vivíais	
hablaban		aprendían		vivían	

As indicated above, the imperfect may be translated in three ways: *was* + the verb in *-ing*; *used to* + the verb; or a simple past in connection with a repeated action, as *I ate there every day.*

27. The Imperfect Indicative of Irregular Verbs

There are only three verbs which are irregular in the imperfect indicative.

Imperfect Indicative of the Irregular Verbs **ir, ser** and **ver**

ir	ser	ver
iba $\begin{cases} \textit{I was going} \\ \textit{I used to go} \\ \textit{I went} \end{cases}$	era $\begin{cases} \textit{I used to be} \\ \textit{I was} \end{cases}$	veía $\begin{cases} \textit{I was seeing} \\ \textit{I used to see} \\ \textit{I saw} \end{cases}$
ibas	eras	veías
iba	era	veía
íbamos	éramos	veíamos
ibais	erais	veíais
iban	eran	veían

28. Use of the Imperfect Tense

The imperfect is used to describe what was happening or used to happen in the past, with no end to the action being stated or implied.

Yo escribía una carta.	*I was writing a letter.*
Me visitaban todos los días.	*They used to visit me every day.*

29. Personal Pronouns

The subject pronouns were presented with the verbs in Lesson 2, and the reflexive pronouns with the reflexive verbs in Lesson 6. This lesson is concerned with the direct object pronouns and their use. The complete table of personal pronouns is given here for reference and to show the relationships between the different forms.

PERSONAL PRONOUNS

Subject	Indirect Object	Direct Object	Reflexive	Object of a Preposition
yo	me	me	me	(a) mí
tú	te	te	te	(a) ti
usted	le	le, lo, la	se	(a) usted
él	le	le, lo	se	(a) él
ella	le	la	se	(a) ella
nosotros, -as	nos	nos	nos	(a) nosotros
vosotros, -as	os	os	os	(a) vosotros
ustedes	les	les, los, las	se	(a) ustedes
ellos	les	les, los	se	(a) ellos
ellas	les	las	se	(a) ellas

NOTE: The personal pronoun forms corresponding to **tú** and **vosotros** will not be used in the exercises in this text, therefore they are omitted in the following discussion of the position and meaning of object pronouns.

30. Direct Object Pronouns: Position and Meaning

Direct object pronouns precede the conjugated forms of the verb. However, they follow and are attached to an infinitive, just as in the case of the reflexive pronouns studied in Lesson 6.

me	*me*	**nos**	*us*
le	*you* (m.), *him*	**les**	*you* (m.), *them* (m. *people*)
lo	*you* (m.), *him, it* (m.)	**los**	*you* (m.), *them* (m. *people and things*)
la	*you* (f.), *her, it* (f.)	**las**	*you* (f.), *them* (f. *people and things*)

Veo a mi amigo. Lo (le) veo.	*I see my friend. I see him.*
Ella me ve. Él no puede verme.	*She sees me. He cannot see me.*
Yo tenía el libro. Yo lo tenía.	*I had the book. I had it.*
Él estudia la lección. La estudia.	*He studies the lesson. He studies it.*
Quiero a mi madre. La quiero.	*I love my mother. I love her.*

EXERCISES

A. Repeat the following, changing the italicized verb to the imperfect tense:

EXAMPLE: Pancho *vive* en el campo.
Pancho vivía en el campo.

1. Pancho *vive* en el campo.
2. Ella siempre *prepara* un buen desayuno.
3. Las lecciones *son* fáciles.
4. No *tengo* que estudiar.
5. Los niños *buscan* los libros.
6. Carlos *va* al cine.
7. La *veo* en la biblioteca.
8. *Jugamos* al fútbol.
9. ¿*Quiere* usted salir?
10. Pedro *llama* a Carlos.

B. Answer the following questions affirmatively, changing noun objects to direct object pronouns.

EXAMPLE: ¿Estudia usted la lección?
Sí, la estudio.

1. ¿Estudia usted la lección?
2. ¿Lee usted los libros?
3. ¿Ve usted a las hermanas?
4. ¿Toma usted café?
5. ¿Tiene usted las naranjas?
6. ¿Llama usted a Pedro?
7. ¿Ve usted a los jóvenes?
8. ¿Tiene usted la carta?
9. ¿Escribe usted los ejercicios?
10. ¿Bebe usted la leche?

X **C.** Change noun objects to direct object pronouns:

EXAMPLE: Yo aprendía la lección.

Yo la aprendía.

1. Yo aprendía la lección.
2. Carlos veía a sus amigos.
3. Los niños comían tocino.
4. Sus padres tomaban café.
5. Anita y yo vemos a María.
6. El señor García enseña las lecciones.
7. Pedro llamaba a Carlos y a Pancho.
8. Los jóvenes veían a sus amigas.
9. La madre llamaba a los niños.
10. Anita toma jugo de naranja.

D. Change noun objects to direct object pronouns, noting position of object pronoun with infinitive.

EXAMPLE: Quiero ver a María.

Quiero verla.

1. Quiero ver a María.
2. No puedo ver a Carlos.
3. Quiero leer las lecciones.
4. No puedo escribir los ejercicios.
5. Ella quiere preparar la comida.
6. No podemos ver a Pancho.
7. Quiere encontrar el diccionario.
8. No puede llevar los libros.

X **E.** Give in Spanish:

1. They used to answer.
2. He was entering.
3. They used to talk.
4. We used to ask.
5. We were writing.
6. They had.
7. I was not going.
8. What were you saying?
9. What was he doing?
10. He was small.

F. Write in Spanish:

1. They went to school every day.
2. Their mother always prepared a good breakfast.
3. I was looking for my books.
4. We used to get up at six o'clock.
5. We always ate breakfast at seven o'clock.
6. Sometimes they went to the movies.
7. They saw her every day in class.
8. There were many students in the library.
9. I always ate in the cafeteria.
10. Pancho would prepare his lessons at school.

58

PRONUNCIATION EXERCISES

DIPHTHONGS:	**ia**	**ie**	**io**	**iu**	**ai**	**au**
	seria	pie	patio	viudo	hay	gaucho
	viaje	siete	sitio	ciudad	aire	autobús
	rubia	miedo	medio	ciudadano	baile	aunque

VOCABULARY

abrir *to open*

acostarse (ue) *to go to bed*

empezar (ie) *to begin*

encontrar (ue) *to find*

entender (ie) *to understand*

esperar *to hope, expect*

pensar (ie) *to think, intend*

prometer *to promise*

pronunciar *to pronounce*

sentarse (ie) *to sit down*

volver (ue) *to return*

cada (*invariable*) *each*

la dificultad *difficulty*

el fin *end*

la gramática *grammar*

mal *badly*

mejor *better*

necesario *necessary*

o *or*

la oficina *office*

la palabra *word*

para *in order to*

la regla *rule*

sobre *about, on*

el tiempo *weather*

al fin	*finally*
dice que sí	*he says yes (so)*
pensar + *inf.*	*to intend, to plan*

pensar en	*to think of, about*
por lo menos	*at least*
salir bien	*to pass* (a course)

MODEL SENTENCES

1. Ella se sienta a la mesa y empieza a comer.
1. *She sits down at the table and begins to eat.*
2. Él me lo lee. Él no se lo lee a usted.
2. *He reads it to me. He does not read it to you.*
3. Hacía mal tiempo pero no hacía mucho frío.
3. *It was bad weather but it wasn't very cold.*
4. Él pensaba escribir los ejercicios. En vez de escribirlos pensaba en María.
4. *He intended to write the exercises. Instead of writing them he thought about Mary.*
5. El profesor iba a dárselos a él.
5. *The professor was going to give them to him.*

EXPRESS IN SPANISH

1. They sit down at the table and begin to eat. We sit down and begin to study.
2. They read it (*m.*) to me. I read it (*m.*) to her. You write it (*f.*) to us. We write them (*f.*) to you.
3. The weather was good. It was not very cold. It was warm (hot).
4. They intended to write their exercises. She was thinking of Peter.
5. They were going to read it (*f.*) to them. He wanted to give them (*m.*) to you.

Una visita al profesor

Pancho va a la oficina del profesor García para hablarle sobre algunas dificultades en la lección de español. Se sienta y le dice al profesor:

—Yo encuentro las lecciones más difíciles cada día. ¿Puede usted
5 ayudarme?

El profesor quiere ayudar a Pancho, y empieza a hablarle de varias reglas de gramática, pero Pancho no las entiende. Al fin el profesor abre el libro de español y se lo da a Pancho. El joven estudia las reglas y después de unos momentos él profesor le pregunta si las

60

10 entiende mejor. ~~Pancho~~ dice que sí. Lee ~~varias palabras en español al~~
~~profesor,~~ pero las pronuncia muy mal.

—¿Lee usted en español o en inglés?—le pregunta el profesor.

—Le digo la verdad, profesor. Leo en español.

Pancho lee otras palabras en español al profesor pero no las
15 pronuncia bien. Al fin el profesor le dice:

—¿Cómo espera usted salir bien si no estudia? Es necesario
estudiar por lo menos dos horas cada día.

Pancho promete estudiar más y sale de la oficina del profesor
García. Hacía buen tiempo y él quería jugar al béisbol, pero en vez de
20 hacerlo vuelve a su casa a estudiar. Estudia muchas horas y se acuesta
muy cansado.

QUESTIONS

A. Answer in complete sentences in Spanish:

1. ¿Por qué va Pancho a la oficina del profesor García?
2. ¿Qué le dice Pancho al profesor?
3. ¿Qué empieza a hacer el profesor?
4. ¿Qué le da el profesor a Pancho?
5. ¿Entiende Pancho las reglas de gramática?
6. ¿Pronuncia bien Pancho?
7. ¿Lee Pancho en español o en inglés?
8. ¿Qué promete Pancho?
9. ¿Qué tiempo hacía?
10. ¿Qué quería hacer Pancho?

B. Personalized questions. Answer in complete sentences in Spanish:

1. ¿Entiende usted bien las preguntas del profesor?
2. ¿A qué hora empieza a estudiar?
3. ¿A qué hora se acuesta usted?
4. ¿Piensa usted estudiar más?
5. ¿Encuentra usted difíciles las lecciones?
6. ¿Cuántas horas es necesario estudiar cada día?
7. ¿Pensaba ir usted a la oficina de su profesor?
8. ¿Qué hace usted cuando se sienta a la mesa?
9. ¿Dice usted la verdad siempre?
10. ¿En qué pensaba usted?

C. Dígale a un amigo:

1. que usted empieza a hablar mejor el español.
2. que usted encuentra fáciles los ejercicios.
3. que no entiende las reglas de gramática.
4. que usted piensa en sus profesores.
5. que pronuncia muy bien el español.

GRAMMAR

31. Present Indicative of Stem-changing Verbs, Class I

Stem-changing verbs are those which change the last vowel of the stem when this vowel is under stress. All Class I verbs end in **-ar** or **-er** and change the vowel **e** to **ie** and the vowel **o** to **ue**. This change occurs in the first, second and third persons singular and the third person plural of the present indicative. Verbs which change in this manner will be indicated in the vocabulary as follows: **pensar (ie), volver (ue).** Stem-changing verbs of Class I are regular in all other tenses of the Indicative Mood.

Present Indicative of Stem-changing Verbs, *Class I*

pensar (ie) *to think, to intend*	**volver (ue)** *to return*	**sentarse (ie)** *to sit down*
pienso	vuelvo	me siento
piensas	vuelves	te sientas
piensa	vuelve	se sienta
pensamos	volvemos	nos sentamos
pensáis	volvéis	os sentáis
piensan	vuelven	se sientan

32. Indirect Object Pronouns

The indirect object of a verb is the person to or for whom something is done. While the word *to* or *for* is not always expressed in English the idea is understood. For example, "I gave Mary the book." = "I gave the book to Mary." The indirect object pronouns in Spanish are:

me	*to me*	**nos**	*to us*
le	*to you*	**les**	*to you*
le	*to him, to her*	**les**	*to them*

Indirect object pronouns follow the same rule as to position as do reflexive pronouns and direct object pronouns; that is, they precede the conjugated forms of the verb but follow and are attached to an infinitive.

Pedro me hablaba.	*Peter was talking to me.*
Voy a darles el libro.	*I am going to give them the book.*

33. Prepositional Phrases for Clearness or Emphasis

Since **le** and **les** may be translated in several ways, a prepositional phrase (**a él, a ella, a usted,** etc.) is often used in addition to the indirect object pronouns in order to make the meaning clear. Sometimes these phrases are used for emphasis, as are the phrases **a mí** and **a nosotros.** (Refer to the table of Personal Pronouns in Lesson 7 for the complete list of pronouns used as the object of a preposition.)

Él les hablaba a ellas.	*He was talking to them.*
Ella me lo daba a mí.	*She was giving it to me.*

34. Direct and Indirect Object Pronouns Used Together

An indirect object pronoun precedes a direct object pronoun. The usual word order is: subject, indirect object, direct object, verb.

Ella me los leía.	*She used to read them to me.*
Carlos nos lo busca.	*Charles looks for it for us.*

Two object pronouns used together are added to an infinitive in the same order: indirect, direct. An accent must be written on the last syllable of the infinitive.

Van a decírmelo.	*They are going to tell me about it.*
¿Quién puede enseñárnosla?	*Who can teach it to us?*

When both object pronouns are in the third person, **se** replaces **le** or **les,** for two object pronouns beginning with "l" cannot be used together. This substitution should not be confused with the reflexive pronoun **se.** This substitute **se** can mean *to him, to her, to you* (*sing.*), *to them* and *to you* (*pl.*) when it is followed by **lo, la, los** or **las.** The following combinations of direct and indirect object pronouns should be memorized. They will occur in these combinations whether they precede the verb or follow and are attached to it.

me lo (la)	*it to me*
me los (las)	*them to me*
nos lo (la)	*it to us*

63

nos los (las)	*them to us*
se lo (la)	*it to him, her, you, them*
se los (las)	*them to him, her, you, them*
Él se lo lleva a ella.	*He is taking it to her.*
Anita se los da a ellos.	*Anne gives them to them.*
Vamos a dárselos a él.	*We are going to give them to him.*
Se lo escribía a usted.	*He was writing it to you.*

35. Expressions of Weather

The verb **hacer** is used with several nouns to express weather conditions. These nouns are modified by **mucho** to express *very*. (Remember that **bueno** and **malo** drop the final **-o** when they come before a masculine singular noun.)

¿Qué tiempo hace? Hace calor.	*How is the weather? It is hot.*
No hacía mucho frío.	*It was not very cold.*
No hace mal tiempo.	*The weather is not bad.*
Hace muy buen tiempo.	*The weather is very good.*

EXERCISES

A. Substitute pronoun or proper name for the italicized subject, making the proper verb changes.

1. *Nosotros* empezamos a comer.
   María, ustedes, el profesor, ellos

2. *Pancho* se acuesta a las once.
   Julio y Carlos, nosotros, usted, yo

3. *María* piensa estudiar la lección.
   yo, Isabel y María, usted, nosotros

4. *La señora Pérez* se sienta a la mesa.
   Anita y yo, ellos, Pedro, usted

5. *Pedro* vuelve a casa.
   nosotros, María y Anita, yo, ustedes

B. Change indirect object pronouns to plural:

EXAMPLE: Me habla.
          Nos habla.

1. Me habla.
2. Le dice la verdad.
3. Me enseñaba las reglas.

4. Empieza a hablarme.
5. Le leían el libro.

C. Add a prepositional phrase for emphasis:

    EXAMPLE: Yo le escribo.

                Yo le escribo a él.

1. Yo le escribo.
2. Ella me lo decía.
3. Él nos los escribía.
4. Usted se lo dice.
5. Carlos le habla.

D. Use **mucho (mucha)** with the following expressions:

    EXAMPLE: Hace frío.

                Hace mucho frío.

1. Hace frío.
2. Tengo hambre.
3. Hace calor.
4. Tenía sed.
5. Tenemos calor.
6. Teníamos frío.
7. Hacía frío.
8. Tengo calor.
9. Tiene... años.
10. Hacía calor.

E. Give in Spanish:

1. We are thinking of Mary.
2. I intend to go.
3. It was good weather.
4. It was bad weather.
5. It is very cold.
6. He was teaching the rules. He was teaching them to him.
7. Who begins the lesson? She begins it. She is going to begin it.
8. They were reading the book to Frank. They were reading it to him.
9. He was giving it (*m.*) to them. (Use a prepositional phrase in this sentence for clarity, and in the next.)
10. I intend to write to you. He wants to write to her.

F. Supply the Spanish verb or verb ending needed to translate *was* or *it was:*

1. _____ mal tiempo, pero no _____ mucho frío.
2. Yo _____ enfermo.
3. Ella le escrib _____ .
4. Pancho _____ mucha hambre.
5. _____ mucho calor.
6. El me habl _____ en inglés.
7. Ella _____ sed.
8. Mi hermano se llam _____ Julio.
9. ¿Cuántos años _____ él?
10. Yo no vivía en el campo cuando _____ niño.

65

PRONUNCIATION EXERCISES

DIPHTHONGS	ua	ue	uo	ui	ei
(*continued*):	cuando	pueblo	cuota	ruido	reina
	cual	puerta	antiguo	cuido	seis
	agua	suerte	averiguo	muy	ley

VOCABULARY

Know

casarse (con) *to marry*
enseñar *to show*
graduarse *to be graduated*
irse *to go away, leave*
ponerse *to put on*
sacar *to take out*
venir *to come*

anoche *last night*
ayer *yesterday*
la camisa *shirt*
el coche *car, automobile*
como *as*
conmigo *with me*

¿cuál? *which (one)?*
el cumpleaños *birthday*
el edificio *building*
el estadio *stadium*
el ex-alumno *alumnus*
el hombre *man*
el hotel *hotel*
hoy *today*
la iglesia *church*
luego *afterwards, later, then*
nuevo, -a *new*
el paquete *package*
la semana *week*

a la iglesia *to church*
en todo el día *all day long*

66

LESSON NINE

hace veinte años	*twenty years ago*
lo que	*what* (that which)
¿qué tal?	*how goes it?*

MODEL SENTENCES

1. Yo iba a la clase cuando él me llamó.
2. Los domingos yo no tenía que trabajar.
3. Eran las seis cuando mis padres salieron.
4. Mi madre quería volver a casa.
5. Ella se casó con mi padre hace veinte y cinco años.

1. *I was going to class when he called me.*
2. *On Sundays I did not have to work.*
3. *It was six o'clock when my parents left.*
4. *My mother wanted to return home.*
5. *She married my father twenty-five years ago.*

EXPRESS IN SPANISH

1. I was in the library when they spoke to me. Julius was playing when Mary arrived at home. What were they doing when you saw them?
2. On Saturdays Julius did not have to go to school. On Mondays I had to study a great deal. On Sundays Mr. Pérez did not have to go to the bank.
3. It was one o'clock when I sat down at the table. It was half past two when my friend called me. What time was it when he left?
4. My father wanted to go to the movies. They knew the lesson well. We thought that Spanish was easy.
5. He married my sister two years ago. When did you write to her? I wrote to her three weeks ago.

Ayer fue domingo

Hoy es lunes. Pedro iba a su clase cuando un amigo le llamó y le preguntó:

—¿Qué tal, amigo? ¿A dónde fue usted ayer? Yo quería decirle algo y no le vi en todo el día.

5   —Usted no me vio porque yo estaba con mis padres—le contestó Pedro. —Ellos llegaron antes de las once y fueron conmigo a la iglesia. Luego fuimos al hotel a comer. Después de la comida mi madre fue a ver a una amiga que vive aquí y yo llevé a mi padre a ver los edificios

nuevos de la universidad. Él se graduó hace veinte y cinco años y quería
10 ver los dormitorios de hombres, la biblioteca, y el nuevo estadio.

—¿Entonces su padre es ex-alumno de la universidad? ¿Estudió
su madre aquí también?

—Sí, los dos estudiaron aquí. Él se casó con ella un mes después
de graduarse.

15 —¿Y cuándo volvieron sus padres a casa?

—Volvieron anoche. Eran las seis cuando se fueron. Como
mañana es el día de mi cumpleaños, antes de salir sacaron un paquete
grande del coche y me lo dieron. ¿Sabe lo que me dieron? Dos camisas
nuevas muy bonitas. Si quiere verlas puede venir a mi cuarto a las doce.
20 Quiero enseñárselas. Luego voy a casa de María y no sé cuál ponerme.

QUESTIONS

A. Answer in complete sentences in Spanish:

1. ¿A dónde iba Pedro?
2. ¿Quién le llamó?
3. ¿Por qué no le vio su amigo?
4. ¿A dónde fue Pedro con sus padres?
5. ¿A dónde fueron luego a comer?
6. ¿Quién fue a ver a una amiga?
7. ¿Cuándo se graduó el padre de Pedro?
8. ¿A qué hora se fueron sus padres anoche?
9. ¿Por qué le dieron a Pedro un paquete grande?
10. ¿Estaba contento Pedro con las camisas?

B. Personalized questions. Answer in complete sentences in Spanish:

1. ¿Dónde comió usted anoche?
2. ¿A dónde fue usted el domingo?
3. ¿A quién vio usted en la biblioteca?
4. ¿Tenía usted que trabajar los domingos?
5. ¿Cuándo volvió usted a casa anoche?
6. ¿Tiene la universidad nuevos edificios?
7. ¿Estudiaba usted cuando llamé?
8. ¿Qué hora era cuando salió usted de casa?
9. ¿Pensó usted ir al cine anoche?
10. ¿Qué quería usted hacer después de comer?

C. Dígale a un amigo:

1. que usted no tiene clases los sábados.
2. que sus padres le dieron un coche.
3. que usted salió de casa muy temprano esta mañana.
4. que anoche usted fue a la biblioteca a estudiar.
5. que vuelve a casa el domingo.

GRAMMAR

36. Preterite Indicative of Regular Verbs

The preterite tense of regular verbs is formed by adding the endings **-é, -aste, -ó, -amos, -asteis, -aron** to the stem of verbs of the first conjugation, and the endings **-í, -iste, -ió, -imos, -isteis, -ieron** to the stem of verbs of the second and third conjugations. Note that the first and third persons singular have an accent. The first person plural forms, **hablamos** and **vivimos,** have the same form in the present and in the preterite tenses, but the meaning is ordinarily clear from the context.

Preterite Tense of **hablar, aprender** and **vivir**

hablé	*I spoke*	aprendí	*I learned*	viví	*I lived*
	I did speak		*I did learn*		*I did live*
hablaste		aprendiste		viviste	
habló		aprendió		vivió	
hablamos		aprendimos		vivimos	
hablasteis		aprendisteis		vivisteis	
hablaron		aprendieron		vivieron	

The preterite is translated as the simple English past tense: *I spoke, he learned, they lived,* etc. The English translation may contain the verb *did* in the interrogative, negative or emphatic forms:

¿Habló ella?	*Did she speak?*
No aprendieron.	*They did not learn.*
Él lo escribió.	*He did write it.*

37. The Preterite of Stem-changing Verbs of Class I

These verbs have no stem change in the preterite and are conjugated like **hablar** and **aprender.**

pensar (ie): pensé, pensaste, pensó, pensamos, pensasteis, pensaron
volver (ue): volví, volviste, volvió, volvimos, volvisteis, volvieron

38. The Preterite of the Irregular Verbs *ser, ir* and *dar*

ir, *to go*	ser, *to be*	dar, *to give*
fui *I went, I did go*	fui *I was*	di *I gave, I did give*
fuiste	fuiste	diste
fue	fue	dio
fuimos	fuimos	dimos
fuisteis	fuisteis	disteis
fueron	fueron	dieron

39. Use of the Preterite Tense

The preterite tense is a tense of action. It is used to describe an act which has begun and ended. The act may have lasted a short or long period of time, but the idea of the completion of the whole act must be implied if the verb is to be in the preterite.

Volvieron a las siete.	*They returned at seven o'clock.*
Yo abrí el libro.	*I opened the book.*
¿Llegó usted ayer?	*Did you arrive yesterday?*
Vivimos dos años en México.	*We lived in Mexico two years.*

40. Preterite and Imperfect Contrasted

(*a*) The preterite expresses the completion of a single act in the past, tells what happened. It is a narrative tense.

Se casaron el lunes.	*They were married on Monday.*
Él se fue a las dos.	*He left at two o'clock.*

(*b*) As stated in Lesson 7, the imperfect is a descriptive tense, and tells what was happening, used to happen, or happened repeatedly, without expressing the completion of the act.

Ella era alta y rubia.	*She was tall and blonde.*
Estudiaba cuando era niña.	*I studied when I was a child.*
Ellos leían la lección.	*They were reading the lesson.*
Comía allí todos los días.	*He ate there every day.*

(*c*) The imperfect is used to express a mental state or action in the past. (Verbs such as **pensar, querer, saber,** etc.)

Anita quería ir al cine.	*Anne wanted to go to the movies.*
Pancho no sabía la lección.	*Frank did not know the lesson.*

(*d*) The imperfect is used to express the time of day in the past.

Eran las cuatro y media.	*It was half past four.*
Era la una y diez.	*It was ten minutes after one.*

(*e*) When the imperfect and preterite are used together, the imperfect tells what was happening when an act took place. This act is expressed by the preterite.

Ella escribía cuando entramos.	*She was writing when we entered.*
Yo hablaba cuando él me llamó.	*I was talking when he called me.*

41. Days of the Week

Know

Sunday	el domingo	*Thursday*	el jueves
Monday	el lunes	*Friday*	el viernes
Tuesday	el martes	*Saturday*	el sábado
Wednesday	el miércoles		

The names of the days of the week are written with small letters. The definite article **el** is used with days of the week except after the verb **ser,** and often is the equivalent of the English *on* (*a certain day*).

Yo voy el lunes.	*I am going on Monday.*
Hoy es sábado.	*Today is Saturday.*

When the days of the week are used in the plural, as *on Mondays*, this is expressed by using the plural article **los** before the name of the day. The words **domingo** and **sábado** add **-s** in the plural, the others do not change.

Los sábados no tenemos clases.	*On Saturdays we do not have classes.*
Anita va a su casa los viernes.	*Anne goes home on Fridays.*

EXERCISES

A. Read in Spanish, then repeat, changing verb to preterite.

EXAMPLE: María se sienta a la mesa.
María se sentó a la mesa.

1. María se sienta a la mesa.
2. Mi madre trabaja en casa.
3. Pancho me enseña el paquete.
4. Las muchachas llegan a la biblioteca.
5. Yo entro en el edificio.
6. Anita no aprende la lección.
7. Carlos y yo comemos a la una.
8. Los profesores salen el martes.
9. Vivimos en el dormitorio.
10. Pancho no entiende las reglas.

71

B. Change the infinitive to proper form of preterite or imperfect.

1. Anita (ver) a María anoche en la biblioteca.
2. Nosotros siempre (comer) en casa. ·
3. Juan y Carlos (llegar) a las ocho.
4. María (estudiar) todas las noches.
5. Ayer Julio y yo (ir) al cine.
6. Cuando yo (ser) niño (jugar) al fútbol.
7. Ella me (dar) el dinero el miércoles.
8. Ellas no (estudiar) mucho anoche.
9. Pedro y Carlos (ir) a la iglesia todos los domingos.
10. Yo no (pensar) ir a la escuela ayer.

C. Complete the following, using a day or days of the week, using the definite article if necessary:

EXAMPLE: Siempre íbamos a la iglesia los domingos.

1. Siempre íbamos a la iglesia _____.
2. No tenemos clase _____.
3. Quiero ir al cine _____.
4. Ayer fue _____.
5. Mañana es _____.
6. ¿Quiere usted comer conmigo _____?
7. Mis padres vienen a verme _____.
8. Tengo mi clase de español _____.

D. Change the following verbs in the present tense to the preterite.

EXAMPLE: llevo — llevé

1. llevo	5. vuelvo	9. escribimos	13. abren
2. da	6. se levanta	10. dan	14. entro
3. vamos	7. soy	11. come	15. se sienta
4. aprenden	8. piensa	12. me acuesto	

E. Write in Spanish:

1. I was writing when they arrived.
2. It was ten o'clock when he finished.
3. They wanted to see her because she was blonde and pretty.
4. My father married my mother twenty-two years ago.
5. I used to work on Saturdays.
6. On Sunday they went to church.
7. My father bought a book and gave it to me.
8. Our university had many new buildings.
9. We were in the library when you arrived.
10. I wanted to see Peter but I knew that he wasn't at home.

PRONUNCIATION EXERCISES

ch	h	x	y
chico	hasta	examen	ya
charlar	hermano	éxito	yerro
Chile	hombre	explicar	yo
charco	huevo	extraño	yugo

VOCABULARY

comprar *to buy*
conocer *to know, be acquainted with*
creer *to believe, think*
dedicar *to devote*
explicar *to explain*
ganar *to win*
gustar *to like, be pleasing to*
jugar (ue) *to play* (a game)
oir *to hear*
presenciar *to see* (be present)
sorprenderse *to be surprised*
traer *to bring*

la banda *band*
el básquetbol *basketball*

bastante *enough*
el campeonato *championship*
casi *almost*
colombiano, -a *Colombian*
los deportes *sports*
emocionante *exciting*
el equipo *team*
el espectáculo *spectacle*
los Estados Unidos *United States*
este, esta *this*
el estudio *study*
la explicación *explanation*
el gusto *pleasure*
José *Joseph, Joe*
el jugador *player*
el lado *side*

el librito *pamphlet, program*
lleno, -a *full*
el mes *month*
mil *thousand*
el mundo *world*
naturalmente *naturally*
el nombre *name*
noviembre *November*
el número *number*
octubre *October*

el otoño *autumn*
la parte *part*
el partido *game*
la persona *person*
pronto *soon*
sentado, -a *seated, sitting*
Tejas *Texas*
la temporada *season*
el tenis *tennis*
el tiempo *time*

a mi lado — *beside me*
con mucho gusto — *gladly*
dedicar su tiempo — *to devote his time*
de lejos — *from a distance*
escuela superior — *high school*
hacer preguntas — *to ask questions*
todo el mundo — *everybody*

MODEL SENTENCES

1. Me gusta jugar al fútbol.
2. A María no le gustaban los libros.
3. Yo no sabía lo que ella quería hacer.
4. ¿Conoce usted a José? Le conocí ayer.
5. Yo supe que él vino anoche.

1. *I like to play football.*
2. *Mary did not like the books.*
3. *I did not know what she wanted to do.*
4. *Do you know Joe? I met him yesterday.*
5. *I found out that he came last night.*

EXPRESS IN SPANISH

1. We like to play baseball. They do not like to study. She likes to teach.
2. Frank likes the pens. Mary didn't like sports (*los deportes*).
3. They didn't know what I was doing. We didn't know what he wanted.
4. Does he know Joe? We met him yesterday. They met her last night.
5. She found out that they came last night. We learned that you brought the book.

Un partido de fútbol

El otoño es la temporada del fútbol. En los meses de octubre y noviembre hay partidos casi todos los sábados y asisten miles de personas. Voy siempre porque me gusta mucho el fútbol y también porque me gusta oir la banda.

LESSON TEN

5   Ayer conocí a un joven de Bogotá, Colombia. Él me dijo que quería hacerme preguntas sobre los deportes y la vida aquí en los Estados Unidos. Se sorprendió cuando le dije que cuando yo estaba en la escuela superior jugaba al fútbol, al béisbol y al tenis. No jugaba al básquetbol porque no era bastante alto. El colombiano me dijo que

10 él no tomaba parte en los deportes porque tenía que dedicar todo su tiempo a sus estudios. Para poder explicarle bien el juego de fútbol compré un librito con los nombres de los jugadores de los dos equipos, y muy pronto los conocíamos a todos por su nombre y número. El joven me hizo muchas preguntas y se las contesté con mucho gusto.

15 Nuestro equipo ganó el partido, y naturalmente creemos que va a ganar el campeonato este año.

      —¿A usted le gustó el partido, José?

      —Sí, me gustó mucho. Es un espectáculo muy emocionante, y ya entiendo algo de lo que hacen los jugadores, gracias a sus explicaciones.

20 Veo que a muchas personas les gusta presenciar el partido. El estadio estaba muy lleno. Hay personas que vienen de lejos, ¿verdad?

      Sí, es verdad. Muchos ex-alumnos vienen y traen a sus familias. El señor que estaba sentado a mi lado me dijo que era de Tejas. Hoy todo el mundo está contento porque tenemos un buen equipo.

QUESTIONS

A. Answer in complete sentences in Spanish:

  1. ¿Cuándo es la temporada del fútbol?
  2. ¿En qué meses hay partidos?
  3. ¿Asisten muchas personas?
  4. ¿Por qué asisten ellas?
  5. ¿Qué quería saber el joven de Bogotá?
  6. ¿Por qué no tomaba parte en los deportes el colombiano?
  7. ¿Cómo se llamaba el joven de Colombia?
  8. ¿Le gustó a él el partido?
  9. ¿Hay personas que vienen de lejos?
  10. ¿Por qué están contentos los alumnos y los ex-alumnos?

B. Personalized questions. Answer in complete sentences in Spanish:

  1. ¿Cuál de los meses le gusta más?
  2. ¿Le gusta a usted más el fútbol o el béisbol?

   3. ¿Ganó nuestro equipo de fútbol el campeonato este año?
   4. ¿Conoce usted a muchos colombianos?
   5. ¿Cómo se llama el estudiante que está a su lado?
   6. ¿A quién conoció usted anoche?
   7. ¿Le hace muchas preguntas a su profesor?
   8. ¿Estudiaba usted mucho cuando estaba en la escuela superior?
   9. ¿Por qué no dedicaba usted todo su tiempo a sus estudios?
10. ¿A qué hora se acostó usted anoche?

C. Dígale a un amigo:

   1. que le gustan a usted los partidos de fútbol.
   2. que usted conoció a un mexicano anoche.
   3. que le gusta a usted mucho el otoño.
   4. que no sabía bien su lección esta mañana.
   5. que usted no sabía que sus padres venían.

GRAMMAR

42. The Present Indicative of the Irregular Verbs *venir*, *conocer* and *traer*

Present of **venir**, *to come*; **conocer**, *to know*; **traer**, *to bring*

vengo	conozco	traigo
vienes	conoces	traes
viene	conoce	trae
venimos	conocemos	traemos
venís	conocéis	traéis
vienen	conocen	traen

43. Irregular Preterites

Three irregular preterites were given in Lesson 9 (**ir, ser** and **dar**). Most other verbs which are irregular in the preterite tense follow a regular pattern. The preterite stem differs from that of the infinitive but these verbs use the same endings, which are:

-e	-imos
-iste	-isteis
-o	-ieron

76

Note that the first and third persons singular do not bear an accent as they do in the regular preterite endings. The other endings are the same as those of regular verbs of the second and third conjugations. (See the preterite of **aprender** and **vivir** in Lesson 9.)

44. The Preterite of *decir, hacer* and *traer*

decir, *to say, to tell*	**hacer,** *to do, to make*	**traer,** *to bring*
dije *I said, I told*	hice *I did, I made*	traje *I brought*
dijiste	hiciste	trajiste
dijo	hizo	trajo
dijimos	hicimos	trajimos
dijisteis	hicisteis	trajisteis
dijeron	hicieron	trajeron

Note that the third person plural of **decir** and **traer** lose the **i** of the verb ending because of a preceding **j.**

45. Other Irregular Preterites

The first person singular forms of other verbs with irregular preterite stems are given below. The other forms follow the pattern given above. (See Cover Chart for these verbs.)

estar	*to be*	estuve	*I was*
poder	*to be able*	pude	*I was able, I could*
poner	*to put*	puse	*I put, I placed*
querer	*to wish*	quise	*I wished, I tried to*
saber	*to know*	supe	*I found out, I learned*
tener	*to have*	tuve	*I had, I received*
venir	*to come*	vine	*I came*

46. *Saber* and *conocer*

Saber means *to know a fact,* or with an infinitive, *to know how to do something.* **Conocer** means *to know* in the sense of *to be acquainted.* In referring to the past these verbs are ordinarily used in the imperfect tense and are translated *I knew.* In the preterite **saber** means *found out* or *learned;* **conocer** means "*met*" ("*became acquainted with*"). **Conocer** is regular in the preterite.

Yo no sé jugar al béisbol.	*I don't know how to play baseball.*
Él sabía bien la lección.	*He knew the lesson well.*

Mi hermano lo supo ayer.	*My brother found it out yesterday.*
Yo no conozco bien a Juan.	*I do not know John well.*
¿Conocía usted a su madre?	*Did you know his mother?*
José la conoció anoche.	*Joe met her last night.*

47. Use of the Verb *gustar*

The English idea of *to like* is expressed in Spanish by the verb **gustar,** *to be pleasing.* An English sentence containing the verb *like* must be reworded to contain an indirect object telling to whom something is pleasing. The subject in English becomes the indirect object in Spanish, and is always expressed in the form of an indirect object pronoun. The subject usually follows the verb in this construction.

> *I like the book. = The book is pleasing to me.*
> Me gusta el libro.
>
> *We like to eat. = It pleases us to eat.*
> Nos gusta comer.
>
> *They like Spanish. = Spanish is pleasing to them.*
> Les gusta el español.
>
> *Do you like tea? = Is tea pleasing to you?*
> ¿Le gusta a usted el té?
>
> *Mary likes Anne and Joe. = Anne and Joe are pleasing to Mary.*
> A María le gustan Anita y José.

EXERCISES

A. Read the following sentences in Spanish, then change the verb to the preterite tense:

EXAMPLE: Hace mucho frío.
Hizo mucho frío.

1. Hace mucho frío.
2. No pueden ganar el partido.
3. Pongo los libros en la mesa.
4. Queremos explicar las reglas.
5. Mi padre está en casa.
6. Los profesores siempre dicen la verdad.
7. Traigo a mi familia a la universidad.
8. Sé los nombres de los jugadores.

9. Venimos a ver los edificios nuevos.
10. Le digo la hora de la clase.
11. Hacen muchas preguntas al profesor.
12. Ponemos un plato de sopa en la mesa.
13. Viene a comer a las seis.
14. Tienen mucha sed.
15. Estoy muy cansado.

B. Supply the proper form and tense of **saber** or **conocer**:

1. Yo _____ al muchacho que viene de México.
2. Nosotros _____ a la señorita García anoche.
3. Ella no _____ que vivíamos en Colombia.
4. Carlos _____ esta mañana que venían.
5. Yo no _____ jugar al fútbol.
6. ¿ _____ usted cómo se llama el joven?
7. Nosotros la _____ bien cuando asistíamos a la universidad.
8. Ellos _____ a María en la casa del señor Blanco.
9. ¿A qué hora _____ ustedes que no podían ir?
10. Él dijo que _____ a la muchacha bonita.

C. Substitute the nouns given below for the italicized subject, making the verb **gustar** agree with subject:

EXAMPLE: Me gusta *el libro*.
Me gustan las camisas, etc.

1. Me gusta *el libro*.
las camisas, el fútbol, la universidad, las tostadas

2. Nos gustan *los huevos*.
la leche, las casas, nuestro profesor, los jóvenes

3. Le gustaba a María *la comida*.
los libros, leer, los muchachos, el artículo

4. Les gustó a los muchachos *la película*.
el partido, los juegos, la clase, las señoritas

5. Me gustan *los coches nuevos*.
la muchacha bonita, las lecciones fáciles,
las buenas comidas, el café negro

6. Nos gustaba *jugar al béisbol*.
levantarnos tarde, los paquetes, ir al cine, los jóvenes

7. A él le gusta *el té*.
los niños, la casa nueva, su profesor, las rubias

79

D. Write a sentence in Spanish, using each of the following recognizable cognates:

1. familia	6. diccionario	11. miembro	16. oficina
2. preparar	7. artículo	12. severo	17. edificio
3. inteligente	8. persona	13. universidad	18. graduarse
4. vocabulario	9. sopa	14. dificultad	19. naturalmente
5. estudio	10. apetito	15. ejercicio	20. noviembre

E. Give in Spanish:

1. We like Spanish.
2. I (emphatic) like to play baseball.
3. Do you like to see the new cars?
4. Joe liked the games because our team won.
5. Frank likes blondes (las rubias).
6. Joe likes brunettes (las morenas).
7. I do not like to get up early.
8. The boys do not like to work.
9. The young man liked to hear the explanations.
10. I like autumn very much.

VOCABULARY

acercarse (a) *to approach*
caminar *to walk*
costar (ue) *to cost*
mirar *to look at*
ofrecer *to offer*
presentar *to introduce*
valer *to be worth*
vender *to sell*
visitar *to visit*

amarillo, -a *yellow*
americano, -a *American*
barato, -a *cheap*
bello, -a *beautiful, lovely*
el camino *road, highway*
el centavo *cent*
la Ciudad de México *Mexico City*
la clase *kind*
el clavel *carnation*
el color *color*
como *like*
el contraste *contrast*
¿cuánto? *how much?*
la docena *dozen*

entre *among, between*
la excursión *trip, excursion*
la flor *flower*
hacia *toward*
hermoso, -a *beautiful, handsome*
histórico, -a *historical*
indio, -a *Indian*
las indias *Indian women*
el mercado *market*
la música *music*
el país *country*
el peso *Mexican dollar*
el precio *price*
el pueblo *town, people, country*
¡qué! *how!*
rojo, -a *red*
la rosa *rose*
el sitio *place, site*
solo, -a *alone*
la vendedora *vendor, seller (f.)*
el verano *summer*
el viaje *trip*
el viajero *traveler*
la visita *visit*

¿cuánto vale?	*what is the price?*
¿cuántos, -as?	*how many?*
el verano que viene	*next summer*
hacer un viaje	*to take a trip*
¡qué barato!	*how cheap!*

MODEL SENTENCES

1. Clara estaba comprando claveles rojos.
2. Me gusta este sitio. No me gusta aquél.
3. Las reglas son difíciles. Estoy leyéndolas.
4. ¡Qué baratas son las flores en México!
5. Estas flores amarillas son bellísimas.

1. *Clara was buying red carnations.*
2. *I like this place. I do not like that one (over there).*
3. *The rules are difficult. I am reading them.*
4. *How cheap flowers are in Mexico!*
5. *These yellow flowers are very beautiful.*

EXPRESS IN SPANISH

1. Mary was looking at the car. The man was selling flowers.
2. He likes this color. He doesn't like that one (*at a distance*).
3. This lesson is interesting. I am studying it. Those books are very easy. My brother is reading them.
4. How beautiful the red roses are! How beautiful that country is!
5. This road is very bad. That music is very beautiful. Those flowers are very cheap.

Una visita a México

Mi amiga Clara fue a México este verano. Le gustó mucho México, porque es un país muy interesante. Ella hizo varias excursiones a los sitios históricos, que le gustaron mucho. También visitó un mercado de flores. Allí vio flores de muchas clases y de todos colores.
5 Cuando Clara estaba mirando las flores la vendedora le dijo:
—Flores, señorita, muy baratas.
—¿Cuánto vale una docena de claveles?—le preguntó Clara.
—Vale tres pesos, señorita—contestó la vendedora.

82

—¡Qué baratas son las flores en México!—pensó Clara. —Tres
10 pesos son treinta y cinco centavos americanos. Claveles como éstos
cuestan muchísimo más en los Estados Unidos. —Y pensando en esto,
Clara compró cuatro docenas de bellísimos claveles rojos.

Otro día en el camino al pueblo de Cuernavaca ella vio algunas
indias que caminaban hacia el pueblo llevando flores. Ellas se acercaron
15 al autobús con sus flores y se las ofrecieron a los viajeros a precios muy
bajos. Había rosas de varios colores, y Clara las compró amarillas y
rojas. Las indias vendieron casi todas sus flores entre los viajeros.

El verano que viene pienso hacer un viaje a México. Quiero
visitar ese país de música y colores y conocer ese pueblo de contrastes.
20 Yo conozco a un joven que vive en la Ciudad de México y él va a
presentarme a otros. Hablando español con ellos todos los días voy a
aprender mucho.

QUESTIONS

A. Answer in complete sentences in Spanish:

1. ¿Cuándo fue Clara a México?
2. ¿A dónde hizo ella varias excursiones?
3. ¿Qué mercado visitó ella?
4. ¿Qué vio allí?
5. ¿Qué le dijo la vendedora?
6. ¿Cuántas docenas de claveles compró?
7. ¿Cuánto vale una docena?
8. ¿Qué vio Clara otro día en el camino a Cuernavaca?
9. ¿De qué color eran las rosas que Clara compró?
10. ¿Quiénes compraron casi todas las flores?

B. Personalized questions. Answer in complete sentences in Spanish:

1. ¿Cuándo piensa usted ir a México?
2. ¿Quiere usted hacer el viaje solo?
3. ¿Conoce usted a alguien en México?
4. ¿Qué quiere usted comprar allí?
5. ¿Es ésta una lección facilísima?
6. Estudiando mucho el español, ¿qué puede usted hacer?
7. ¿Cuáles le gustan más a usted, las rosas o los claveles?
8. ¿A dónde quiere ir usted el verano que viene?
9. ¿Qué compró usted ayer?
10. ¿Cuánto vale una docena de huevos?

C. Pregúntele a un amigo: (Ask a friend) Use **usted** in your question.
1. si piensa hacer un viaje a México este verano.
2. si está estudiando el español ahora.
3. si es dificilísimo el español.
4. si le gustaba la música de México.
5. si estaba comprando un coche amarillo

GRAMMAR

48. The Present Participle

The present participle is formed by adding **-ando** to the stem of **-ar** verbs and **-iendo** to the stem of **-er** and **-ir** verbs. This form is invariable.

INFINITIVE	PRESENT PARTICIPLE	
hablar	hablando	*speaking*
aprender	aprendiendo	*learning*
vivir	viviendo	*living*

Irregular present participles of verbs used in previous lessons are:

decir	diciendo	*saying, telling*
poder	pudiendo	*being able*
venir	viniendo	*coming*
ir	yendo	*going*
creer	creyendo	*believing*
leer	leyendo	*reading*
oir	oyendo	*hearing*
traer	trayendo	*bringing*

49. Uses of the Present Participle

(*a*) The present participle is used with **estar** to form the progressive forms of tenses. Object pronouns follow and are attached to the present participle. An accent is required to maintain the original stress.

Juan está leyéndomelos.	*John is reading them* (m.) *to me.*
Ellos estaban acercándose.	*They were approaching.*

The progressive forms are used to intensify and emphasize the action. For example: **Estoy comiendo.** *I am* (in the act of) *eating*; **Él estaba leyendo.** *He was reading* (right then). If this meaning is absent a simple tense is used. The progressive forms of **ir** and **venir** are seldom used in Spanish.

(*b*) The present participle is used as in English to replace an adverbial phrase, especially when *by, because of* or *while* is implied. It is also used to express an action that occurs at the same time as the main verb.

> Estudiando mucho él aprendió los verbos.
> (*By*) *studying a great deal he learned the verbs.*
> Caminaban hacia el pueblo llevando flores.
> *They were walking toward the town carrying flowers.*

(*c*) The present participle is not used after a preposition. As has been shown in Lesson 5 the infinitive is used.

> antes de casarse   *before getting married*
> después de comprarlos   *after buying them*

50. Use of -*ísimo*

The ending -**ísimo** (-**a, -os, -as**) is added to an adjective to express a high degree of the quality with no comparison. An adjective ending in a vowel drops the vowel. With an adverb the ending -**ísimo** is invariable.

difícil	dificilísimo, -a	*very difficult*
hermoso	hermosísimo, -a	*extremely or very beautiful*
importante	importantísimo, -a	*very or most important*
mucho (*adverb*)	muchísimo	*very much, a great deal*

51. Demonstrative Adjectives and Pronouns

(*a*) The demonstrative adjectives in English are *this, that, these* and *those*. In Spanish there is an additional word for *that* (**aquel**) meaning *that* at a distance. Since the Spanish demonstrative adjectives agree in gender and number with the noun modified, each adjective will have four forms.

	SINGULAR			PLURAL	
m.	*f.*		*m.*	*f.*	
este	esta	*this*	estos	estas	*these*
ese	esa	*that*	esos	esas	*those*
aquel	aquella	*that* (*yonder*)	aquellos	aquellas	*those*

> este camino, estas flores   *this road, these flowers*
> esa flor   *that flower* (*near you*)
> aquellas indias   *those Indian women* (*yonder*)

(b) The demonstrative pronouns have the same forms as the demonstrative adjectives except that they have a written accent on the stressed vowel.

éste	ésta	*this one*		éstos	éstas	*these*
ése	ésa	*that one*		ésos	ésas	*those*
aquél	aquélla	*that one (far away)*		aquéllos	aquéllas	*those*

este joven y ése	*this young man and that one*
estas casas y aquéllas	*these houses and those (over there)*

Each demonstrative pronoun has a neuter form which refers to an idea, phrase or clause, rather than to an object which has gender. These forms, **esto, eso, aquello,** do not bear a written accent.

Esto es interesante.	*This is interesting.*
¿Qué es eso? ¿Qué es aquello?	*What is that? What is that (at a distance)?*

EXERCISES

A. Change the verb in each sentence to the progressive form:

EXAMPLE: Yo leo la lección.
Yo estoy leyendo la lección.

1. Yo leo la lección.
2. El hombre vendía flores.
3. Clara compraba claveles.
4. Yo hablaba con la vendedora.
5. El americano visitaba el mercado.
6. Yo digo la verdad.
7. El niño no aprende mucho.
8. José no juega al béisbol.

B. Add **-ísimo, -a** to each adjective to express a high degree of the quality:

EXAMPLE: una flor bella
una flor bellísima

1. una flor bella
2. una lección importante
3. un día hermoso
4. un momento difícil
5. un pueblo pequeño
6. un desayuno barato
7. un joven alto
8. libros interesantes
9. un río grande
10. una explicación fácil

C. Give in Spanish, noting position of object pronouns:

1. bringing it to us
2. believing it
3. reading them to him
4. looking at her
5. selling them to us
6. hearing us
7. buying them
8. telling it to her
9. offering it to me
10. opening it

D. Supply proper demonstrative adjective or pronoun and read in Spanish:

EXAMPLE: (These) flores y (those)
Estas flores y ésas

1. (These) flores y (those).
2. (This) camisa y (that one).
3. (These) lápices y (those).
4. (This) hotel y (that one over there).
5. (These) libros y (those).

6. (This) lección y (that one).
7. (This) profesor y (that one).
8. ¿Qué es (this)?
9. No creíamos (that).
10. (These) casas y (those over there).

E. Write in Spanish:

1. (By) writing the exercises he learns a great deal.
2. (By) working on Saturdays I can take a trip next summer.
3. Next Saturday is Charles' birthday.
4. After studying the lesson he thought that it was very easy.
5. He entered the house eating an orange.
6. Joe thinks that all his lessons are very difficult.
7. What is the price of a dozen carnations?
8. That building over there is our new dormitory.
9. What were you doing when I entered?
10. This is very interesting. How many towns did you visit?

VOCABULARY

cometer *to commit*
confundir *to confuse*
haber *to have* (auxiliary)
practicar *to practice*
recitar *to recite*

el adjetivo *adjective*
la comparación *comparison*
la cosa *thing*
cubano, -a *Cuban*
el dinero *money*
el dólar *dollar*
e *and* (before i or hi)
el error *error, mistake*
el examen *examination*
los exámenes *examinations*
el favor *favor, kindness*
la frase *sentence*

mayor *greater, older; greatest, oldest*
mejor *better, best*
menor *younger, youngest*
peor *worse, worst*
que *than* (after a comparison)
rápido, -a *rapid*
rápidamente *rapidly*
rico, -a *rich*
la sonrisa *smile*
la suerte *luck*
tampoco *neither*
tan *so, as*
tanto, -a *as (so) much; pl. as (so) many*
la tía *aunt*
el trabajo *work*
triste *sad*

¿Cómo le va a usted? *How are you getting along?*
de veras *really*
de visita *on a visit*
encontrarse con *to meet*
eso no *not that*
hágame el favor de + *inf.* *please* + verb

¡hasta luego!	*see you later*
hoy mismo	*this very day*
tal vez	*perhaps*
tener suerte	*to be lucky*
¡ya lo creo!	*of course*

MODEL SENTENCES

1. Rosita me ha ayudado mucho.
2. Ella es más alta que María.
3. ¿Es el señor García el hombre más rico de la ciudad?
4. Carlos tiene tantos amigos como María, pero no tiene tanto dinero como ella.
5. Hágame el favor de presentarme a Rosita.

1. *Rose has helped me a great deal.*
2. *She is taller than Mary.*
3. *Is Mr. García the richest man in the city?*
4. *Charles has as many friends as Mary, but he doesn't have as much money as she.*
5. *Please introduce me to Rose.*

EXPRESS IN SPANISH

1. They have helped me a great deal. Mr. Martínez has written me in Spanish. Have you met them?
2. Charles is taller than Joseph. We are richer than you. Anne is more charming than Mary.
3. My English professor is the largest man in the town. John is the worst student in the class. Rose is the best teacher that I have.
4. Do you have as many friends as he? I haven't made as many errors as you. They don't have as much money as I.
5. Please introduce me to Charles. Please do not ask me (*any*) more questions. Please practice the adjectives.

¿ Quiere usted conocer a Rosita?

El otro día me encontré con un amigo que no había estudiado mucho. Él estaba triste porque se acercaba el fin del curso e iba a tener los exámenes pronto. Me preguntó:

—Carlos, ¿cómo le va a usted en la clase de español? ¿Ha
5 aprendido mucho? ¿Ha escrito todos los ejercicios? ¿Ha recitado todas

las frases? ¿Ha leído algo en español todos los días? ¿Ha hablado
español siempre en la clase?

Naturalmente yo no había hecho todas esas cosas. —Haga el
favor de no hacerme más preguntas—le dije. —Usted sabe bien que
10 no he hecho todo mi trabajo. Pero yo voy a salir bien en los exámenes
porque una amiga me ha ayudado con las cosas difíciles. Ella es Rosita
Torres, una señorita cubana que está aquí de visita. La conocí hace un
mes. Antes vivía en la Habana, pero ahora vive en México con su
familia. Es una muchacha muy simpática y es tal vez la más bonita de
15 todas mis amigas.

—De veras, Carlos, usted ha tenido suerte. ¿Cómo le ayuda ella?
¿Le escribe los ejercicios?

—No, eso no. Hablamos en español y si cometo un error ella me
lo dice. Ayer yo estaba aprendiendo la comparación de los adjetivos y
20 le dije: —Yo soy el mejor de mi familia. (Yo había confundido "mejor"
y "mayor.") Con una sonrisa ella me dijo: —¿Y quién es el peor de su
familia? —Luego me hizo practicar frases como éstas: "Mi padre es
mayor que mi madre. Ella es menor que él. Yo no soy el mejor estudiante de la clase, tampoco soy el peor. Este libro es más grande que
25 ése." Me gusta estudiar con una profesora tan simpática como ella.
¿No quiere usted conocerla?

—¡Ya lo creo! Hágame el favor de presentarme a ella hoy mismo.

—Muy bien. Si quiere conocerla puede venir a mi casa a las
cuatro para ir conmigo a la casa de la tía de Rosita. ¡Hasta luego!

QUESTIONS

A. Answer in complete sentences in Spanish:

1. ¿Con quién se encontró Carlos el otro día?
2. ¿Por qué estaba triste el amigo?
3. ¿Qué preguntas le hizo él a Carlos?
4. ¿Cómo le contestó Carlos?
5. ¿Quién es Rosita?
6. ¿Cómo es ella?
7. ¿Por qué va a salir bien Carlos en los exámenes?
8. ¿Cómo le ayuda Rosita?
9. ¿Por qué le gusta a Carlos estudiar con ella?
10. ¿A qué hora van los muchachos a la casa de la tía de Rosita?

B. Personalized questions. Answer in complete sentences in Spanish:

1. ¿Ha escrito usted todos los ejercicios?
2. ¿Ha recitado todas las frases?
3. ¿Tiene usted exámenes pronto?
4. ¿Va usted a salir bien?
5. ¿Es usted el mejor estudiante de la clase?
6. ¿Quién es el joven más alto de su clase?
7. ¿Quién es el más rico de sus amigos?
8. ¿Es usted el (la) mayor de su familia?
9. ¿Tiene usted tanto dinero como su profesor?
10. ¿Ha escrito usted más ejercicios que yo?

C. Pregúntele a un amigo:

1. si ha conocido a una muchacha simpática.
2. si ha salido bien en los exámenes.
3. si es más alto que su padre.
4. si ha aprendido todas las reglas.
5. si es el peor estudiante de la clase.

GRAMMAR

52. *Haber* as Auxiliary Verb

Haber, *to have*, is used an an auxiliary verb to form the perfect tenses. Remember that **tener** is always used to translate *to have* in the sense of *to possess.*

PRESENT INDICATIVE		IMPERFECT INDICATIVE	
he	hemos	había	habíamos
has	habéis	habías	habíais
ha	han	había	habían

53. Past Participles

Regular past participles are formed by adding **-ado** to the stem of **-ar** verbs, and **-ido** to the stem of **-er** and **-ir** verbs.

hablar	hablado	*spoken*
comer	comido	*eaten*
vivir	vivido	*lived*

91

Verbs in previous lessons which have irregular past participles are:

abrir	abierto	*opened*	decir	dicho	*said, told*
creer	creído	*believed*	escribir	escrito	*written*
hacer	hecho	*done, made*	poner	puesto	*put, placed*
ir	ido	*gone*	traer	traído	*brought*
leer	leído	*read*	ver	visto	*seen*
oir	oído	*heard*	volver	vuelto	*returned*

54. The Present Perfect Indicative

The present perfect indicative is formed with the present tense of **haber** plus a past participle.

AUXILIARY VERB NEVER USED ALONE HELPER.

he		*I have spoken*
has	hablado	*you have spoken*
ha		*you have, he or she has spoken*
hemos		*we have spoken*
habéis	hablado	*you have spoken*
han		*you, they have spoken*

55. The Pluperfect Indicative

The pluperfect indicative is formed with the imperfect tense of **haber** plus a past participle.

había		*I had eaten*
habías	comido	*you had eaten*
había		*you, she, he had eaten*
habíamos		*we had eaten*
habíais	comido	*you had eaten*
habían		*you, they had eaten*

Note that in the perfect tenses the past participle always ends in **-o**. Object pronouns, reflexive pronouns, and the word **no** always precede the auxiliary verb.

¿La ha abierto Vd.?	*Have you opened it?*
Se había levantado.	*He had gotten up.*
No he escrito.	*I have not written.*

56. Comparison of Adjectives

In English the comparative and superlative degrees are ordinarily expressed by the endings *-er* and *-est* (*taller, tallest*). The words *more* and *most* are used with some adjectives (*more interesting, the most interesting*). Spanish expresses the comparative by the use of the word **más,** translated *more* or *most* according to the context.

> Carlos es alto.
> *Charles is tall.* (*positive*)
> Carlos es más alto que Pancho.
> *Charles is taller than Frank.* (*comparative*)
> Carlos es el joven más alto de la clase.
> *Charles is the tallest young man in the class.* (*superlative*)

To form the comparative, **más** (*more*) or **menos** (*less*) is placed before an adjective. *Than* is translated by **que,** except when *than* is followed by a number, in which case it is expressed by **de.**

> Carlos es más rico que yo.   *Charles is richer than I.*
> Son menos altos que él.   *They are less tall than he.*
> BUT:
> Tengo más de cinco dólares.   *I have more than five dollars.*

The superlative degree is expressed by using the proper definite article or possessive pronoun with the comparative form. After a superlative *in* is translated by **de.**

> San Antonio no es la ciudad más grande del mundo.
> *San Antonio is not the largest city in the world.*
> Él es el muchacho más inteligente de la clase.
> *He is the most intelligent boy in the class.*

Note the word order — *The boy most intelligent.*

57. Irregular Comparisons

bueno	*good*	mejor	*better*	el mejor	*best*
malo	*bad*	peor	*worse*	el peor	*worst*
grande	*large*	más grande	*larger*	el más grande	*largest*
		mayor	*older, larger*	el mayor	*oldest*
pequeño	*small*	más pequeño	*smaller*	el más pequeño	*smallest*
		menor	*younger, smaller*	el menor	*youngest*

In referring to persons, **mayor** and **menor** indicate *age* rather than size. **Mejor** and **peor** precede the noun as do **bueno** and **malo.**

Mi hermano mayor tiene treinta años.
My older brother is thirty years old.

Su hermana menor estudia el inglés.
His younger sister is studying English.

Es el mejor estudiante de la clase.
He is the best student in the class.

Ella es la peor profesora de la universidad.
She is the worst teacher in the university.

58. Comparison of Equality

To express an equal quality (*as rich as*) use **tan... como** (**tan** rico **como**). **Tan** always precedes adjectives.

Él es tan rico como ella.   *He is as rich as she.*

To express an equal quantity, use **tanto (-a), tantos (-as)... como.**

Ella tiene tantos libros como él.   *She has as many books as he.*
Hay tantas muchachas como muchachos.   *There are as many girls as boys.*
Yo no tengo tanto dinero como usted.   *I haven't as much money as you.*

59. Adverbs ending in *-mente*

In Spanish the adverbial ending **-mente** is added to the feminine singular of an adjective to form an adverb. This corresponds to *-ly* in English.

rápido, -a *rapid*   rápidamente *rapidly*
fácil   *easy*   fácilmente   *easily*

60. Comparison of Adverbs

Adverbs are compared by placing **más** or **menos** before the adverb.

Ella habla más rápidamente que él.   *She speaks more rapidly than he.*

61. Adverbs that are Compared Irregularly are:

mucho *much*   más   *more*   bien *well*   mejor *better*
poco *little* menos *less*   mal *badly*   peor *worse*

Él lo entiende bien.   *He understands it well.*
Yo lo entiendo mejor.   *I understand it better.*

EXERCISES

A. Change the verb in each sentence to the corresponding perfect tense:

EXAMPLE: Escribo los ejercicios.

He escrito los ejercicios.

1. Escribo los ejercicios.
2. No lo hago bien.
3. Ella se levanta tarde.
4. ¿Se acuesta él temprano?
5. Yo confundo las frases.
6. Yo le escribía.
7. Tienen un examen.
8. Ellos miraban las flores.

B. Change these adjectives to adverbs by adding **-mente** to the feminine form:

1. difícil	5. triste	8. severo
2. fácil	6. solo	9. necesario
3. malo	7. nuevo	10. natural
4. rápido		

C. Change the italicized verbs with irregular past participles to the present perfect, then to the pluperfect:

EXAMPLE: *Veo* a Rosita.

He visto a Rosita.

Había visto a Rosita.

1. *Veo* a Rosita.
2. ¿*Escribe* usted muchas veces a su madre?
3. Ella *pone* la mesa.
4. Carlos y Pancho *vuelven* temprano de sus clases.
5. *Hacemos* muchos errores en español.
6. Él *dice* que es más rico que usted.
7. No *traigo* mis libros.
8. Lo *leen* en inglés.
9. María *se va* a México.
10. Clara y Anita *abren* sus libros.

D. Give in Spanish:

1. My younger brothers.
2. Your older sisters.
3. Mary is taller than Anne.
4. This lesson was easier than that one.
5. Those exercises are not as difficult as these.

95

6. He is the best student in the class.
7. I have recited as many sentences as you.
8. They have worked more than three years.
9. Professor García speaks more rapidly than Miss White.
10. There were as many Cubans as Mexicans.

E. Write in Spanish:

1. They have opened their books and have written the exercises.
2. She had told me that she was going to take an examination.
3. Please help me with the most difficult sentences.
4. Anne is the prettiest girl in the class.
5. I had not asked as many questions as you.
6. Those men over there are shorter than these.
7. We have studied more than eleven lessons.
8. They have given me more than ten dollars.
9. I didn't write as much as Frank.
10. The professor used to speak more rapidly than the students.

VOCABULARY

alegrarse (de)   *to be glad to*
amar   *to love*
celebrar   *to celebrate*
celebrarse   *to be celebrated*
deber (*inf.*)   *ought, must*
decidir   *to decide*
divertirse (ie)   *to have a good time*
durar   *to last*
escoger   *to choose, select*
invitar   *to invite*
necesitar   *to need*
pasar   *to spend* (*time*), *pass*
perder (ie)   *to lose, miss*
permitir   *to permit*
quedarse   *to stay, remain*
reunirse   *to get together*
usar   *to use*
viajar   *to travel*

abril   *April*
agosto   *August*
alegre   *happy, gay*
alegremente   *happily, gaily*
así   *so, thus*
el avión   *airplane*
azul   *blue*

el baño   *bath*
diciembre   *December*
la diversión   *amusement*
enero   *January*
el equipaje   *baggage*
la estación   *season*
febrero   *February*
la fiesta   *celebration, party*
el francés   *French*
Francia   *France*
el invierno   *winter*
julio   *July*
junio   *June*
largo, -a   *long*
la mano   *hand*
marzo   *March*
mayo   *May*
la Navidad   *Christmas*
negro, -a   *dark, black*
norteamericano, -a   *North American*
el ojo   *eye*
el pelo   *hair*
el pie   *foot*
la playa   *beach*
la primavera   *spring*

primero, -a *first*
el rey *king*
los Reyes Magos *Wise Men*
la ropa *clothes*
septiembre *September*

el sombrero *hat*
el traje *suit*
las vacaciones *vacation*
el vestido *dress*
ya *presently, later*

avión a reacción — *jet plane*
¿Cómo sola? — *Why alone?*
el día de los Reyes Magos — *Twelfth Night, January 6*
espero que no (sí) — *I hope not (so)*
mucho tiempo — *a long time*
quince días — *two weeks*
traje de baño — *bathing suit*
vamos a ver — *let's see*

MODEL SENTENCES

1. Ellos irán a México el lunes.
2. Dijeron que pasarían quince días en la ciudad.
3. Anita tiene los ojos negros.
4. La Navidad se celebra el veinte y cinco de diciembre.
5. ¿Quiere usted comer conmigo mañana?

1. *They will go to Mexico on Monday.*
2. *They said that they would spend two weeks in the city.*
3. *Anne has dark eyes.*
4. *Christmas is celebrated on December twenty-fifth.*
5. *Will you have dinner with me tomorrow?*

EXPRESS IN SPANISH

1. We shall go to Mexico on Friday. He will arrive home on Wednesday. They will be here on Sunday.
2. He said that he would spend two weeks in Mexico. We would buy many things there. They decided that they would not go to Cuba.
3. Charles has blue eyes. He has large feet. Do you have dark eyes?
4. The Fourth of July is not celebrated in Mexico. Spanish is spoken in Colombia. Books will be sold here.
5. Will you go to the movies with me? He refuses to study the lesson.

Anita pasará las vacaciones en México

Anita ha pensado muchas veces en hacer un viaje a México. Ha hablado varias veces con Rosita Torres de la vida y las diversiones allí. Un día Rosita fue a casa de Anita.

ANITA: Buenas tardes, Rosita. Me alegro de verla. Mi madre y yo
5 hemos estado hablando de las vacaciones de Navidad. Tengo quince días libres y he decidido ir a México; pero, naturalmente, ella no me permitirá ir sola.

ROSITA: ¿Cómo sola? Yo volveré a casa el diez y ocho, y la invito a acompañarme y también a pasar las vacaciones en mi casa. A
10 mis padres les gustará tenerla con nosotros.

ANITA: ¡Qué buenos son ustedes! ¿Cómo viajaremos?

ROSITA: Iremos en avión de Atlanta a la ciudad de México. El viaje no es largo, es de unas cuatro horas en un avión a reacción.

ANITA: Yo creo que así mis padres me permitirán ir.

15 ROSITA: ¡Espero que sí! ¡Ya verá! Se reunirán en casa algunos amigos cubanos y se celebrarán muchas fiestas alegres.

ANITA: ¿Cree que me tomarán por norteamericana? Espero que no.

ROSITA: Con el pelo negro, los ojos negros y los pies tan pequeños
20 usted pasará por cubana; pero al hablar, todos van a saber que usted es norteamericana. Ese acento que tiene es muy simpático, pero muy norteamericano.

ANITA: Me gustaría quedarme en México hasta la fiesta de los Reyes Magos, pero no debo perder los primeros días de clases.

25 ROSITA: Las fiestas del día de los Reyes Magos son para los niños. Los jóvenes celebramos más el día de Año Nuevo, el primero de enero, cuando las fiestas duran día y noche. ¡Nos divertiremos mucho!

ANITA: ¿Qué ropa debo llevar? No se permite llevar mucho equipaje en el avión.

30 ROSITA: En la ciudad de México se usa ropa de invierno; pero como iremos a Acapulco, a la playa, necesitaremos, también, ropa de primavera y trajes de baño. Ahora vamos a ver qué vestidos debemos escoger. Me gusta ese azul que tiene en la mano.

Así, hablando alegremente, las muchachas escogieron la ropa que
35 Anita debía llevar.

QUESTIONS

A. Answer in complete sentences in Spanish:

1. ¿En qué ha pensado Anita?
2. ¿Dónde pasará ella las vacaciones de Navidad?
3. ¿Con quién irá Anita?
4. ¿Cómo viajarán las muchachas?
5. ¿Es largo el viaje?
6. ¿Tiene Anita los pies grandes o pequeños?
7. ¿Cómo es el acento de ella?
8. ¿Qué ropa se usa en la ciudad de México?
9. ¿Por qué debe llevar el traje de baño?
10. ¿Qué día de enero se celebra el día de los Reyes Magos?

B. Personalized questions. Answer in complete sentences in Spanish:

1. ¿En qué mes estamos?
2. ¿Qué día es su cumpleaños?
3. ¿Quiere usted ir a la playa en el verano o en el invierno?
4. ¿Qué estación del año le gusta más?
5. ¿A qué hora volverá usted a casa?
6. ¿Tiene usted los ojos azules o negros?
7. ¿Cuánto tiempo le gustaría quedarse en México?
8. ¿Cuándo se celebra nuestro día de Independencia?
9. ¿A dónde quiere usted hacer un viaje este verano?
10. ¿Cómo viajaría a México?

C. Pregúntele a un amigo:

1. si ha pasado algún tiempo en México.
2. a dónde viajará este verano.
3. si le gustaría ir a Acapulco.
4. cuándo se celebra su cumpleaños.
5. si tiene los pies grandes.

GRAMMAR

62. Future Indicative of Regular Verbs

The future indicative of all regular verbs, whether ending in **-ar, -er** or **-ir,** is formed by adding the following endings to the infinitive:

SINGULAR	PLURAL
-é	-emos
-ás	-éis
-á	-án

Note that these endings are approximately the same as the present indicative of **haber,** from which they are derived.

Future of hablar, to speak

hablaré	*I shall speak*	hablaremos	*we shall speak*
hablarás	*you will speak*	hablaréis	*you will speak*
hablará	*you will speak*	hablarán	*you will speak*
hablará	*he, she will speak*	hablarán	*they will speak*

In the same way the future of **aprender** is **aprenderé,** etc., and of **vivir, viviré,** etc. Note the written accent over each of the endings except the first person plural.

63. Conditional Indicative of Regular Verbs

The conditional tense is formed by adding the following endings to the infinitive of all regular verbs. Note that these endings are the same as those used in forming the imperfect tense of **-er** and **-ir** verbs, and every form has a written accent on the **i.**

SINGULAR	PLURAL
-ía	**-íamos**
-ías	**-íais**
-ía	**-ían**

Conditional of hablar, to speak

hablaría	*I should speak*	hablaríamos	*we should speak*
hablarías	*you would speak*	hablaríais	*you would speak*
hablaría	*you would speak*	hablarían	*you would speak*
hablaría	*he, she would speak*	hablarían	*they would speak*

64. Use of the Future and Conditional Tenses

(*a*) The future and conditional tenses in Spanish are generally used as in English. The conditional may be thought of as a past future.

Él dice que irá.	*He says that he will go.*
Él dijo que iría.	*He said that he would go.*

(*b*) In Spanish the future tense may be used to indicate probability or conjecture in the present. The conditional indicates these ideas in the past.

¿Qué hora es?	*What time is it?*
Serán las once.	*It is probably (must be) eleven o'clock.*
¿Qué hora era?	*What time was it?*
Serían las tres.	*It must have been (probably was) three o'clock.*

101

65. Other Translations of *will* and *would*

Will and *would* in English may express ideas other than those given above. *Will*, expressing *to be willing*, is translated by **querer,** which in the negative may mean *to refuse to*. *Would not* (<u>*refused to*</u>) is expressed by the <u>preterite of **querer.**</u> However *would* meaning *used to* is expressed by the imperfect tense in Spanish. (See Lesson 7.)

¿Quiere usted ir conmigo?	*Will you go with me?*
Él no quiere hacerlo.	*He will not (refuses to) do it.*
Él no quiso entrar.	*He would not (refused to) enter.*
Yo la veía todos los días.	*I would (used to) see her every day.*

66. Special Uses of *se*

(*a*) **Se** is sometimes used with a verb as a substitute for the passive voice. This construction is often used when a thing is the subject of a verb in the passive voice in English. The subject usually follows the verb, which must agree with it in number.

En esta clase **se** habla español.	*Spanish is spoken in this class.*
Aquí **se** venden sombreros.	*Hats are sold here.*

(*b*) The reflexive third person **se** corresponds to indefinite subjects in English such as: *one, people, you, they.*

¿Cómo **se** dice en inglés?	*How do you say it in English?*
Se va por aquí.	*One goes (you go) this way.*
Se dice que lo ha vendido.	*People say that he has sold it.*
	(They say that he has sold it.)

67. Uses of the Definite Article

As has been learned previously, the definite article is used in Spanish with titles and names of languages (Lesson 1), hours of the day (Lesson 4) and days of the week (Lesson 9).

El doctor González vive aquí.	*Doctor González lives here.*
El francés se habla en Francia.	*French is spoken in France.*
Tomaremos el avión a las ocho.	*We shall take the plane at eight o'clock.*
Volveremos el lunes.	*We shall return on Monday.*

The definite article is also used with parts of the body, articles of clothing, seasons, dates and meals, and with nouns used in a general or abstract sense.

Ella tiene el pelo negro.	*She has dark (black) hair.*
Él levantará la mano.	*He will raise his hand.*
Ella llevará el traje de baño.	*She will take her bathing suit.*
Me gusta la primavera.	*I like spring.*
Llegaré el tres de enero.	*I shall arrive on January third.*
Tomo café en el desayuno.	*I drink coffee for breakfast.*
A ella le gustan los niños.	*She likes children.*
Los americanos aman la libertad.	*Americans love liberty.*

68. Seasons, Months and Days of the Month

la primavera	*spring*	el otoño	*autumn*
marzo	*March*	septiembre	*September*
abril	*April*	octubre	*October*
mayo	*May*	noviembre	*November*
el verano	*summer*	el invierno	*winter*
junio	*June*	diciembre	*December*
julio	*July*	enero	*January*
agosto	*August*	febrero	*February*

The cardinal numerals are used to express the days of the month, except the first (**primero**).

El primero de enero es el día de Año Nuevo.	*January first is New Year's Day.*
El dos de marzo es el día de mi cumpleaños.	*March second is my birthday.*

69. Expressions of Time

Tiempo is used to express time in a *general sense*; **hora,** to express *time of day*; and **vez** to express *time in a series.*

No tenemos tiempo.	*We don't have time.*
Es hora de comer.	*It is time to eat.*
La he visto una vez.	*I have seen her once.*
Habló muchas veces del viaje.	*She spoke often of the trip.*

EXERCISES

A. Change the italicized verb to the future, then to the conditional:

EXAMPLE: *Va* a México.
Irá a México.
Iría a México.

1. *Va* a México.
2. *Viajan* en avión.
3. *Compra* un sombrero.
4. *Aman* la libertad.
5. *Ven* a Anita.
6. A ella le *gusta* el viaje.
7. *Llevo* el traje de baño.
8. *Llevamos* poco equipaje.
9. Rosita *llega* el jueves.
10. Me *gusta* el pelo negro.

B. Change the date to a day later:

EXAMPLE: el treinta de abril
el primero de mayo

1. el treinta de abril
2. el primero de junio
3. el doce de agosto
4. el catorce de octubre
5. el treinta y uno de diciembre
6. el once de julio

C. Fill in the definite article when it is needed, and read in Spanish:

1. Viajaremos con _____ señor Martínez.
2. Iremos mañana a _____ ocho.
3. Estábamos hablando de _____ vida en México.
4. Ella no habla _____ inglés, pero habla bien _____ francés.
5. _____ jóvenes celebran más _____ primero de enero.
6. ¿Cuál le gusta más a usted, _____ verano o _____ otoño?
7. Hoy es _____ lunes. Voy a casa _____ sábado.
8. Los meses de _____ primavera son _____ marzo, _____ abril y _____ mayo.

D. Complete the following sentences by using one of the expressions in the column at the right:

1. Es ___8___ de levantarse.
2. No puedo ir a la playa porque no tengo ___5___.
3. Le he visto varias ___1___ esta semana.
4. ¿ ___2___ usted acompañarme a mi casa?
5. ¿Qué hora ___1___?
6. ___4___ las doce.

1. veces
2. quiere
3. se hace
4. serán
5. tiempo
6. se dice

7. Ella tiene ___10___ pequeñas.   7. será
8. Aquí ___9___ libros franceses y españoles.   8. hora
9. En la playa no ___3___ eso.   9. se venden
10. ¿Cómo ___6___ "summer" en español?   10. las manos

E. Write in Spanish, using the **se** construction as a substitute for the passive voice:

1. French is not spoken in this class.
2. The door was closed at five o'clock.
3. It is known that Charles will arrive tomorrow.
4. The letters were written yesterday.
5. The houses will be sold on Saturday.
6. Many errors are made.
7. Many cars are seen on the streets.
8. It is said that Spanish is easy.

F. Write in Spanish:

1. Anne will like Mexico.
2. She will have a good time.
3. Rose said that they would go to parties every night.
4. Let's take this blue dress.
5. Frank says it is probably nine o'clock.
6. Anne has dark eyes and hair.
7. Will Anne return (on) January first? She hopes so.
8. Will you come with me?
9. The house will be sold next Friday.
10. One sees many Cubans in Miami.

VOCABULARY

conseguir (i) *to get, obtain*
engañar *to deceive, cheat*
gastar *to spend*
pagar *to pay*

alguien *someone*
el baile *dance*
el billete *ticket*
ciento (cien) *a hundred*
la compra *purchase*
el cuidado *anxiety, worry*
durante *during*
el esposo *the husband*
el habitante *inhabitant*
los informes *information*
jamás *never, ever*
la joya *jewel*

el mediodía *noon*
nada *nothing*
nadie *no one*
ni... ni *neither . . . nor*
ninguno, -a *no one, none, no*
nunca *never, not . . . ever*
o... o *either . . . or*
el pasaporte *passport*
el perfume *perfume*
la plata *silver*
seguro, -a *sure*
la tarjeta *card*
la tarjeta de turista *tourist card*
tercero, -a *third*
típico, -a *typical*
u *or (before o or ho)*
el valor *value*

billete de ida y vuelta	*round trip ticket*
esta noche	*tonight*
habrá	*there will be*
los señores Walker	*Mr. and Mrs. Walker*
más tarde	*later*
no tendrán cuidado	*they will not be anxious or worried*
tener preguntas que hacer	*to have questions to ask*

LESSON FOURTEEN

MODEL SENTENCES

1. Los padres de Anita no sabían nada del viaje a México.
2. Nadie habría creído eso.
3. Carlos nunca vendrá los sábados. Ni Pancho tampoco.
4. Llegaremos el primer día de enero. Hará buen tiempo en México.
5. Ningún estudiante llegó tarde.

1. *Anne's parents didn't know anything about the trip to Mexico.*
2. *No one would have believed that.*
3. *Charles will never come on Saturdays. Neither will Frank.*
4. *We shall arrive on January first. The weather will be good in Mexico.*
5. *No student arrived late.*

EXPRESS IN SPANISH

1. I didn't know anything about Cuba. She will not buy anything in Mexico. She gave me nothing.
2. No one would have gone early. No one would have deceived Rose.
3. Charles will never do it. I shall not either. They will never be worried. Neither will Anne.
4. The first day of class will be difficult. The weather will be cold.
5. No Spanish book is easy. No flower is more beautiful than the rose.

Anita se divertirá mucho en México

Los padres de Anita, los señores Walker, tenían muchas preguntas que hacer a Rosita sobre el viaje a México. Dijeron que no sabían nada de ese país. Rosita vino a su casa a darles todos los informes que querían.

5   —¿Cuánto costará el billete de avión?—preguntó el señor Walker.
—Estoy seguro de que será más barato comprar un billete de ida y vuelta.

    —Un billete de ida y vuelta costará ciento ochenta dólares y noventa centavos. Saldremos de Atlanta a las once y cinco de la
10 mañana, estaremos en Nueva Orleans al mediodía y en la ciudad de México a la una y veinte y dos de la tarde. Anita no tendrá que llevar pasaporte, puede conseguir una tarjeta de turista.

    —Yo le daré a Anita cien dólares para gastar en México—dijo el señor Walker. —¿Qué podrá comprar ella?

15   —Anita podrá comprar artículos de plata, joyas, perfumes y cosas típicas de México. Querrá comprar de todo, pero yo la ayudaré en sus

compras. Nadie podrá engañarla, porque yo sé muy bien el valor de las cosas.

—¿Qué harán ustedes por la noche?—preguntó la madre de Anita.

20 —Habrá bailes u otras fiestas—explicó Rosita. —Anita estará conmigo o con algún miembro de mi familia todo el tiempo.

Los esposos Walker están muy contentos porque saben que Anita se divertirá mucho en México. Ellos no tendrán cuidado porque su hija estará con la familia Torres durante su visita.

QUESTIONS

A. Answer in complete sentences in Spanish:
1. ¿Quién vino a casa de los señores Walker?
2. ¿Cuánto costará el billete de ida y vuelta a la ciudad de México?
3. ¿A qué hora saldrán las muchachas de Atlanta?
4. ¿A qué hora llegarán a México?
5. ¿Se necesita pasaporte para el viaje?
6. ¿Cuánto dinero llevará Anita para gastar allí?
7. ¿Qué cosas podrá comprar ella?
8. ¿Quién le ayudará en sus compras?
9. ¿Qué harán las jóvenes por la noche?
10. ¿Por qué están contentos los señores Walker?

B. Personalized questions. Answer in complete sentences in Spanish:
1. ¿Cuándo irá usted a México?
2. ¿Cuánto le costaría un billete de ida y vuelta?
3. ¿Conoce usted a algún colombiano?
4. ¿Qué tiempo hará mañana?
5. ¿Cuándo saldrá usted de vacaciones?
6. ¿Quién tendrá que estudiar mucho el mes que viene?
7. ¿Ha llegado tarde a la clase su profesor?
8. ¿Cuándo se celebra el día de Año Nuevo?
9. ¿Qué compraría usted con cien dólares?
10. ¿A qué hora habrá entrado él en la clase?

C. Pregúntele a un amigo:
1. si vendrá temprano a la clase mañana.
2. si ha ido a México.

3. cuánto dinero gastaría para ir a un baile.
4. si pagaría veinte pesos por un sombrero en México.
5. cuánto cuesta un billete de ida y vuelta de aquí a su casa.

GRAMMAR

70. Irregular Future and Conditional Forms

All Spanish verbs use the regular future and conditional endings. However a few verbs form the future and conditional tenses on an irregular infinitive stem. These verbs may be divided into three groups according to the changes that occur in the infinitive.

(*a*) Two verbs have retained an old Spanish infinitive:

decir	diré	*I shall tell*	diría	*I should tell*
hacer	haré	*I shall do (make)*	haría	*I should do (make)*

(*b*) In the following verbs the **e** of the infinitive is dropped:

haber	habré	*I shall have*	habría	*I should have*
poder	podré	*I shall be able*	podría	*I should be able*
querer	querré	*I shall wish*	querría	*I should wish*
saber	sabré	*I shall know*	sabría	*I should know*

(*c*) In the following verbs a **d** is substituted for the vowel of the infinitive ending:

poner	pondré	*I shall put*	pondría	*I should put*
salir	saldré	*I shall leave*	saldría	*I should leave*
tener	tendré	*I shall have*	tendría	*I should have*
valer	valdré	*I shall be worth*	valdría	*I should be worth*
venir	vendré	*I shall come*	vendría	*I should come*

71. Future Perfect and Conditional Perfect Indicative

The future perfect is formed with the future of **haber** and a past participle; the conditional perfect is formed with the conditional of **haber** and a past participle.

FUTURE PERFECT

habré ⎫
habrás ⎬ hablado
habrá ⎭

habremos ⎫
habréis ⎬ hablado
habrán ⎭

CONDITIONAL PERFECT

habría ⎱		habríamos ⎱	
habrías ⎬ hablado		habríais ⎬ hablado	
habría ⎰		habrían ⎰	

The future perfect is translated *shall* or *will have spoken*. The conditional perfect is translated *should* or *would have spoken*.

Habré terminado antes de las ocho.	*I shall have finished before eight.*
Ella habría ido pero estaba enferma.	*She would have gone but she was sick.*

72. Indefinite and Negative Expressions

alguien	*someone, anyone*	nadie	*no one, nobody*
alguno, -a	*some, any*	ninguno, -a	*none, not any, no* for nouns
algo	*something, anything*	nada	*nothing*
también	*also*	tampoco	*neither*
o... o	*either . . . or*	ni... ni	*neither . . . nor*
		nunca, jamás	*never*

The indefinite expressions listed in the first column are used only in positive statements. In a negative statement the corresponding negative expression is used.

Creo que alguien ha venido.	*I think that someone has come.*
No vi a nadie.	*I did not see anyone.*
¿Sabe usted algo?	*Do you know something?*
Ella tampoco lo sabe.	*Neither does she know it.*
Nadie me lo ha dicho.	*No one has told me about it.*

In Spanish **no** or another negative expression must precede the verb in a negative sentence. Double negatives are common in Spanish, contrary to English usage. The following examples show that a negative sentence may be written in two ways.

No sé nada. Nada sé.	*I know nothing.*
Nadie vendrá. No vendrá nadie.	*No one will come.*
Nunca estudian. No estudian nunca.	*They never study.*

The PERSONAL ~~preposition~~ **a** is used with **nadie** and **alguien** when they are direct objects of a verb.

¿Conoció usted a alguien en la fiesta?
Did you meet anyone at the party?

No, yo no conocí a nadie.
No, I did not meet anyone.

73. Shortened Forms of Adjectives

(*a*) The final **-o** of certain adjectives is lost before masculine singular nouns. The most common of these adjectives are: **alguno, bueno, malo, ninguno, primero, tercero, uno. Algún** and **ningún** require an accent.

El martes es el tercer día.	*Tuesday is the third day.*
algún día... veinte y un días	*some day . . . twenty-one days*

(*b*) **Grande** shortens to **gran** before any singular noun, and **ciento** becomes **cien** before a noun or a number larger than itself.

Ella es una gran mujer.
She is a great woman.

Le daré cien dólares.
I shall give her a hundred dollars.

Vivo en una ciudad de cien mil habitantes.
I live in a city of a hundred thousand people.

EXERCISES

A. Change the italicized verb to the future, then to the conditional tense:

EXAMPLE: *Tengo* frío.
Tendré frío.
Tendría frío.

1. *Tengo* frío.
2. *Tiene* hambre.
3. No *tenemos* calor.
4. No *vale* nada.
5. Ella no *puede* hacerlo.
6. Lo *pongo* aquí.
7. Él no *quiere* ir.
8. *Hace* buen tiempo.
9. *Hay* tres aquí.
10. ¿Qué *dicen* ustedes?

B. Answer in the negative, using the words **nada, nadie, ninguno, -a, ni... ni** and **nunca:**

EXAMPLE: ¿Quería usted comprar algo?
No quería comprar nada.

1. ¿Quería usted comprar algo?
2. ¿Podrá ir alguien?
3. ¿Escribió usted algo en español?
4. ¿Conoce usted a alguien en México?

III

5. ¿Conoció Carlos a alguna muchacha en el baile anoche?
6. ¿Tiene María el libro o el cuaderno?
7. ¿Quién irá conmigo?
8. ¿Vendrá algún alumno antes de las ocho?
9. ¿Pagaría usted mucho por ese perfume?
10. ¿Cuándo aprenderán ustedes todos los verbos?

C. Use a shortened form of the adjective in the following sentences:

EXAMPLE: The weather will be good.
Hará buen tiempo.

1. The weather will be good.
2. Tomorrow we study the third chapter.
3. She would have been a great woman.
4. No student will arrive before eight.
5. Some Mexican would have understood it.
6. This month has thirty-one days.
7. He would have given me a hundred dollars.
8. The weather was bad yesterday.
9. She will arrive on the first day of the month.
10. Our president is a great man.

D. Give the proper form of **ser, estar, tener, hacer,** or **haber**:

1. (We will be) cansados.
2. Ella (was) alta y rubia.
3. (They were) en casa.
4. La señorita Blanco (is a) profesora.
5. (There would be) veinte alumnos.
6. Él (is) treinta años.
7. (They were) mucha hambre.
8. (We will be) mucho frío.
9. (I used to be) frío.
10. (It is) mucho calor.
11. (It was) mal tiempo.
12. (It will be) buen tiempo.

E. Write in Spanish:

1. No one had read the first chapter.
2. He said that the weather would be bad.
3. Tomorrow will be a great day.
4. Some day they will know something.
5. He wouldn't have done it either.
6. Someone will take a trip.
7. No student will come before eight.
8. Santa Teresa was a great woman.
9. He will not know anyone at the dance.
10. They will never say it.

[handwritten annotations:]
La palma real — the Royal Palm
humano, a — human
el isla — island
el general — general

VOCABULARY

acordarse (ue) (de) *to remember*
bailar *to dance*
comprender *to understand*
discutir *to discuss*
encantar *to charm, to fascinate*
preferir (ie) *to prefer*

el abanico *fan*
la belleza *beauty*
el cigarrillo *cigarette*
el concierto *concert*
cuarto, -a *fourth*
décimo, -a *tenth*
delante de *in front of*
despacio *slowly*
detrás de *behind*
la impresión *impression*
la luna *moon*
la luz (*pl.* luces) *light*
magnífico, -a *magnificent*
el mar *sea*
la montaña *mountain*
noveno, -a *ninth*
octavo, -a *eighth*

la página *page*
el parque *park*
el paseo *boulevard, walk*
el patio *courtyard, yard*
la pirámide *pyramid*
la pizarra *blackboard*
pobre *poor*
la prenda *piece of jewelry*
quinto, -a *fifth*
quisiera *should, would like*
la razón *reason*
romántico, -a *romantic*
el sarape *Mexican blanket*
segundo, -a *second*
séptimo, -a *seventh*
sexto, -a *sixth*
sin *without*
el sol *sun*
la tierra *land, country*
verde *green*
viejo, -a *old*
el viento *wind*
el volcán *volcano*
la voz (*pl.* voces) *voice*

[handwritten annotations:]
parecer — to seem
tratar to try
bajar to get down off

descubrir — to discover
amable — pleasant
el Capitolio

113

[handwritten: por todas partes - everywhere]
[handwritten: yo quisiera - I might (would should) like]

a la luz de la luna	*in the moonlight*
había luna	*the moon was shining*
había (hacía) sol	*the sun was shining*
hacía viento	*it was windy*
tienen razón	*they are right*
tomar baños de mar	*to go swimming*

[handwritten: a la vez - at the same time]
[handwritten: al mediodía - at noon]

MODEL SENTENCES

1. Ese joven leyó el primer capítulo.	1. *That young man read the first chapter.*
2. La señora trajo su abanico nuevo consigo. *[handwritten: ella]*	2. *The lady brought her new fan with her.*
3. El gran general no era un hombre grande.	3. *The noted general was not a large man.*
4. Ésta no es la décima lección; es la (lección) quince.	4. *This is not the tenth lesson; it is the fifteenth.*
5. Yo quisiera comprar flores para ella.	5. *I should like to buy flowers for her.*

EXPRESS IN SPANISH

1. Those blonde girls are good friends. That old woman lives in the third house.
2. The gentleman gave the poor boy a hundred dollars. The boy will go with him to buy new shoes and a new hat.
3. Charles and I have the same professor. The professor himself has never been in Spain.
4. This is my third cigarette today. That is the fifth for you.
5. I should like to dance with her. I should like to sit in front of him. I should like to return without them.

Impresiones de México

Anita volvió de México el dos de enero, trayendo muchas cosas bonitas. Entre ellas trajo un abanico y prendas de plata para su madre y un sarape verde y rojo para su padre. Estaban muy contentos.

El primer día Anita llegó tarde a la clase de español y no quería
5 entrar, porque oyó la voz del profesor García y comprendió que había empezado la clase. Cuando él la vio, la llamó y le dijo:

—Vd. puede entrar, señorita Walker. Hoy hablaremos sobre lo
que cada uno hizo durante las vacaciones de Navidad. Hágame el favor
de pasar a la pizarra y de escribir algo de sus impresiones de México.

10   Esto es lo que Anita escribió en la pizarra. Después todos lo
leyeron y lo discutieron con ella.

     —Las personas que dicen que México es una tierra de mucha
belleza tienen razón. Las altas montañas y los volcanes me encantaron,
como también las bellas flores que se ven en los parques, en los paseos,
15 en los patios y en el campo.

     Un día fuimos a Acapulco, donde tomamos baños de mar. En la
playa hacía mucho sol y mucho viento.

     El sitio histórico que más me gustó fue la magnífica Pirámide del
Sol. ¿Sabían Vds. que hay muchas pirámides en México?

20   Asistíamos por la noche a conciertos y bailes. Me acuerdo de que
una noche no bailé mucho porque había luna y yo preferí sentarme en
el patio a la luz de la luna—con un joven romántico. Ya Vds. ven que
me gustó mucho México y quisiera volver algún día.

QUESTIONS

A. Answer in complete sentences in Spanish:

    1. ¿Qué día volvió Anita de México?
    2. ¿Qué compró para su madre?
    3. Y ¿para su padre?
    4. ¿Por qué no quería entrar en la clase el primer día?
    5. ¿De qué tenía que escribir Anita en la pizarra?
    6. ¿Quiénes leyeron lo que ella escribió?
    7. ¿Dónde se ven flores?
    8. ¿Qué tiempo hacía en la playa?
    9. ¿Qué sitio histórico le gustó más a Anita?
   10. ¿A qué asistía por la noche?

B. Personalized questions. Answer in complete sentences in Spanish:

    1. ¿Cuántas páginas leyó usted anoche?
    2. ¿Trajo usted muchas cosas a la clase hoy?
    3. ¿Qué libro leyó usted la semana pasada?
    4. ¿Qué le gustaría escribir en la pizarra?
    5. ¿Quisiera usted asistir al concierto?

6. ¿Cuántos cigarillos ha fumado usted hoy?
7. ¿Prefiere usted las montañas o el mar?
8. ¿Cuál es el tercer día de la semana?
9. ¿Ha visto usted un volcán?
10. ¿Qué lección estamos estudiando ahora?

C. Pregúntele a un amigo:

1. quién está sentado cerca de él o de ella.
2. qué quisiera hacer esta noche.
3. si ha gastado mucho dinero hoy.
4. qué día será mañana.
5. quién está delante de la clase.

GRAMMAR

74. Preterite of *creer, leer* and *oir*

In Spanish an unaccented **i** between vowels is written **y.** The preterite of these verbs will contain a **y** in the third person singular and plural. Note the use of accents on the **i** so that the stress may fall on the preterite ending.

creer, *to believe*		**leer,** *to read*		**oir,** *to hear*	
creí	creímos	leí	leímos	oí	oímos
creíste	creísteis	leíste	leísteis	oíste	oísteis
creyó	creyeron	leyó	leyeron	oyó	oyeron

75. Prepositional Forms of Object Pronouns

Pronouns used as the object of a preposition were listed in the table of personal pronouns in Lesson 7, and have been used for clearness or emphasis in succeeding lessons. Note again that they have the same forms as the subject pronouns except in the first and second person singular forms.

mí	*me* or *myself*	nosotros, -as	*us* or *ourselves*
ti	*you* or *yourself*	vosotros, -as	*you* or *yourselves*
usted (Vd.)	*you*	ustedes (Vds.)	*you*
él	*him*	ellos	*them*
ella	*her*	ellas	*them*
sí	{ *yourself* *himself* *herself*	sí	{ *yourselves* *themselves*

Special forms with **con** are:

conmigo	*with me*
contigo	*with you*
consigo (*reflexive*)	*with himself, herself, yourself, themselves,* etc.

Some prepositions commonly used are:

para	*for* (destination, purpose)	lejos de	*far from*
por	*by, through, for the sake of*	menos	*except, but*
cerca de	*near*	detrás de	*behind*
entre	*between*	delante de	*in front of*
sin	*without*		

Lo trajeron para mí.	*They brought it for me.*
Se sentaron cerca de nosotros.	*They sat down near us.*
Él estaba sentado entre ellos.	*He was seated between them.*
Él lo hizo por ella.	*He did it for her sake.*

Exceptions to the above usage are:

entre usted y yo	*between you and me*
menos yo	*except me*

76. Ordinal Numbers

"o"
drop m.s.
before m.s.
nouns

1st	primero, -a	4th	cuarto, -a	8th	octavo, -a
2nd	segundo, -a	5th	quinto, -a	9th	noveno, -a
3rd	tercero, -a	6th	sexto, -a	10th	décimo, -a
		7th	séptimo, -a		

The ordinal numbers agree in number and gender with the nouns which they modify. They are used with chapters of books, names of streets, titles of royalty, etc., but are ordinarily not used above the tenth. Above this they are replaced by cardinal numbers, which follow the noun. Remember that **primero** and **tercero** drop the final **o** before masculine singular nouns.

la primera vez, el primer libro	*the first time, the first book*
el segundo capítulo	*the second chapter*
Carlos Quinto	*Charles the Fifth*
la calle veinte y dos	*twenty-second street*
la página catorce	*the fourteenth page*

117

Remember that **primero** is used with the first day of the month, and that cardinal numbers are used with the other days. (Lesson 13.)

77. Notes on the Position of Adjectives

(*a*) An adjective precedes the noun that it modifies (1) if it tells how many or which; (2) if it describes qualities which the noun is expected to have:

(1) cuatro sombreros, muchas plumas	*four hats, many pens*
esos hombres	*those men*
(2) las altas montañas	*the high mountains*
mis buenos amigos	*my good friends*

(*b*) An adjective follows the noun it modifies if it distinguishes it from another of the same class.

un libro azul	*a blue book* (not a red one)
una muchacha rubia	*a blonde* (not a brunette)

(*c*) A few adjectives change their meaning according to whether they precede or follow the nouns they modify. Preceding a noun, these adjectives have a subjective or figurative meaning, and following the noun they have the literal or objective meaning. Illustrations of a few of these are:

el gran hombre	*the great man*
un hombre grande	*a large man*
el Nuevo Mundo	*the New World*
un sombrero nuevo	*a new hat* (just bought)
el pobre niño	*the poor boy* (unfortunate)
el niño pobre	*the poor boy* (not rich)
el mismo profesor	*the same professor*
el profesor mismo	*the professor himself*

78. Adjectives as Nouns

An adjective may be used as a noun when it is preceded by an article or a demonstrative adjective.

el viejo	*the old man*
esa joven	*that young girl*

118

EXERCISES

A. Supply the proper Spanish prepositional form for the English pronouns in parentheses:

EXAMPLE: Anita compró perfume para (me).
Anita compró perfume para mí.

1. Anita compró perfume para (me).
2. Yo iré al cine con (him).
3. ¿Quisiera usted comer con (me)?
4. Carlos dijo que no saldría sin (her).
5. María prefería sentarse detrás de (us).
6. Estábamos sentados delante de (you, *fam.*).
7. Su padre siempre hizo mucho por (him).
8. Vivimos lejos de (them).
9. ¿Quién es ese muchacho delante de (you)?
10. Nuestro profesor vive cerca de (you, *pl.*).

B. Give the proper form of **grande**:

1. Nueva York es una ciudad muy _____.
2. Alfonso Décimo fue un _____ rey.
3. Nuestros dormitorios son edificios _____.
4. España ha tenido muchos _____ hombres.
5. Creo que tenemos un _____ profesor.

C. Substitute pronoun or proper name for italicized subject, making proper verb change:

EXAMPLE: *Yo* lo leí bien.
María lo leyó bien.

1. *Yo* lo leí bien.
María, nosotros, ustedes

2. *Él* lo oyó muchas veces.
yo, usted, Carlos y Pancho

3. *Ellos* no creyeron nada.
él y yo, usted, yo

4. *Ella* está leyendo ahora.
María y él, yo, Anita y yo

5. *María* no ha oído al profesor.
ustedes, nosotros, yo

6. *Julio* nunca habría creído eso.
María y yo, el señor Pérez, ellos

7. *Rosita* no había leído el primer capítulo.
nosotros, ellos, él

8. *José* vendrá el primero de enero.
Anita y yo, sus padres, María

9. *La señora Pérez* habrá llegado a las diez.
nosotros, yo, ustedes

10. *El viejo* quería hablar conmigo.
la joven, los viejos, el pobre

For Friday **D.** Give the Spanish for the following expressions, then use each expression in a short sentence in Spanish:

1. see you later
2. I hope so
3. two weeks
4. let's see

5. everywhere
6. perhaps
7. next summer

8. at the same time
9. of course
10. please help me

E. Write in Spanish:

(a)
1. the 15th of February
2. the 4th of July
3. the first of March
4. the third man
5. the seventh lesson

6. the thirteenth page
7. Fifteenth Street
8. the first day
9. first impressions
10. the second dance

(b)
1. At three o'clock they heard the plane.
2. Yesterday they read the article.
3. That young girl dances well.
4. In the winter the sun does not shine every day.
5. It is windy at night.
6. I like to sit in the yard in the moonlight.
7. The fifth book was more difficult than this one.
8. You are right; it was much more difficult.
9. Those old men like to go to the park.
10. Charles and Frank will have the same professor.

Monday test Ch. # 14 -15

invitar (a + inf.) to invite (a person to do something)

VOCABULARY

alegre happy

aceptar	*to accept*	arriba	*up, upstairs*
bajar	*to come down*	el biftec	*steak*
desear	*to desire, to want*	la bondad	*kindness*
despedirse de (i, i)	*to say good-bye*	el café	*café*
despertarse (ie)	*to wake up*	el cheque	*check*
divertirse (ie, i)	*to have a good time*	divertido, -a	*amusing*
dormir (ue, u)	*to sleep*	excelente	*excellent*
dormirse (ue, u)	*to go to sleep*	la función	*performance*
importar	*to matter*	el helado	*ice cream*
morir (ue, u)	*to die*	la heroína	*heroine*
parecer	*to seem*	el maíz	*corn*
pedir (i, i)	*to ask for, order*	la película	*film*
preferir (ie, i)	*to prefer*	la roseta de maíz	*popcorn*
recibir	*to receive*	el saco	*sack, bag*
repetir (i, i)	*to repeat*	la sorpresa	*surprise*
sentir (ie, i)	*to be sorry, regret,* to feel	el taxi	*taxicab*
sentirse (ie, i)	*to feel* (well, etc.)	el teatro	*theater*
servir (i, i)	*to serve*	el teléfono	*telephone*
vestirse (i, i)	*to dress*	todavía	*still, yet*

en seguida	*at once*
lo siento	*I am sorry*
llamar por teléfono	*to telephone*
no le importó mucho	*it didn't matter much to him*
para gran sorpresa suya	*to his great surprise*
tenga la bondad de + *inf.*	*please* + verb

have the ↑ kindness of

121

MODEL SENTENCES

1. Se divirtieron mucho en el café.	1. *They had a very good time in the café.*
2. Pedro pidió un biftec pero María pidió helado.	2. *Peter ordered a steak but Mary ordered ice cream.*
3. Ella saldrá a las nueve para comprar algo para su madre.	3. *She will leave at nine in order to buy something for her mother.*
4. No podemos pasar por Nueva Orleans. Lo siento mucho.	4. *We can't go through New Orleans. I am very sorry.*
5. Pedro se acostó y se durmió en seguida.	5. *Peter went to bed and went to sleep at once.*

EXPRESS IN SPANISH

1. She had a good time at (**en**) the dance. Did you have a good time last night? Yes, we had a very good time.
2. They ordered a steak. They served good ice cream in that restaurant.
3. I shall leave early in order to buy something for my father. Will he buy cigarettes for you?
4. We cannot go through New York. We are very sorry. They could not go through San Antonio. He was very sorry.
5. They went to bed and went to sleep. I went to bed and went to sleep.

Una noche de diversión

Pedro estaba muy alegre porque había recibido un cheque de su padre. En seguida llamó a María por teléfono para invitarla a ir al cine con él aquella noche. María aceptó con mucho gusto, y a las siete y media Pedro llegó a su casa. Él encontró a la madre de María en la
5 puerta.

—María está todavía arriba vistiéndose, Pedro. Lo siento, pero Vd. sabe bien que las muchachas necesitan mucho tiempo para vestirse. Creo que ella bajará en un momento.

Después de media hora María y Pedro salieron para ir al cine.
10 María quería ir en taxi y esto no le importó mucho a Pedro porque él se sentía rico. Pedro deseaba ver una película divertida, pero María prefirió una muy triste en que la heroína murió. Durante la función María comió dos sacos de rosetas de maíz y tomó dos coca colas.

LESSON SIXTEEN

Al salir del teatro Pedro le preguntó a María si quería ir a un café
15 antes de volver a casa. Para gran sorpresa suya ella le contestó que
tendría mucho gusto en acompañarle. Fueron a un café donde se
servían helados excelentes. María pidió un biftec pequeño y un helado.
Todo el mundo en el café parecía divertirse mucho menos Pedro, que
ya no se sentía rico.
20   Cuando María se despidió de Pedro le dijo: —Muchas gracias
por todo. Me divertí muchísimo. Tenga la bondad de llamarme otra
vez muy pronto.

QUESTIONS

A. Answer in complete sentences in Spanish:

    1. ¿Por qué estaba alegre Pedro?
    2. ¿Por qué llamó a María?
    3. ¿A qué hora llegó Pedro a casa de María?
    4. ¿Quién estaba en la puerta?
    5. ¿Dónde estaba María?
    6. ¿Bajó ella en seguida?
    7. ¿Qué clase de película prefirió María?
    8. ¿Qué comió ella durante la función?
    9. ¿Qué pidió en el café?
    10. ¿Quién no parecía divertirse en el café?

B. Personalized questions. Answer in complete sentences in Spanish:

    1. ¿A qué hora se durmió usted anoche?
    2. ¿Pagaría usted cinco dólares por un biftec?
    3. ¿Cuándo quisiera usted salir para México?
    4. ¿Ha visto usted una película divertida?
    5. ¿Se siente usted bien esta mañana (tarde)?
    6. ¿Dónde se sirven helados excelentes?
    7. ¿Se visten rápidamente las señoritas?
    8. ¿Qué hace usted para divertirse?
    9. ¿Viene usted a la escuela en taxi?
    10. ¿Compró usted algo para su madre?

C. Pregúntele a un amigo:

    1. si se divirtió anoche.   4. si ha recibido un cheque.
    2. a qué hora se acostó.   5. qué pide en un café.
    3. si se duerme en seguida.

123

GRAMMAR

79. Stem-changing Verbs

(a) *Class I* (Review Lesson 8). Common verbs in this class are:

acordarse (de) (ue)	*to remember*	entender (ie)	*to understand*
acostarse (ue)	*to go to bed*	jugar (ue)	*to play* (a game)
cerrar (ie)	*to close*	llover (ue)	*to rain*
contar (ue)	*to tell, count*	pensar (ie)	*to think, plan, intend*
comenzar (ie)	*to begin*	perder (ie)	*to lose*
costar (ue)	*to cost*	rogar (ue)	*to beg*
despertarse (ie)	*to wake up*	sentarse (ie)	*to sit down*
empezar (ie)	*to begin*	sonar (ue)	*to sound, ring*
encontrar (ue)	*to find*	volver (ue)	*to return*

(b) *Class II.* Class II stem-changing verbs have the infinitive ending **-ir**, and the present indicative changes as do verbs of Class I; that is, **e** to **ie** and **o** to **ue** when the vowel is under stress.

PRESENT TENSE

sentir (ie, i), *to feel, regret*		**dormir (ue, u)**, *to sleep*	
siento	sentimos	duermo	dormimos
sientes	sentís	duermes	dormís
siente	sienten	duerme	duermen

Verbs of this class have an additional change in the preterite. The last vowel of the stem changes **e** to **i** and **o** to **u** in the third person singular and plural. The preterite endings are regular.

PRETERITE

sentir (ie, i)		**dormir (ue, u)**	
sentí	sentimos	dormí	dormimos
sentiste	sentisteis	dormiste	dormisteis
sintió	sintieron	durmió	durmieron

Verbs in Class II are indicated in the vocabulary as follows: **(ie, i)**, **(ue, u)**. Common verbs in this class are:

divertirse (ie, i)	*to have a good time*	morir (ue, u)	*to die*
dormir (ue, u)	*to sleep*	preferir (ie, i)	*to prefer*
dormirse (ue, u)	*to go to sleep*	sentir (ie, i)	*to feel, to regret*
mentir (ie, i)	*to lie*		

(c) *Class III.* Class III stem-changing verbs also have the infinitive ending **-ir,** and change in the same persons in the present and preterite indicative as do Class II verbs. The difference is that the change is **e** to **i** always.

pedir (i, i), *to ask for, to request, to order*

PRESENT		PRETERITE	
pido	pedimos	pedí	pedimos
pides	pedís	pediste	pedisteis
pide	piden	pidió	pidieron

Verbs in this class are indicated as follows: **(i, i).** Common verbs are:

conseguir (i, i) *to get, to obtain*

despedirse (i, i) de *to say goodbye, to take leave of*

pedir (i, i) *to ask for, to order* (a meal, etc.)

reírse (i, i) *to laugh*

repetir (i, i) *to repeat*

seguir (i, i) *to continue, to follow*

servir (i, i) *to serve*

vestir (i, i) *to dress*

vestirse (i, i) *to dress* (one's self)

(d) The present participles of the verbs of Class II and Class III take the same change as is found in the third person plural of the preterite tense of the verb.

divertirse (ie, i)	(se divirtieron)	divirtiéndose	*having a good time*
dormir (ue, u)	(durmieron)	durmiendo	*sleeping*
morir (ue, u)	(murieron)	muriendo	*dying*
pedir (i, i)	(pidieron)	pidiendo	*asking for, ordering*
sentir (ie, i)	(sintieron)	sintiendo	*feeling, regretting*
vestirse (i, i)	(se vistieron)	vistiéndose	*dressing* (one's self)

80. Uses of *para* and *por*

(a) *The preposition **para** is used:*

(1) before the person for whom something is intended

Traje un vestido para Anita.   *I brought a dress for Anne.*

(2) to express purpose or use

Estudio para aprender.   *I study in order to learn.*

Quiero un vaso para agua.   *I want a water glass.*

(3) to express destination

Salen mañana para Cuba.   *They are leaving tomorrow for Cuba.*

(4) <u>to express a fixed time in the future</u>

Estarán aquí para las seis.   *They will be here <u>by</u> six o'clock.*

(*b*) *The preposition <u>**por** is used to express</u>:*

(1) <u>duration of time</u>

Llovió por cuarenta días.   *It rained for forty days.*

(2) <u>*for* in the sense of *because of, in exchange for, for the sake of*</u>

No compró nada por falta de dinero.
She didn't buy anything because of lack of money.

Di cinco pesos por el sombrero.
I gave five dollars for the hat.

Lo harán por él.
They will do it for his sake.

(3) <u>agency</u>

El libro fue escrito por Martí.   *The book was written <u>by</u> Martí.*

(4) <u>along, by, through, around</u>

Íbamos por la Calle Quince.	*We were going along Fifteenth Street.*
Viajarán por avión.	*They will travel by plane.*
Pasarán por Miami.	*They will pass through Miami.*
María está por aquí.	*Mary is around here.*

EXERCISES

A. Substitute pronoun or proper name for the italicized subject, making the necessary verb changes.

EXAMPLE: *Yo* me despedí de ellos.
           Pedro se despidió de ellos.

1. *Yo* me despedí de ellos.
   Pedro, ella, nosotros, usted

2. *El niño* durmió ocho horas.
   María, ustedes, yo, Carlos y yo

3. *Ellos* repitieron la palabra.
   Anita, nosotros, usted, yo

4. *Los jóvenes* se divirtieron en el baile.
   José, mi madre, María y yo

5. *María* prefirió una película triste.
   yo, Pancho, nosotros, ellos

B. Change the following verbs to the preterite tense:

1. pido	5. pierden	8. me despierto
2. se siente	6. nos vestimos	9. prefiere
3. duermo	7. se sirve	10. se ríe
4. se divierten		

C. Give in Spanish:

1. four difficult rules	5. her good friends	8. a red flower
2. many blonde girls	6. the 20th of July	9. the third house
3. the same day	7. that poor boy (unfortunate)	10. a new dress
4. these young men		

D. Complete these sentences by using **para** or **por**:

1. El helado es _____ María.
2. ¿Cuánto pagó Ud. _____ el billete de ida y vuelta?
3. Salgo mañana _____ México.
4. Estarán aquí _____ las cinco.
5. Durmió _____ ocho horas.
6. Caminábamos _____ la calle.
7. Ellos querían pasar _____ Jacksonville.
8. Este cheque fue escrito _____ mi padre.
9. No pude jugar con ellos _____ falta de tiempo.
10. Ellos viajan _____ divertirse.

E. Write in Spanish:

1. Feeling rich, Charles ordered a steak.
2. Charles said good-bye to Mary and returned home.
3. She awoke and dressed before seven o'clock.
4. We will leave tomorrow for New Orleans.
5. I sat down at the table and asked for bacon and eggs.
6. She would have paid fifty dollars for that dress.
7. Please give us our money.
8. The professor himself repeated the sentence.
9. I preferred to dance, but she preferred to eat.
10. Frank went to sleep immediately but he didn't sleep well.

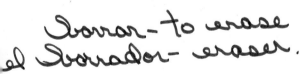

borrar - to erase
el borrador - eraser.

VOCABULARY

cultivar *to cultivate, raise*
dejar *to leave*
gritar *to shout*
interesar *to interest*
llover (ue) *to rain*
olvidarse (de) *to forget*
ordeñar *to milk*
responder *to reply*
sonar (ue) *to ring, sound*

la abuela *grandmother*
el abuelo *grandfather*
la abundancia *abundance*
amable *pleasant, kind*
el animal *animal*
el árbol *tree*
la bienvenida *welcome*
el caballo *horse*
la cámara fotográfica *camera*
el comedor *dining room*
chico, -a *little, small*
Chico *name of a dog*

el deseo *desire, wish*
el despertador *alarm clock*
especialmente *especially*
la finca *farm*
la fruta *fruit*
el gato *cat*
las legumbres *vegetables*
listo, -a *ready*
la maleta *suitcase*
la manzana *apple*
la máquina *machine*
Misi *name of a cat*
el paseo *walk or ride*
la pera *pear*
el perro (perrito) *dog (little dog)*
el pollo *chicken*
el regalo *present, gift*
la sala *living room*
la silla *chair*
temprano *early*
la uva *grape*
la vaca *cow*

al día siguiente *on the following day*
a mano *by hand*
dar la bienvenida *to welcome*

la cámara — chamber

dar un paseo	*to take a walk or ride*
fin de semana	*weekend*
hacer la maleta	*to pack the suitcase*
por eso	*for that reason, therefore*
tener deseos de	*to be eager to*

MODEL SENTENCES

1. Levántese Vd. y venga conmigo.
2. Enséñenme Vds. las vacas. Enséñen-melas Vds.
3. No se olvide Vd. de comprar la cámara fotográfica.
4. Carlos tiene dinero, que lo compre él.
5. Hablemos español en esta clase. Hablémoslo siempre.

1. *Get up and come with me.*
2. *Show me the cows. Show them to me.*
3. *Don't forget to buy the camera.*
4. *Charles has some money, let him buy it.*
5. *Let's speak Spanish in this class. Let's speak it always.*

EXPRESS IN SPANISH

1. Get up and give me the book. Read the verbs and write them.
2. Show us the chickens. Show them to us. Bring me the grapes. Bring them to me.
3. Do not forget to bring the present. Do not forget to bring it.
4. Joe is coming soon, let him bring it. Frank has time, let him do it.
5. Let's visit your grandfather's farm. Let's visit it.

En la finca

José Montenegro, de Bogotá, Colombia, tiene muchos deseos de visitar una casa de campo en los Estados Unidos. Por eso Pancho le ha invitado a ir con él a la finca de sus abuelos cerca del pueblo donde ellos estudian. Harán el viaje en autobús. Como tendrán que salir temprano
5 por la mañana, los muchachos hacen las maletas antes de acostarse.

A las siete de la mañana suena el despertador. —Levántese Vd., José,—gritó Pancho. —¡Ya es hora de vestirnos! No se olvide de poner la cámara fotográfica en la maleta. Y déme el paquete que está en esa silla, es un regalo que llevo a mis abuelos. ¿Ya está listo? ¡Venga!
10 Traiga la maleta.

Cuando ellos llegaron a la finca la abuela les dio la bienvenida y los hizo pasar al comedor para tomar un buen desayuno, diciéndoles:

—Dejen Vds. las maletas en la sala. Vengan a desayunarse. Vds. habrán tomado el desayuno muy temprano y tendrán hambre. Coman
15 bien y después vayan a buscar al abuelo. Y lleven el perrito con Vds. Se llama Chico y le gustará mucho acompañarles. Este gato se queda conmigo, ¿no es verdad, Misi?

A José le interesaron mucho los animales de la finca, especialmente las vacas y los pollos. Había miles de éstos, todos blancos.
20 —Abuelo—dijo Pancho—enseñe a José cómo se ordeñan las vacas con máquina. En la finca de sus padres todo el trabajo se hace a mano.

—Con mucho gusto—respondió el abuelo. —Luego vayan Vds. por la finca para ver los árboles y las legumbres. Se cultivan las legum-
25 bres que necesitamos para la mesa, y hay abundancia de peras, uvas, manzanas y otras frutas. Pancho, lleve a su amigo a ver los caballos. Si no llueve pueden dar un paseo por la tarde.

Al día siguiente cuando Pancho y José se despidieron de los abuelos, José les dijo:
30 —Muchísimas gracias por una visita muy interesante. Vengan Vds. a verme en nuestra finca en Colombia algún día. ¡Adiós!

—¡Adiós, José! Venga Vd. con Pancho otro fin de semana—le contestaron.

QUESTIONS

A. Answer in complete sentences in Spanish:

1. ¿De dónde es José Montenegro?
2. ¿A dónde van él y Pancho?
3. ¿Cómo harán el viaje?
4. ¿Cuándo hicieron las maletas?
5. ¿A qué hora se levantaron ellos el día del viaje?
6. Cuando llegaron a la finca, ¿quién les dio la bienvenida?
7. ¿Dónde dejaron las maletas?
8. ¿Qué animales le interesaron mucho a José?
9. ¿Qué frutas se cultivaban en la finca?
10. ¿Cómo se llama el perro del abuelo de Pancho?

B. Personalized questions. Answer in complete sentences in Spanish:

1. ¿Vive su abuelo en el campo?
2. ¿Tiene Vd. animales en casa?
3. ¿Prefiere Vd. un perro o un gato?
4. ¿Le gustaría visitar una finca en el invierno?
5. ¿Qué hace Vd. cuando llueve?
6. ¿Quisiera Vd. hacer un viaje en autobús?
7. ¿A qué hora suena su despertador?
8. ¿Qué hará Vd. este fin de semana?
9. ¿Qué frutas le gustan a Vds.?
10. ¿Por qué son importantes las vacas?

C. Pregúntele a un amigo:

1. cómo se llama su perro o gato.
2. si come legumbres todos los días.
3. si ha escrito todos los ejercicios.

4. si se levantará temprano mañana.
5. qué se cultiva en una finca.

GRAMMAR

81. The Present Subjunctive of Regular Verbs

The present subjunctive of regular verbs is formed from the first person singular of the present indicative. Drop the **-o** and add the following endings:

For **-ar** verbs: **-e, -es, -e, -emos, -éis, -en**
For **-er** and **-ir** verbs: **-a, -as, -a, -amos, -áis, -an**

Present Subjunctive of **hablar** and **aprender**

hablar		**aprender**	
(que) hable	(que) hablemos	(que) aprenda	(que) aprendamos
(que) hables	(que) habléis	(que) aprendas	(que) aprendáis
(que) hable	(que) hablen	(que) aprenda	(que) aprendan

The subjunctive has so many uses that there is no regular translation for the present subjunctive. A single verb form may be translated thus:

(que) hable   (*that*) *I may speak*
(que) aprendan   (*that*) *they may learn*

131

82. The Present Subjunctive of Irregular Verbs

(*a*) The present subjunctive of most irregular verbs is formed in the same way as is shown above.

INFINITIVE	PRESENT INDICATIVE	PRESENT SUBJUNCTIVE
conocer	conozco	conozca, conozcas, conozca, conozcamos, etc.
decir	digo	diga, digas, diga, digamos, etc.
hacer	hago	haga, hagas, haga, hagamos, etc.
oir	oigo	oiga, oigas, oiga, oigamos, etc.
poner	pongo	ponga, pongas, ponga, pongamos, etc.
tener	tengo	tenga, tengas, tenga, tengamos, etc.
ver	veo	vea, veas, vea, veamos, etc.

(*b*) Irregular verbs which do not follow this form are:

dar	dé, des, dé, demos, deis, den
estar	esté, estés, esté, estemos, estéis, estén
haber	haya, hayas, haya, hayamos, hayáis, hayan
ir	vaya, vayas, vaya, vayamos, vayáis, vayan
saber	sepa, sepas, sepa, sepamos, sepáis, sepan
ser	sea, seas, sea, seamos, seáis, sean

83. Uses of the Present Subjunctive

The present subjunctive is used:

(*a*) In direct commands.

The third person singular or plural is used with **Vd.** or **Vds.** to express the polite or formal commands. Object pronouns and reflexive pronouns follow and are attached to an affirmative command, but precede a negative command. Thus the polite command forms of (1) **aprenderla,** (2) **levantarse** and (3) **decírmelo** are:

(1) Apréndala Vd.	Apréndanla Vds.	*Learn it.*
No la aprenda Vd.	No la aprendan Vds.	*Do not learn it.*
(2) Levántese Vd.	Levántense Vds.	*Get up!*
No se levante Vd.	No se levanten Vds.	*Don't get up!*
(3) Dígamelo Vd.	Díganmelo Vds.	*Tell me about it.*
No me lo diga Vd.	No me lo digan Vds.	*Don't tell me about it.*

(See Appendix, § 110, for the familiar commands or imperatives.)

(*b*) In indirect commands.

Que + the third person singular or plural of the present subjunctive expresses an indirect command, translated variously as *let, have,* or *may*. In indirect commands object pronouns and reflexive pronouns precede the verb. A noun or pronoun used as the subject will follow the verb.

Que lo haga él.	*Let him do it.*
Que los compre Anita.	*Have Anne buy them.*
Que tenga Vd. suerte.	*May you be lucky. (I hope you are lucky.)*
Que no vaya a la escuela hoy.	*Don't have him go to school today.*

(*c*) To express *let us.*

The first person plural of the present subjunctive, without **que**, expresses *let us*. Since this is a direct command, object pronouns follow the rule given in (*a*) above. In reflexive verbs the final **-s** of the verb is dropped before **-nos**.

Escribamos los ejercicios.	*Let's write the exercises.*
Escribámoslos.	*Let's write them.*
No los escribamos.	*Let's not write them.*
Sentémonos.	*Let's sit down.*
No nos levantemos.	*Let's not get up.*

Remember (Lesson 13) that *let us* may also be expressed by **vamos a** + the infinitive.

Vamos a abrir la ventana.	*Let's open the window.*

EXERCISES

A. Read in Spanish, then add a formal or polite command:

EXAMPLE: Quiero comerlas.   ¿Puedo venderlos?
           Pues, cómalas Vd.   Sí, véndalos.

1. Quiero comerlas.
2. Quiero dárselas a Vds.
3. Quiero escribirlos.
4. Quiero hacerlo.
5. Queremos levantarnos.

6. ¿Puedo venderlos?
7. ¿Puedo enseñárselas a él?
8. ¿Puedo decírselo a Vds.?
9. ¿Puedo dejarla?
10. ¿Puedo llevarlo?

133

p. 110-115 in lab. manual

B. In these negative commands substitute object pronouns for noun objects:

> EXAMPLE: No dé el paquete a José.
>   No se lo dé.

1. No dé el paquete a José
2. No grite su nombre.
3. No deje a su amiga.
4. No me traiga el gato.
5. No ponga los libros aquí.
6. No compre flores para mí.
7. No invite a Carlos.
8. No lea las palabras.
9. No abra la puerta.
10. No compre las legumbres.

C. Change the following commands to the plural:

> EXAMPLE: Ponga sus libros aquí.
>   Pongan sus libros aquí.

1. Ponga sus libros aquí.
2. Haga bien su trabajo.
3. Déme cincuenta dólares.
4. Tenga la bondad de venir.
5. Oiga la música.
6. Vaya al concierto.
7. Esté aquí para las siete.
8. Salga de casa ahora.
9. Traiga a su amigo.
10. Venga a la clase temprano.

D. Write in Spanish:

1. Study the lessons. Study them.
2. Eat the vegetables. Eat them.
3. Let Joe do it. Have him come tonight.
4. Let's sit down. Let's get up.
5. Let's take the dog with us.
6. Tell it to me. Don't tell it to her.
7. After eating breakfast, pack the suitcases.
8. He is eager to see the horses.
9. There were thousands of white chickens.
10. Many vegetables are raised here.

learn

VOCABULARY

acabar   *to finish, end*
comenzar (ie)   *to begin*
limpiar   *to clean*
llevar   *to wear*
mandar   *to command, send,* ORDER
molestar   *to trouble*
notar   *to notice, note*
quedar   *to remain, be left*
temer   *to be afraid*
Miado - FEAR

la carne   *meat*
la carnicería   *butcher shop*

la cocina   *kitchen*
corto, -a   *short*
cualquier(a)   *any*
especial   *special*
la esposa   *wife*
el huésped   *guest*
inesperado, -a   *unexpected*
limpio, -a   *clean*
el negocio   *business*
nervioso, -a   *nervous*
las noticias   *news*
la toalla   *towel*
la venida   *arrival, coming* (llegada)

acabar de + *inf.*   *to have just*
lo mismo   *the same thing*
no tenga cuidado   *don't worry*
pase Vd.   *come in*
ponerse nervioso   *to become nervous*
quedarle (a ella)   *to be left* (for her)
todo lo necesario   *all that is necessary*
Vd. está en su casa   *you are welcome here,*
   make yourself at home

135

MODEL SENTENCES

1. Queremos que el Sr. González coma con nosotros.
2. Siento que Vds. no estén aquí.
3. Ella le pide a María que sirva la comida.
4. Mi madre no quiere que yo duerma tarde.
5. Él se alegrará de que yo venga.

1. *We want Mr. González to eat with us.*
2. *I am sorry that you are not here.*
3. *She asks Mary to serve the meal.*
4. *My mother doesn't want me to sleep late.*
5. *He will be glad that I am coming.*

EXPRESS IN SPANISH

1. She wants Mary to eat with them. Do you want us to do it?
2. She is sorry that they are not here. They are sorry that Charles doesn't study. We are sorry that no one is coming.
3. They ask Anne to return early. She tells us to buy it. I shall tell them to do it.
4. They don't want us to sleep late. He doesn't want Rose to read it.
5. We are glad that you are coming. She hopes that I will understand it. I am afraid that he will leave.

Un huésped inesperado

A las cuatro de la tarde el señor Pérez llamó a su esposa para decirle que iba a traer un huésped a casa a comer aquella noche. Un hombre de negocios muy importante acababa de llegar y el señor Pérez no quiere que este señor coma en un restaurante su primera noche en la
5 ciudad.

—Siento que tú no tengas más tiempo para preparar la comida— le dijo el señor Pérez a su esposa. —No quiero que prepares una comida especial. Lo mismo que comemos cualquiera otra noche.

Con estas noticias la señora Pérez se ha puesto muy nerviosa.
10 Naturalmente ella quiere servir una comida excelente y desea que su casa esté muy limpia para este huésped importante. Por eso comienza a hacer todo lo necesario en el corto tiempo que le queda antes de la comida. Le dice a Julio que vaya a una carnicería donde se vende carne muy buena; manda a María que limpie la sala y que ponga toallas
15 limpias en el cuarto de baño. Isabel le ayudará en la cocina.

136

—Espero que este señor no entre en la cocina ni en los otros cuartos. No tenemos tiempo para limpiar toda la casa—pensó la señora Pérez.

A las seis el señor Pérez llega con el huésped. No nota que la casa
20 está muy limpia y que su esposa lleva un vestido nuevo.

—Pase Vd., señor González. Vd. está en su casa.

—Muchas gracias. Vd. es muy amable. Me alegro mucho de estar aquí. Espero que mi venida no le moleste.

—No tenga cuidado—dijo el señor Pérez. —Mi esposa no ha
25 hecho nada especial. Ella dice siempre que una persona más no importa.

QUESTIONS

A. Answer in complete sentences in Spanish:

    1. ¿Por qué llamó el Sr. Pérez a su esposa?
    2. ¿Por qué quiere traer al huésped a casa?
    3. ¿Cómo se ha puesto la señora Pérez con estas noticias?
    4. ¿Qué le dice ella a Julio?
    5. ¿Qué quiere ella que haga María?
    6. ¿Qué hará Isabel?
    7. Al llegar a la casa, ¿qué le dice el señor Pérez al huésped?
    8. ¿Qué contesta el señor González?
    9. ¿Qué lleva la señora Pérez?
    10. ¿Es verdad que la señora no ha hecho nada especial?

B. Personalized questions. Answer in complete sentences in Spanish:

    1. ¿Se alegraría Vd. de ir al baile?
    2. ¿Quiere Vd. que su profesor vaya también?
    3. ¿Teme Vd. no salir bien en esta clase?
    4. ¿A qué hora prefiere Vd. que se sirva la comida?
    5. ¿Qué cosa quiere Vd. que sus padres le compren?
    6. ¿Qué prohibe su profesor?
    7. ¿Siente Vd. que su amigo esté enfermo?
    8. ¿Quisiera Vd. dormir tarde mañana?
    9. ¿Cuánto dinero le quedó a Vd. después de comer?
    10. ¿Se pone Vd. nervioso antes de los exámenes?

137

C. Pregúntele a un amigo:

1. si acaba de llegar a esta universidad.
2. si quiere que su padre le mande un cheque.
3. qué pediría en un café.
4. si prefiere que las lecciones sean fáciles.
5. cuántas horas tendrá que estudiar esta noche.

GRAMMAR

84. Stem-changing Verbs in the Present Subjunctive

(*a*) Class I stem-changing verbs, such as **pensar (ie)** and **volver (ue)** change in the present subjunctive in the same persons as in the present indicative.

pensar (pienso)   **piense, pienses, piense,** pensemos, penséis, **piensen**
volver (**vuelvo**)   **vuelva, vuelvas, vuelva,** volvamos, volváis, **vuelvan**

(*b*) Class II stem-changing verbs, such as **sentir (ie, i)** and **dormir (ue, u)** have the same changes. In addition they have a second change, **e** to **i** or **o** to **u,** in the first and second persons plural of the present subjunctive.

sentir (siento)   **sienta, sientas, sienta, sintamos, sintáis, sientan**
dormir (duermo)   **duerma, duermas, duerma, durmamos, durmáis, duerman**

(*c*) Class III stem-changing verbs such as **pedir (i, i)** change **e** to **i** in all six forms of the present subjunctive.

pedir (pido)   **pida, pidas, pida, pidamos, pidáis, pidan**

85. The Subjunctive in Dependent Clauses

The subjunctive is seldom used in English, but in Spanish it is used not only in direct and indirect commands (Lesson 17) but also in dependent clauses. The indicative mood usually states or asks for facts, while in general the subjunctive mood expresses an attitude of uncertainty, doubt or emotion, or a desire on the part of one person to influence the action of another. Examples in this and in following chapters show when and how the subjunctive is used in noun clauses, adjective clauses and adverbial clauses.

86. The Subjunctive in Dependent Noun Clauses

Whether the subjunctive is used in a dependent noun clause (that is, a clause used as the object of a verb) depends upon the verb in the main clause. The subjunctive mood is used in clauses following verbs of volition or influence, verbs of emotion, verbs of doubt or uncertainty, and most impersonal expressions.

(*a*) Subjunctive after verbs of *volition* or *influence*.

Some common Spanish verbs of this type are:

querer	*to wish, want*	mandar	*to order, command*
decir	*to tell, order*	preferir (ie, i)	*to prefer*
pedir (i, i)	*to ask (a favor), request*	prohibir	*to prohibit, forbid*

In English the idea of influencing another person is usually expressed by an infinitive: "Charles wants me to go with him." In Spanish such a sentence must be rephrased so that it will contain a noun clause.

We want Mary to do it. = We want that Mary do it.
Queremos que María lo haga.

They tell Anne to buy them. = They tell Anne that she buy them.
Le dicen a Anita que los compre.

Verbs such as **decir, pedir** and **mandar** require an indirect object pronoun, even if the sentence contains an indirect noun object as seen in the last sentence above.

(*b*) When there is only one person involved in a sentence expressing a wish the infinitive is used in Spanish as in English.

She wants to buy it.   Ella quiere comprarlo.

(*c*) Subjunctive after verbs of *emotion*.

Examples of verbs or expressions of emotion are:

sentir (ie, i)	*to regret, to be sorry*	esperar	*to hope*
alegrarse de	*to be glad*	temer	*to be afraid*
es lástima	*it is a pity*		

I am sorry that your mother is sick.	Siento que su madre esté enferma.
She is afraid that they will do it.	Ella teme que lo hagan.
We are glad that he is coming.	Nos alegramos de que él venga.
It is a pity you don't study more.	Es lástima que Vd. no estudie más.

Note that the present subjunctive is sometimes translated in English as a future tense.

EXERCISES

A. Substitute a noun or pronoun subject for the italicized subject of the dependent clause, making proper verb changes in the present subjunctive.

EXAMPLE: Pancho prefiere que *ella* no lo compre.
Pancho prefiere que *ustedes* no lo compren.

1. Pancho prefiere que *ella* no lo compre.
   ustedes, nosotros, yo

2. Mis padres quieren que *yo* estudie más.
   Carlos, María y yo, ellos

3. Sienten que *José* no diga la verdad.
   yo, Anita y usted, nosotros

4. Esperamos que *Rosita* duerma bien.
   ellos, nosotros, el señor Pérez

5. Anita le pide a *María* que lo haga.
   usted, su padre, el profesor

6. Quieren que *Pancho* vuelva temprano.
   José y yo, ellos, nosotros

7. Me alegro de que *Carlos* venga.
   mis amigos, él, ustedes

8. El profesor quiere que *nosotros* repitamos la frase.
   los estudiantes, ustedes, yo

B. Write **Siento mucho que** before each of the following sentences, making proper verb changes.

EXAMPLE: Usted no lo hace.
Siento mucho que no lo haga.

1. Usted no lo hace.
2. María no piensa en mí.
3. Los niños no piden legumbres.
4. José está enfermo.
5. Las noticias son malas.

C. Place **queremos que** before each of the following sentences, making proper verb changes.

EXAMPLE: Julio cierra la puerta.
Queremos que Julio cierre la puerta.

1. Julio cierra la puerta.
2. Viene un huésped.
3. Los muchachos se divierten.
4. José se acuesta temprano.
5. María se viste rápidamente.

D. Use the following phrases to form indirect commands in the plural.

    EXAMPLE: estar bien pronto

            Que estén Vds. bien pronto.

      1. estar bien pronto   4. ver la película
      2. dormir bien   5. no perderla
      3. despertarse temprano

E. Write in Spanish:

      1. They want to sleep well.
      2. They want the guests to sleep well.
      3. We want to have a good time.
      4. We want Anne to have a good time.
      5. I am sorry not to go with you.
      6. I am sorry that Joe is not going with you.
      7. Who has just arrived? It is Mr. González.
      8. Mr. Pérez tells his wife not to prepare a special meal.
      9. She tells Julius to go to the meat market.
    10. He wants Frank to return on Saturday.

I have spoken — he hablado
I had spoken — yo había hablado
I will have spoken — habré hablado
I would have spoken — yo habría hablado
I may have spoken — yo haya hablado

Acabar de
used in present
and imperfect, only!

LESSON **19**

VOCABULARY

tener prisa—to have haste

apurarse *to hurry*	dobles *doubles*
charlar *to chat*	la invitación *invitation*
descansar *to rest*	la lástima *pity*
dudar *to doubt*	el modo *manner*
seguir (i, i) *to continue, follow*	la pareja *couple*
	Pepe *Joe*
la cancha *tennis court*	posible *possible*
cierto, -a *certain*	probable *probable*
dentro de *within*	pues *since*
desocupado, -a *vacant*	la raqueta *tennis racket*

creo que no (sí)	*I think not (so)*
de modo que	*so that*
es lástima	*it is a pity*
ir a buscar a	*to pick up* (a person)
tomar el sol	*to enjoy the sunshine*

MODEL SENTENCES

1. Dudan que Carlos se haya despertado.
2. Un amigo suyo le llamaba por teléfono.
3. Pídale a Pepe que traiga una raqueta mía.
4. Es probable que lleguen temprano.
5. ¿Quieren Vds. que yo les explique las reglas?

1. *They doubt that Charles has waked up.*
2. *A friend of his was calling him on the phone.*
3. *Ask Joe to bring a racket of mine.*
4. *It is probable that they will arrive early.*
5. *Do you want me to explain the rules to you?*

142

LESSON NINETEEN

EXPRESS IN SPANISH

1. I doubt that they have waked up. I don't think that he is sorry (*that he regrets it*). We don't believe that they have gotten up.
2. A friend of theirs was calling them. I was reading a book of yours. Some friends of ours are coming. They have a book of mine.
3. Tell Joe to bring a friend of his. Ask Mary to bring a book of mine.
4. It is possible that Joe will arrive late. It is probable that they will play tennis. It is not possible for Charles to come today.
5. Do you want the boys to explain the rules? I doubt if they know them. I hope that they get a court.

El tenis

Son las ocho de la mañana. Como no hay clases Carlos está durmiendo todavía. Su madre no le ha llamado porque quiere que duerma y descanse. De pronto suena el teléfono. Carlos se despierta y oye la voz de su madre.

5 —¿Quién habla?... Creo que no... Dudo que Carlos se haya despertado. ¿Quiere Vd. que yo le llame?

Oyendo esto, Carlos se levanta y grita: —Mamá, si es un amigo mío dígale que me espere un momento. Voy al teléfono.

CARLOS: —Oiga. ¿Es Vd., Pepe? ¿Qué tal? ¿Por qué me ha llamado
10 tan temprano?

PEPE: —Es un día muy bonito, ¿no quiere jugar al tenis esta mañana?

CARLOS: —¡Ya lo creo! ¿Podremos conseguir una cancha?

PEPE: —Creo que sí. Es probable que consigamos una si vamos
15 temprano. Por eso tenemos que apurarnos. ¿Quiere Vd. que yo le vaya a buscar?

CARLOS: —Sí, Pepe, venga dentro de media hora y tráigame una raqueta mía que dejé en su cuarto. Me vestiré y me desayunaré en seguida.... ¿Y no quiere llamar a María? Dígale que vengan ella y su
20 hermana a jugar con nosotros.

PEPE: —Ya la llamé y nadie me contestó. No seguí llamando porque es probable que la familia de María haya ido a la casa del abuelo, que está enfermo. ¡Apúrese, Carlos!

A las nueve los muchachos llegaron a las canchas de tenis.
25 Muchas parejas ya estaban jugando, pero ellos encontraron una cancha desocupada.

143

—Me gusta jugar dobles—dijo Carlos—pero no veo a ningún amigo nuestro. Es lástima que María e Isabel no estén aquí. Busquemos otra pareja.

30 —Mire, allí vienen los dos hermanos mexicanos. Vamos a invitarles a jugar con nosotros.

Los jóvenes mexicanos aceptaron la invitación, diciendo: —Es posible que no sepamos algunas reglas, pues ésta es la primera vez que jugamos al tenis con norteamericanos, de modo que será necesario 35 que Vds. nos expliquen las reglas antes de empezar. Es posible que no juguemos bastante bien para jugar con Vds.

—Eso no importa—contestaron Carlos y Pepe. Y la verdad es que pasaron dos horas muy agradables jugando, charlando y tomando el sol.

QUESTIONS

A. Answer in complete sentences in Spanish:

1. ¿Por qué está durmiendo Carlos a las ocho?
2. ¿Por qué no le ha llamado su madre?
3. ¿Quién llama a Carlos por teléfono? ¿Por qué?
4. ¿Por qué es necesario que Carlos se vista en seguida?
5. ¿Qué le pide a Pepe que traiga?
6. ¿Jugarán María e Isabel al tenis con los jóvenes?
7. ¿Cuándo llegaron a las canchas de tenis?
8. ¿A quiénes encontraron Carlos y Pepe?
9. ¿Qué era necesario hacer antes de empezar el partido?
10. ¿Cómo se divirtieron los jóvenes?

B. Personalized questions. Answer in complete sentences in Spanish:

1. ¿Es necesario que aprenda Vd. los verbos?
2. ¿Es posible jugar al béisbol en el invierno?
3. ¿Viene un amigo suyo este fin de semana?
4. ¿Duda Vd. que todos hayan llegado a la clase?
5. ¿Es probable que juegue Vd. al tenis esta tarde?
6. ¿Es necesario que compre Vd. más libros para este curso?
7. ¿Siente Vd. que la temporada de fútbol haya acabado?
8. ¿Es verdad que no le gusta a Vd. mirar la televisión?
9. ¿Es probable que el profesor llegue a tiempo?
10. ¿Está seguro Vd. de despertarse temprano?

144

C. Pregúntele a un amigo:

1. si es posible que duerma hasta las nueve.
2. si tiene algunos libros suyos.
3. si prefiere jugar al tenis o al béisbol.
4. si es probable que haya gastado todo su dinero.
5. dónde buscaría a un buen amigo.

GRAMMAR

87. Spelling Changes

Changes in spelling are necessary in certain verbs in order to retain the pronunciation of the final consonant of the stem. This occurs when the consonants have two different sounds. Note how the sounds are represented in the following chart.

	a	e	i	o	u
Sound of **k**	ca	que	qui	co	cu
Sound of hard **g**	ga	gue	gui	go	gu
Sound of **s** (or *th*)	za	ce	ci	zo	zu
Sound of **h**	ja	ge, je	gi, ji	jo	ju

By reference to this chart it can be seen that verbs ending in

-car change **c** to **qu** before **-e**
-gar change **g** to **gu** before **-e**
-zar change **z** to **c** before **-e**
-ger change **g** to **j** before **-o** and **-a**
-guir change **gu** to **g** before **-o** and **-a**

These changes will occur in **-ar** verbs in the preterite and in the present subjunctive; in **-er** and **-ir** verbs in the present indicative and the present subjunctive. Some stem-changing verbs have spelling changes also.

88. Typical Verbs with Spelling Changes

buscar	Preterite	busqué, buscaste, buscó, buscamos, etc.
to look for	Pres. Subj.	busque, busques, busque, busquemos, etc.
llegar	Preterite	llegué, llegaste, llegó, llegamos, etc.
to arrive	Pres. Subj.	llegue, llegues, llegue, lleguemos, etc.

jugar (ue)	Preterite	jugué, jugaste, jugó, jugamos, etc.
to play	Pres. Subj.	juegue, juegues, juegue, juguemos, etc.
comenzar (ie)	Preterite	comencé, comenzaste, comenzó, comenzamos,
to begin		etc.
	Pres. Subj.	comience, comiences, comience, comencemos,
		etc.
escoger	Pres. Ind.	escojo, escoges, escoge, escogemos, etc.
to choose	Pres. Subj.	escoja, escojas, escoja, escojamos, etc.
seguir (i, i)	Pres. Ind.	sigo, sigues, sigue, seguimos, seguís, siguen
to continue,		
follow	Pres. Subj.	siga, sigas, siga, sigamos, sigáis, sigan

(See Appendix, § 111 for a list of other verbs conjugated like the above.)

89. The Present Perfect Subjunctive

The present perfect subjunctive of all verbs is formed by the present subjunctive of **haber** + a past participle.

haya ⎫
hayas ⎬ hablado   *I may have spoken*   hayamos ⎫
haya ⎭   hayáis ⎬ hablado
                                           hayan ⎭

This tense is often translated like the present perfect indicative. The same rules apply for its use as have been learned for the use of the present subjunctive.

| *I am sorry that Mary has gone.* | Siento que María se haya ido. |
| *They doubt that he has arrived.* | Dudan que él haya llegado. |

90. Subjunctive Used in Noun Clauses (*continued*)

(*a*) Following verbs of *doubt* or *uncertainty.*

I don't believe that he has come.	No creo que él haya venido.
They doubt that she is rich.	Dudan que ella sea rica.
We are not sure that he will do it.	No estamos seguros de que lo haga.

Note that the indicative is used after **creer** in the affirmative.

I believe that he will come.   Creo que vendrá.

146

(*b*) Following *impersonal expressions*, if a subject is mentioned.

It is necessary for Mary to study. (*that Mary study*)	Es necesario que María estudie.
It is probable that he will leave.	Es probable que él salga.
BUT:	
It is necessary to study.	Es necesario estudiar.

Note that the indicative is used in noun clauses after expressions of certainty, such as **es verdad** and **es cierto.**

It is true that Anne has arrived today.
Es verdad que Anita ha llegado hoy.

91. Possessive Adjectives

Possessive adjectives have two forms, the short forms, which precede nouns (Lesson 5), and the long forms, which follow the nouns. The following table shows both forms.

The forms that follow the nouns are used in direct address and to translate the English *of mine, of yours, of his,* etc.

Possessive Adjectives

BEFORE NOUNS		AFTER NOUNS	
mi, mis	*my*	mío, -a, -os, -as	*my, of mine*
tu, tus	*your*	tuyo, -a, -os, -as	*your, of yours*
su, sus	*your, his, her, its*	suyo, -a, -os, -as	*his, hers, its, your, of his, hers, its, yours*
nuestro, -a, -os, -as	*our*	nuestro, -a, -os, -as	*our, of ours*
vuestro, -a, -os, -as	*your*	vuestro, -a, -os, -as	*your, of yours*
su, sus	*your, their*	suyo, -a, -os, -as	*your, their, of yours, of theirs*

Remember that possessive adjectives in Spanish agree with the thing possessed, NOT with the possessor as in English.

¿Cómo está, amigo mío?	Un buen amigo nuestro viene.
How are you, my friend?	*A good friend of ours is coming.*
Padre nuestro, que estás en los cielos...	Dos primos suyos llegaron ayer.
Our Father who art in heaven . . .	*Two cousins of his arrived yesterday.*

Since all forms of **suyo** may have so many translations, a prepositional phrase such as **de él, de ustedes,** etc., may be used instead of **suyo** to make the meaning clear.

Yo leía un libro de ella.   *I was reading a book of hers.*
Un amigo de Vd. ha llamado.   *A friend of yours has called.*

EXERCISES

A. Substitute pronoun or proper name for the italicized subject, making the proper verb and adjective changes.

EXAMPLE: Es lástima que *Pepe* esté enfermo.
              Es lástima que Vds. estén enfermos.

1. Es lástima que *Pepe* esté enfermo.
   ustedes, yo, nosotros
2. Es posible que *Carlos* haya salido.
   ellos, ella, Pedro y Pancho
3. Ellos dudan que *Anita* sea rica.
   yo, ustedes, nosotros
4. Es necesario que *Vd.* busque otra casa.
   Carlos, Carlos y Pepe, yo
5. Es probable que *Rosita* llegue el domingo.
   unos amigos suyos, un hermano mío, un hijo suyo

B. Place **no creo que** before each of the following sentences, making the proper verb changes.

EXAMPLE: Hará buen tiempo.
              No creo que haga buen tiempo.

1. Hará buen tiempo.
2. Carlos se ha despertado.
3. Las señoritas juegan bien.
4. Pepe ha llegado.
5. Son las nueve.

C. Give the polite commands, singular and plural:

EXAMPLE: buscarle   búsquele Vd., búsquenle Vds.

1. buscarle
2. no llegar tarde
3. comenzar (ie) pronto
4. repetirlo (i, i)
5. seguirme (i, i)
6. explicármelo
7. escogerlos
8. sacarlas
9. escogerla
10. jugarlo

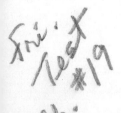

148

D. Write in Spanish:

(*a*) 1. Two friends of mine are here.
    2. A student of hers is waiting.
    3. She used to be a teacher of ours.
    4. How are you, my friend?
    5. Sit down and study, my son.

(*b*) 1. I will pick up Charles at six-thirty.
    2. It is a pity that the game begins so late.
    3. Please hurry so that we may arrive early.
    4. The students want the teacher to explain the rules clearly.
    5. He doubts that we will be able to go.
    6. It is necessary to choose a new book.
    7. It is certain that they are coming today.
    8. They are sorry that he has received bad news.

VOCABULARY

añadir *to add*
aparecer *to appear*
contar (ue) *to tell, recount*
dejar de + *inf.* *to cease, stop*
entregar *to hand over*
escuchar *to listen*
exclamar *to exclaim*
reírse (i, i) *to laugh*
rogar (ue) *to beg*

el administrador de correos
　　　　　　postmaster
el apartado *P.O. Box*
el apellido *surname*
¡ay! (*an exclamation*) *oh!*
la carta *letter*
la causa *cause*

certificado, -a *registered*
completo, -a *complete*
el correo *post office*
la costumbre *custom*
el cuento *story*
la duda *doubt*
el empleado *clerk, employee*
la experiencia *experience*
el futuro *future*
la gana *desire, inclination*
el interés *interest*
latino, -a *Latin*
parecido, -a *similar*
pasado, -a *past, last*
la risa *laughter*
según *according to –*
sólo *only*

al casarse con él　　*when she married (marries) him*
¡cuánto me alegro!　*how glad I am!*
el verano pasado　　*last summer*
es que　　　　　　*the fact is that*
hace días que espero　*for some days I have been expecting*
por fin　　　　　　*finally*
por supuesto　　　　*of course*
tener ganas de + *inf.*　*to be anxious to*

150

MODEL SENTENCES

1. ¿Conoce Vd. a alguien que hable español?	1. *Do you know anyone who speaks Spanish?*
2. No hay nadie aquí que pueda hacerlo.	2. *There is no one here who can do it.*
3. Buscaban una casa que estuviera cerca de la universidad.	3. *They were looking for a house which was near the university.*
4. Dudaban que la carta fuese de él.	4. *They doubted that the letter was his.*
5. Sentía que Roberto no la hubiera recibido.	5. *He was sorry that Robert had not received it.*
6. Traeré mis libros y los de Vd.	6. *I will bring my books and yours.*
7. Sus amigos y los míos querían que viniéramos.	7. *Your friends and mine wanted us to come.*

EXPRESS IN SPANISH

1. Do you know anyone who reads Spanish? Is there a person here whom (**a quién**) he knows? She is looking for someone who learns easily.
2. I don't know anyone who wants to study. They don't have anything that I like.
3. They were looking for a student who knew the lesson. Mary wanted a book that was easy.
4. We doubted that the letter was hers. I doubted if that house was yours.
5. They were sorry that Mary had not done it. We were afraid that you had gone out.
6. He will bring your books and mine. She will drink her coffee and yours. We will write with his pen and hers.
7. Your father and mine wanted us to go to Cuba. Robert wrote his mother to use his first surname and not to use hers.

Los apellidos

El Sr. García entró en la clase riéndose. Cuando Pepe le rogó que nos contara la causa de su risa nos dijo:

—Cuando entré en el correo esta mañana, Roberto Gómez, ese joven de Costa Rica, estaba hablando con el administrador de correos
5 y parecía que no se entendían muy bien. Me acerqué a ellos, y Roberto, al verme, exclamó:

—¡Ay, señor! ¡Vd. no sabe cuánto me alegro de que Vd. haya llegado! Hace días que espero un cheque. Esta mañana llegó una carta certificada para mí y no quieren dármela.

10 —Vamos a ver, Roberto—le dije. ¿Por qué no quieren dársela?
¿Dudan que sea de Vd.?

—Vd. verá, señor. Es que mi madre escribió mi nombre "Roberto
Gómez Díaz." El señor administrador de correos cree que ése no es mi
nombre, y me dijo que buscase una persona que me conociera, ¡y Vd.
15 apareció!

El administrador escuchó con mucho interés cuando yo le
expliqué que en la América Latina cada persona tiene dos apellidos, y
que "Gómez" era el apellido del padre de Roberto y "Díaz" el de su
madre. Como una persona puede usar los dos apellidos o sólo el de su
20 padre, le dije que sin duda la carta era de Roberto y que podía dársela.
Dice Roberto que va a escribirle a su madre que en el futuro ponga sólo
el apellido de su padre y no el de ella.

El profesor García, viendo que a todos les había gustado el
cuento, preguntó si algún alumno sabía de otra persona que hubiera
25 tenido una experiencia parecida a la de Roberto. En seguida Clara
levantó la mano y dijo que durante los primeros días que ella pasó en
México el verano pasado no había recibido cartas. Por fin ella le dio al
empleado del hotel su nombre completo, y él le entregó varias cartas.
Su nombre es Clara Martin Durham, y el empleado había puesto sus
30 cartas en el apartado de la "M," creyendo que Martin era su apellido.

Anita tenía ganas de hablar de los apellidos de la familia Torres,
para explicar lo que se hace cuando una muchacha se casa. Dijo, que la
señora de Torres, la madre de Rosita, antes de casarse se llamaba Rosa
Sánchez y Pérez. Al casarse con el Sr. Omar Torres dejó de usar el
35 apellido Pérez, que era el de su madre, y añadió el de su esposo, llamán-
dose entonces Sra. Rosa Sánchez de Torres. Rosita, por supuesto, es
Rosita Torres y Sánchez, pero al casarse perderá el apellido Sánchez y
tomará el de su esposo.

QUESTIONS

A. Answer in complete sentences in Spanish:

1. ¿Qué le rogó Pepe al Sr. García?
2. ¿Quiénes estaban hablando en el correo?
3. ¿Qué esperaba Roberto hace días?
4. ¿Qué había llegado para Roberto?

5. ¿Por qué no quieren dársela?
6. ¿Cuántos apellidos tiene cada persona en la América Latina?
7. ¿Cuál era el apellido del padre de Roberto?
8. ¿Cuál era el de su madre?
9. ¿Es necesario usar siempre los dos apellidos?
10. ¿Qué le escribirá Roberto a su madre?

B. Personalized questions. Answer in complete sentences in Spanish:

1. ¿Usa Vd. un apellido o dos?
2. ¿Cuál es su apellido?
3. ¿Cuál era el apellido de su madre antes de casarse?
4. ¿Cómo sería su nombre completo según la costumbre española?
5. ¿Qué apellido pierde una muchacha al casarse?
6. ¿Quería Vd. que su padre le mandara un cheque?
7. ¿Conoce Vd. a alguien que haya viajado a Costa Rica?
8. ¿Quién le mandó a Vd. que escribiera en la pizarra?
9. ¿Es necesario que compremos un billete para el partido de básquetbol?
10. ¿Preferiría Vd. que tuviésemos la clase a otra hora?

C. Pregúntele a un amigo:

1. si conoce a jóvenes de la América Latina.
2. si puede explicar los apellidos que usan en la América Latina.
3. si tiene ganas de ir al cine.
4. si vive en una casa que está cerca de la escuela.
5. si quisiera casarse con alguien de la América Latina.

GRAMMAR

92. Imperfect Subjunctive

All verbs in Spanish form the imperfect subjunctive by dropping the **-ron** of the third person plural of the preterite indicative and adding either of the following sets of endings:

-ra, -ras, -ra, -ramos, -rais, -ran
OR   -se, -ses, -se, -semos, -seis, -sen

153

Sin embargo — however
hay que — one must

(*a*) Regular verbs.

hablar		comer	
3RD PERS. PL. PRET.—hablaron		3RD PERS. PL. PRET.—comieron	
-ra	-se	-ra	-se
hablara	hablase	comiera	comiese
hablaras	hablases	comieras	comieses
hablara	hablase	comiera	comiese
habláramos	hablásemos	comiéramos	comiésemos
hablarais	hablaseis	comierais	comieseis
hablaran	hablasen	comieran	comiesen

Note that the first person plural form has an accent. Although the imperfect subjunctive may have several translations, a single verb form may be translated with the word *might*: (**que**) **hablara,** (*that*) *I might speak*.

(*b*) Some irregular verbs.

INF.	3RD PL. PRET.	IMPERFECT SUBJUNCTIVE
dar	dieron	diera (diese), etc.
decir	dijeron	dijera (dijese), etc.
estar	estuvieron	estuviera (estuviese), etc.
hacer	hicieron	hiciera (hiciese), etc.
ir	fueron	fuera (fuese), etc.
leer	leyeron	leyera (leyese), etc.
poder	pudieron	pudiera (pudiese), etc.
saber	supieron	supiera (supiese), etc.
ser	fueron	fuera (fuese), etc.
venir	vinieron	viniera (viniese), etc.

(*c*) Stem-changing verbs.

Since stem-changing verbs of Class II and Class III have the change **e** to **i** or **o** to **u** in the third person plural of the preterite indicative, verbs of these classes will contain such a change in all forms of the imperfect subjunctive.

INF.	3RD PL. PRET.	IMPERFECT SUBJUNCTIVE
dormir	durmieron	durmiera (durmiese), etc.
sentir	sintieron	sintiera (sintiese), etc.
pedir	pidieron	pidiera (pidiese), etc.

(See Cover Chart for a review of all tenses affected by stem changes in verbs of Classes I, II and III.)

93. **The Pluperfect Subjunctive** is formed with either of the imperfect subjunctive forms of **haber** and a past participle.

hubiera (hubiese)⎫
hubieras (hubieses)⎬hablado
hubiera (hubiese)⎭

hubiéramos (hubiésemos)⎫
hubierais (hubieseis)⎬hablado
hubieran (hubiesen)⎭

This tense may be translated as the pluperfect indicative, *I had spoken*, etc.

94. Use of the Imperfect and Pluperfect Subjunctive

The present and present perfect subjunctive are ordinarily used in dependent clauses following a main verb in the present, future or present perfect indicative. (Lesson 19.)

The imperfect and pluperfect subjunctive are required after a main verb in any past tense, that is, in the imperfect, preterite, conditional, pluperfect and conditional perfect tenses.

Él quiere que yo lo compre.   *He wants me to buy it.*
Él quería que yo lo comprase.   *He wanted me to buy it.*

No creen que él haya salido.   *They don't believe that he has gone.*
No creían que él hubiese salido.   *They didn't believe that he had gone.*

At times a past subjunctive tense will follow a present or future tense in the indicative, but when this is true the tenses in English will indicate it.

Siento que Anita esté enferma.
I am sorry that Anne is sick.

Siento que Anita estuviese enferma ayer.
I am sorry that Anne was sick yesterday.

95. The Subjunctive Mood in Adjective Clauses

The key to the use of the subjunctive in adjective clauses is the antecedent, or word modified by the clause. The subjunctive is used in an adjective clause if the noun or pronoun modified is *negative, non-existent,* or *indefinite.* In general, the antecedent refers to a person, characteristic or object being sought, but not yet found; or to a person or thing not existing, as in the case of negative antecedents.

Busco un estudiante que estudie. (*subjunctive*)
I am looking for a student (any student) who studies.

No hay nadie aquí que hable español. (*subjunctive*)
There is no one here who speaks Spanish. (*negative*)

Deseo una gramática que sea fácil. (*subjunctive*)
I want a grammar which is easy. (*not yet found*)

BUT:

Busco al estudiante que me llamó. (*indicative*)
I am looking for the student who called me. (definite person)

Note in the first of the above sentences that the preposition **a** is not used before a noun object which does not refer to a definite person. However this personal **a** is always used with **nadie, alguien** and other indefinite or negative pronouns referring to persons. (See Lesson 14.)

No conozco a nadie que sepa leerlo.
I don't know anyone who can read it.

¿Conoce Vd. a alguien que baile mejor que ella?
Do you know anyone who dances better than she?

96. The Possessive Pronouns

The possessive pronouns, *mine, yours, his, hers,* etc., are formed by using the definite article with the long forms of the possessive adjectives given in Lesson 19. The definite article must agree in number and gender with the thing possessed.

su casa y la (casa) mía
su casa y la mía } *your house and mine*

sus libros y los (libros) nuestros
sus libros y los nuestros } *their books and ours*

mis plumas y las (plumas) suyas
mis plumas y las suyas } *my pens and his*

The third person form **suyo, suya,** etc., may be clarified by a prepositional phrase, **de Vd., de él, de ella,** etc.

Tengo mis plumas y las de él.   *I have my pens and his.*
Él tiene mi libro y el de Vd.   *He has my book and yours.*

The definite article is omitted after **ser** unless used for emphasis or contrast, or after the question, *which one?*

La casa es de él.   *The house is his.*
El coche es mío.   *The car is mine.*
Este libro es el mío.   *This book is mine* (*not yours*).

97. The Definite Article as a Demonstrative Pronoun

As may be observed in the above section, the definite article acts as a demonstrative pronoun.

su casa y la mía   *your house and mine* (*that of mine*)

The definite article is used instead of a demonstrative pronoun before **de** and **que.** (See Chapter 22 for use of definite article with **que.**)

su apellido y el de su esposo
her surname and that of her husband

una experiencia parecida a la de Roberto
an experience similar to that of Robert

EXERCISES

A. Change the main verb to a past tense and make the necessary change in the dependent verb.

EXAMPLE: Quiero que ella vaya.
Quería que ella fuera.

1. Quiero que ella vaya.
2. Dudan que la carta sea de Roberto.
3. Siento que Roberto no la haya recibido.
4. Busco a alguien que me cuente lo que pasó.
5. No hay nadie que sepa jugarlo bien.
6. No creo que Roberto haya llegado.
7. Es posible que él vaya.
8. Quiero un libro que sea fácil.
9. Nos pide que lo compremos.
10. No conozco a nadie que hable español.

B. Substitute pronoun or proper name for italicized subject, making the proper verb changes:

EXAMPLE: Es probable que *Roberto* reciba una carta.
Es probable que yo reciba una carta.

1. Es probable que *Roberto* reciba una carta.
   yo, Pepe y María, nosotros
2. Era posible que *el Sr. García* lo conociera.
   Clara, la señora de Torres, ellos

3. No era necesario que *la madre* lo hiciese.
   nosotros, yo, ellos

4. El profesor sintió que *los alumnos* no viniesen temprano.
   yo, nosotros, Vds.

5. Pepe se alegra de que *ustedes* lo hayan hecho.
   Clara, nosotros, yo

C. Use **yo sentí que** before the following statements, making the proper change in the verb.

EXAMPLE: Roberto no recibió su carta.
                   Yo sentí que Roberto no recibiera su carta.

1. Roberto no recibió su carta.
2. Pepe no la había visto.
3. El profesor no había vuelto.
4. Nadie sabía las lecciones.
5. El hombre hablaba mal el español.

D. Change the following expressions by converting the noun to a possessive pronoun.

EXAMPLE: su casa   la suya (la de él)

1. su casa (his)
2. mi amigo
3. sus flores (your)
4. nuestra universidad
5. mis lápices
6. sus abuelos (her)
7. nuestro libro
8. su patio (their)
9. sus plumas (your, *pl.*)
10. mis padres

E. Write in Spanish:

1. His friends and yours will arrive tomorrow.
2. Let's read your letters and mine.
3. There was no one who knew it.
4. We would like to visit her house and theirs.
5. Robert explained that the letter was his.
6. We were sorry that he had done it.
7. There isn't anyone here who knows me.
8. They wanted a teacher who spoke Spanish.
9. I didn't believe that you understood.
10. They were sorry that she had not written to them.

Learn

VOCABULARY

anunciar   *to announce, advertise*
aprovecharse de   *to take advantage of*
detenerse   *to stop* (ONES SElF)
nacer   *to be born*
quejarse   *to complain*
querer   *to love* — a
tratar   *to treat*

la blusa   *blouse*
bondadoso, -a   *kind* • gentle
caro, -a   *expensive*
el centro   *downtown district*
claro, -a   *light* (color)

la dependiente   *clerk*
el espejo   *mirror*
el estilo   *style*
marino, -a   *navy* (Adj.)
el millonario   *millionaire*
el nilón   *nylon*
el par   *pair* — (FoR objects; Not pEOplE)
satisfecho, -a   *satisfied*
sino   *but* — (dIREct contRAdictionu)
la sombrerería   *hat shop* (AFteR NEgAtivE)
el surtido   *stock*
la tienda   *store*
la venta   *sale*
la zapatería   *shoe store*
el zapato   *shoe*

El DERECho — lAW

a la derecha   *to the right* (hand)
a la izquierda   *to the left* (hand)
¿en qué puedo servirle?   *what can I do for you?*
estar de venta   *to be for sale*
ir de compras   *to go shopping*
le queda bien   *it is becoming to her*
por aquí   *here, around here*
venir bien con   *to look well with*

MODEL SENTENCES

1. Esperará hasta que su padre le mande un cheque.	1. *She will wait until her father sends her a check.*
2. María no irá de compras sin que Anita lo sepa.	2. *Mary will not go shopping without Anne's knowing it.*
3. Anita gasta su dinero como si fuera rica.	3. *Anne spends her money as if she were rich.*
4. María saldrá tan pronto como se vaya Anita.	4. *Mary will leave as soon as Anne goes away.*
5. Aunque no tenía dinero, fui de compras.	5. *Although I didn't have any money I went shopping.*
6. No hablé con Carlos sino con Pancho.	6. *I didn't speak to Charles but to Frank.*

EXPRESS IN SPANISH

1. They will wait until Mary comes. We shall wait until they do it.
2. They will go without your knowing it. Mary will not go without my seeing her.
3. My son spends his money as if he were rich. I speak Spanish as if I were a Cuban.
4. They will go as soon as Joe arrives. He will do it as soon as he sees you.
5. Although the shoes were expensive I bought them. Although the weather was bad I left the house.
6. We didn't speak to Anne but to Mary. I didn't want this hat but that one.

De compras

Un día de primavera María y Anita deciden ir de compras. Anita no puede comprar nada hasta que su padre le mande un cheque, pero acompaña a María para ver las cosas nuevas y bellas que están de venta. María busca una sombrerería que tenga sombreros bonitos y a la vez
5 baratos. Siguen caminando hasta encontrar una sombrerería a la derecha del correo.

Una dependiente les dice: —¿En qué puedo servirles, señoritas?

—Quisiera ver un sombrero chico que venga bien con este vestido.

—Tenemos un buen surtido, señorita. ¿De qué color lo prefiere?
10 —Azul marino. Mire, permítame ver ése, el primer sombrero en esa mesa.

—Tenga Vd. la bondad de sentarse delante de este espejo.... Le queda muy bien... ¿Quiere Vd. que le traiga otros del mismo estilo?

—No—contestó María,—me gusta éste, y voy a comprarlo si no 15 es muy caro. ¿Cuánto vale?

—El precio es de cinco dólares hoy. Tenemos una venta especial.

María pagó los cinco dólares y salió muy satisfecha. Al entrar en una tienda de ropa ella dijo a Anita: —Aquí buscaré una blusa para mi madre. Quisiera dársela el día de su cumpleaños, para que ella sepa 20 cuánto la quiero.

—¿Cuándo es el cumpleaños de su madre?

—Es el martes. Ella nació el diez de abril y mi cumpleaños es el once, de modo que las dos celebramos el mismo día. (*A la dependiente*) —¿Tiene Vd. blusas de nilón por menos de $8.00? Quiero una de color 25 claro. Déjeme ver aquélla allí a la izquierda... ¿Tiene esta misma blusa en el número 36?

Como la blusa le parecía bonita y no muy cara, María la compró. La pobre Anita sentía mucho no poder aprovecharse de las ventas especiales que se anunciaban por todas partes. Se detuvieron delante de 30 una zapatería:

—Mire, María, tan pronto como reciba el dinero de casa, vuelvo por aquí para comprarme un par de zapatos como ésos, aunque cuesten más que los que vi el otro día. Dice mi padre que aunque me mandara cien dólares al mes para gastar en ropa yo nunca tendría bastante; dice 35 también que yo le pido dinero como si él fuera millonario. Yo le contesto que él me trata como si yo fuera una niña. Pero él es muy bondadoso; aunque se queja, siempre me manda lo que yo le pido. En cuanto llegue mi cheque, Vd. vendrá conmigo para hacer las compras que necesito, ¿verdad, María?

QUESTIONS

A. Answer in complete sentences in Spanish:

    1. ¿Cuándo deciden María y Anita ir de compras?

    2. ¿Por qué no puede Anita comprar nada?

    3. Entonces ¿por qué acompaña ella a María?

    4. ¿Dónde encontraron las muchachas una sombrerería?

    5. ¿Cuánto pagó María por el sombrero?

    6. ¿Le parecía caro?

7. ¿Por qué quiere María comprar una blusa bonita?
8. ¿Qué días son los cumpleaños de María y su madre?
9. ¿Qué sentía mucho Anita?
10. ¿Cuándo podrá ella comprar los zapatos que quiere?

B. Personalized questions. Answer in complete sentences in Spanish:

1. ¿Cuándo tienen las tiendas ventas especiales?
2. ¿A dónde iría Vd. de compras?
3. ¿Es el padre de Vd. millonario?
4. ¿Cuánto dinero le manda cada mes?
5. ¿Gasta Vd. dinero como si fuera rico?
6. ¿En qué gasta Vd. más, en libros o en diversiones?
7. ¿Paga Vd. las compras con un cheque?
8. ¿Cuándo celebra Vd. su cumpleaños?
9. ¿Qué quiere Vd. que sus padres le den ese día?
10. ¿Qué hará Vd. para que su amiga salga bien en la clase?

C. Pregúntele a un amigo:

1. si se aprovecha de las ventas especiales.
2. qué recibió para el cumpleaños.
3. cuándo le gusta ir de compras.

4. si hay tiendas grandes por aquí.
5. si se queja cuando hace mal tiempo.

GRAMMAR

98. The Subjunctive in Adverbial Clauses

The subjunctive is used in an adverbial clause when the action of the verb in this clause has not yet taken place or there is doubt that it will take place.

(*a*) The following conjunctions automatically introduce the subjunctive. Memorize this list.

antes (de) que	*before*	para que	*in order that, so that*
con tal que	*provided that*	sin que	*without*
a menos que	*unless*	como si	*as if*

Lo haré antes de que Vd. llegue.
I shall do it before you arrive.

Le escribiré en inglés para que me entienda bien.
I shall write to you in English so that you will understand me well.

Salieron sin que yo lo supiera.
They left without my knowing it.
Ella me hablaba como si yo fuera (un) niño.
She was speaking to me as if I were a child.

Note that **como si,** which introduces a condition contrary to reality or fact, is always followed by the imperfect or pluperfect subjunctive.

(*b*) The subjunctive is used in time clauses which refer to a future time. Common conjunctions which introduce clauses of time are:

cuando	*when*	tan pronto como	*as soon as*
hasta que	*until*	mientras	*while*
en cuanto	*as soon as*		

Se lo diré a él cuando venga.
I shall tell it to him when he comes.

Él dijo que esperaría hasta que yo llegara.
He said he would wait until I arrived.

Ellos los comprarán tan pronto como su padre les mande el dinero.
They will buy them as soon as their father sends them the money.

If the time clause refers to something which *is* happening, *does* happen, or *did* happen, then the indicative is used.

No escucho cuando el profesor habla.   *I don't listen when the professor is speaking.*
Le veo cuando viene a la clase.   *I see him when he comes to class.*
Él me esperó hasta que yo llegué   *He waited for me until I arrived.*

(*c*) The subjunctive is used in adverbial clauses introduced by conjunctions of purpose, concession, proviso, etc., if the action is to take place in the future. Conjunctions of this type are:

aunque	*although, even though*	de modo que	*so that*
como (*manner*)	*as*	de manera que	*so that*

Aunque sea caro, lo compraré.
Although it may be expensive I shall buy it.
Hablaban despacio de modo que (para que) yo pudiera entender.
They spoke slowly so that I might be able to understand.

If the adverbial clause refers to a completed or definite action, the indicative is used.

Aunque la blusa era cara, la compré.
Although the blouse was expensive I bought it.
Siempre habla despacio, de modo que le entiendo.
He always speaks slowly so that I understand him.

99. *Pero* and *sino*

Sino is used instead of **pero** when a negative statement is contrasted with a positive one. (*Not this, but that.*) No conjugated verb form may be used after **sino.**

No hablamos español sino inglés.	*We don't speak Spanish but English.*
No me gusta este libro sino ése.	*I don't like this book but that one.*
No quiero hablar sino bailar.	*I don't want to talk but to dance.*

If this contrast is not present **pero** is used.

No tengo bastante dinero, pero iré.   *I don't have enough money but I shall go.*

EXERCISES

A. Substitute pronoun or noun for the italicized subject, making the proper verb changes:

EXAMPLE: Anita estudiará hasta que *Carlos* la llame.
                Anita estudiará hasta que yo la llame.

1. Anita estudiará hasta que *Carlos* la llame.
   yo, su madre, nosotros, las muchachas
2. El señor Pérez habla lentamente para que *nosotros* le entendamos.
   Carlos, yo, usted, los estudiantes
3. María saldrá antes de que *Anita* llegue.
   Carlos e Isabel, Pancho, yo, José
4. José dormirá cuando *el niño* se vaya.
   las mujeres, el niño y yo, Carlos
5. En cuanto *Pancho* vea a Carlos le invitará a la fiesta.
   yo, nosotros, Rosita, sus amigos

B. Change the main verb to the future and the dependent verb to the present subjunctive:

EXAMPLE: Anita compra muchas cosas cuando recibe un cheque.
                Anita comprará muchas cosas cuando reciba un cheque.

1. Anita compra muchas cosas cuando recibe un cheque.
2. Vamos de compras cuando hace buen tiempo.
3. Hablamos español cuando vemos a los jóvenes mexicanos.
4. Llamo a casa por teléfono cuando termino mi trabajo.
5. Escribo cartas cuando tengo tiempo.

C. Change the verbs in parentheses to the proper tense of the indicative or subjunctive as required by the sense:

    EXAMPLE: Me senté allí antes de que Vd. (entrar).
                 Me senté allí antes de que Vd. entrara.

    1. Me senté allí antes de que Vd. (entrar).
    2. Roberto le dará el dinero tan pronto como lo (recibir).
    3. Pedro estuvo en la sala hasta que Isabel (bajar).
    4. Asistiremos al partido de béisbol aunque (hacer) mal tiempo.
    5. La señora Pérez esperó hasta que su esposo (venir).
    6. Carlos siempre ve a Pancho cuando (ir) a la clase.
    7. Compré un coche nuevo aunque (ser) caro.
    8. Julio leyó la carta sin que lo (saber) su madre.
    9. José abrirá la puerta para que nosotros (entrar).
   10. Carlos se levantó cuando yo (comenzar) a hablar.

D. Give the English for the following expressions, then form a short sentence using each expression:

1. tener ganas de	5. quedarle (a uno)	8. dar un paseo
2. el verano pasado	6. acabar de	9. fin de semana
3. hace días que	7. lo mismo	10. en seguida
4. tomar el sol		

E. Write in Spanish:

  (a) 1. You will learn provided that you study.
       2. Although it may be bad weather I shall go out.
       3. My father will work so that I may have money.
       4. They bought a new home without my knowing it.
       5. He will not find it unless he goes to the left.
       6. They will do it when you come.
       7. He didn't buy it although he had the money.
       8. I always see her when she enters the library.
       9. He left the house as soon as we had breakfast.
     10. They will wait until you arrive.

  (b) 1. I don't want this book but that one.
       2. He doesn't have the money but he will buy it.
       3. He will not write these exercises but those.
       4. I wasn't speaking to Mary but to Professor García.
       5. He didn't know the lesson but he went to class.

VOCABULARY

bastar *to be enough*
dejar *to let*
faltar *to lack*
figurarse *to imagine*
pasar *to happen*
tocar *to play* (an instrument)

el billete *bill* (money)
la capital *capital* (city)
la carrera *profession*
correctamente *correctly*
la cuestión *question*
los dulces *candy*
la Facultad de Leyes *Law School*

famoso, -a *famous*
el gasto *expense*
el grupo *group*
latinoamericano, -a *Latin American*
la ley *law*
el médico *doctor, physician*
la novia *sweetheart*
la obligación *debt*
la oportunidad *opportunity*
la orquesta *orchestra*
práctico, -a *practical*
el programa *program*
la televisión *television*
tonto, -a *foolish*
verdaderamente *really, truly*

¡figúrese! *imagine it!*
ganar algo así *to win something in that way*
hacer una excursión al campo *to go on a picnic*
nos falta dinero *we lack money*
¡qué lástima! *what a pity!*
¡qué tontos somos! *how foolish we are!*
van caminando *are walking along*

LESSON TWENTY-TWO

MODEL SENTENCES

1. Si yo tuviera tiempo iría al campo.
2. Si él tiene dinero comprará dulces.
3. ¡Qué día más hermoso! ¿Qué haremos?
4. ¿De quién es este sombrero? Dudo que sea de él.
5. ¡Qué bonita! Es la muchacha de quien yo hablaba.
6. ¿Con qué muchacho irá María al baile?

1. *If I had time I would go to the country.*
2. *If he has money he will buy candy.*
3. *What a beautiful day! What shall we do?*
4. *Whose hat is this? I doubt if it is his.*
5. *How pretty! She is the girl I was talking about (of whom I was talking).*
6. *With what boy will Mary go to the dance?*

EXPRESS IN SPANISH

1. If they had time they would go to the movies. If Mary were here she would do it.
2. If he has the book he will study. If it is good weather they will go.
3. What a pretty house! What a big man! What shall I say to him?
4. Whose book is this? It is yours. Whose pen is that? It is Joe's.
5. How easy it is! How foolish he is! Is she the lady you were talking about?
6. With what girl will you go? What book are you reading?

¿ Qué haría usted?

Dos jóvenes que trabajan en una cafetería van caminando hacia el centro.

—¡Qué día más hermoso!—exclamó uno. —Quisiera ir con un grupo de amigos míos que van a hacer una excursión al campo esta
5 tarde. Si no tuviera que trabajar iría con ellos.

—¡Qué lástima!—exclamó su amigo. —Si yo tuviera tiempo y dinero asistiría al baile que dan esta noche. Va a tocar una orquesta famosa.

—Lo que pasa, chico, es que a los dos nos falta tiempo y dinero.
10 Mire, el mes pasado una señora a quien yo conozco ganó mil dólares en un programa de televisión. Figúrese, los ganó por haber contestado correctamente a la pregunta "¿Cuál es la capital de El Salvador?" ¡Qué fácil! Yo sé las capitales de todos los países latinoamericanos.

—Entonces es posible que algún día Vd. tenga la oportunidad de
15 ganar algo así. ¿Qué haría Vd. si ganara mil dólares?

167

—¿Qué haría yo? Si yo recibiera mil dólares pagaría todas mis obligaciones y no trabajaría más hasta gastar lo que me quedara. Con lo que me manda mi padre cada mes me bastaría para pagar la comida y los libros y para divertirme con mi novia, a quien yo daría flores y
20 dulces y otros regalos. Y Vd., ¿qué haría?

—Si yo tuviera tan buena suerte pondría todo el dinero en el banco hasta septiembre, cuando entro en la Facultad de Leyes. Entonces lo usaría para pagar todos mis gastos, y no trabajaría. Dicen que la carrera de leyes es muy difícil.... Pero ¡qué tontos somos! No nos
25 han invitado a tomar parte en ningún programa de televisión. La cuestión prática es: ¿Cuánto dinero tenemos ahora y qué haremos con él? Déjeme ver. Yo tengo un billete de un dólar y uno de cinco dólares, pero el de cinco dólares no es mío verdaderamente.

—¿De quién es?

30 —Es del médico que vino a verme el mes pasado cuando estuve enfermo. ¿Cuánto dinero tiene Vd.?

—Yo tengo más de dos dólares, y hay una película muy buena que quisiera ver. Aprovechemos bien el tiempo y el dinero que tenemos, y no pensemos en lo que haríamos si tuviéramos más.

QUESTIONS

A. Answer in complete sentences in Spanish:

1. ¿Dónde trabajan los dos jóvenes?
2. ¿Qué exclamó uno?
3. ¿Qué haría él si no tuviera que trabajar?
4. ¿Qué haría el amigo por la noche si tuviera tiempo y dinero?
5. ¿Cuánto ganó una señora en un programa de televisión?
6. ¿Cuál es la capital de Cuba?
7. ¿Qué haría uno de los jóvenes si recibiera mil dólares?
8. Y, ¿el otro?
9. ¿Cuál es la cuestión práctica para ellos?
10. ¿A dónde van los muchachos, por fin, esa noche?

B. Personalized questions. Answer in complete sentences in Spanish:

1. ¿A dónde iría Vd. si tuviera mil dólares?
2. ¿Cuál es la capital del estado en que vive Vd.?

3. ¿Qué hará Ud. si tiene diez dólares?
4. ¿Que haría Vd. si tuviera cien dólares?
5. ¿Con quiénes habla Vd. en la cafetería?
6. ¿A quiénes visitaría Vd. si hubiera vacaciones?
7. ¿Con qué escribiría si tuviera un examen?
8. Si Vd. fuera rico, ¿qué compraría?
9. ¿Se quedará Vd. en casa si llueve?
10. ¿Hablaría Vd. español si estuviera en México?

C. Pregúntele a un amigo:

1. qué vería si fuera a Acapulco.
2. si se pondría nervioso si tuviera un examen.
3. qué haría si hiciera buen tiempo.
4. si irá al cine si hay una buena película.
5. cuánto pagaría si comprara una casa.

GRAMMAR

100. Conditional Sentences

A conditional sentence contains an *if clause* and a *result clause*. The indicative mood is used in both clauses when the action in the result clause is habitual, actually occurred, or is likely to occur.

Si él va a la clase la ve.	*If he goes to class he sees her.*
Si él fue a la clase la vio.	*If he went to class he saw her.*
Si él va a la clase la verá.	*If he goes to class he will see her.*

When the action of a result clause is contrary to fact or reality, or if it is doubtful that the action will take place, the imperfect subjunctive (or pluperfect subjunctive) is used in the *if clause*, and the conditional (or conditional perfect) in the *result clause*. English sentences of this type contain the word *would* or *should* in the *result clause*.

Si tuviera el libro lo leería.	*If I had the book I would read it.*
Si ella lo hubiera sabido, habría ido.	*If she had known it she would have gone.*

The present subjunctive and the future indicative are seldom used in an if clause.

169

101. Relative Pronouns

The most common relative pronoun in Spanish is **que** (*that, which, who, whom*). It may be used as the subject or object of a verb, and refers to both persons and things.

La muchacha que sale es Rosita. *The girl who is leaving is Rose.*
El libro que estudiamos es fácil. *The book that we study is easy.*
El hombre que veo es el Sr. García. *The man whom I see is Mr. García.*

The relative pronoun is often omitted in English but *must* be expressed in Spanish.

Los libros que Vd. tiene son míos. *The books you have are mine.*

When a relative pronoun is separated from its antecedent by another noun, possible confusion between antecedents is clarified by using **el que (la que, los que, las que)** or **el cual (la cual, los cuales, las cuales)** to show gender and number of the antecedent.

La madre de Pepe, la que Vd. conoció anoche, va a Cuba.
Joe's mother, whom you met last night, is going to Cuba.

Los padres de Juan, los cuales están aquí, hablan inglés.
John's parents, who are here, speak English.

After prepositions **quien** refers to *persons*, while **que** usually refers to *things*.

La muchacha de quien Vd. habla es de México.
The girl you are speaking of is from Mexico.

La pluma con que escribe es mía.
The pen you are writing with is mine.

After **por, sin,** and long or compound prepositions **el cual, la cual, los cuales, las cuales** are used instead of **que**. (**Que** is used after **a, con, de** and **en**.)

la ventana por la cual miro *the window through which I look*
las casas delante de las cuales vivo *the houses in front of which I live*

El que, la que, los que, las que may be translated as *he who, the one who, the one which*, etc.

El que habla es Carlos.
The one who is talking is Charles.

Las que vienen son María y Rosita.
Those who are coming are Mary and Rose.

José quiere mi lápiz y el que Vd. tiene.
Joseph wants my pencil and the one that you have.

Lo que refers to an idea or statement rather than to a specific antecedent.

No entiendo lo que Vd. dijo.   *I do not understand what you said.*

102. Interrogative Words

The most common interrogative words have been used in the text in the questionnaires. Remember that an interrogative word always has a written accent.

¿Quién? refers *only* to persons. As the object of a verb it requires the personal **a.**

¿Quién va a hacerlo?	*Who is going to do it?*
¿A quién vio Vd. anoche?	*Whom did you see last night?*

The interrogative *whose* is expressed by **de quién** with the verb **ser.**

¿De quién es este sombrero?   *Whose hat is this?*
    (Of whom is this hat?)

¿Qué? (*what? which?*) when used as a *pronoun* refers to things; when used as an *adjective*, to persons or things.

¿Qué quiere Vd.?	*What do you want?*
¿Qué libro lee Carlos?	*What (which) book is Charles reading?*

With the verb **ser, ¿qué?** asks for a definition or identification.

¿Qué es un gaucho?	*What is a gaucho?*
¿Qué es eso?	*What is that?*

¿Cuál?, ¿cuáles? (*which?, what?*) are used before **ser** and **de** when the meaning *which?* or *which one?* is expressed or implied.

¿Cuál es el mejor teatro?	*Which is the best theater?*
¿Cuál de los sombreros prefiere?	*Which of the hats do you prefer?*
¿Cuál es la capital de Cuba?	*What is the capital of Cuba?*

103. Exclamatory Words

(a) ¡**Qué** + a noun! = *What a ...!*

¡**Qué mujer**!	*What a woman!*	¡**Qué vida**!	*What a life!*

An adjective may precede the noun, but frequently the adjective follows the noun reinforced by the word **tan** or **más** to intensify the meaning of the adjective.

¡Qué magnífica vista!	*What a magnificent view!*
¡Qué hombre tan rico!	*What a rich man!*
¡Qué muchacha más bonita!	*What a pretty girl!*

(b) ¡**Qué**! + an adjective = *How ...!*

¡**Qué fácil es**!	*How easy it is!*	¡**Qué cansado estoy**!	*How tired I am!*

EXERCISES

A. Change the following sentences to indicate doubt or a situation contrary to fact:

EXAMPLE: Si voy al baile me divertiré.
Si fuera al baile me divertiría.

1. Si voy al baile me divertiré.
2. Si Carlos tiene dinero irá a la excursión.
3. Si hace frío no saldremos.
4. Si tengo buena suerte ganaré algo.
5. Si escucho al profesor entiendo las reglas.
6. Si el programa es interesante invitaré a María.
7. Si tenemos la oportunidad la veremos.
8. Si los jóvenes tienen tiempo irán a las fiestas.
9. Si Vd. gana mil dólares los gastará.
10. Si escribimos en español cometemos muchos errores.

B. Change each statement to an exclamation:

EXAMPLE: Es difícil.   ¡Qué difícil es!

1. Es difícil.	4. Son bondadosos.	7. Estamos nerviosos.
2. Es caro.	5. Estoy cansada.	8. Es chico.
3. Están satisfechos.	6. Está limpio.	

C. Compose and answer ten questions in Spanish using the following interrogative words:

1. ¿Quién?	5. ¿A quién?	8. ¿Por qué?
2. ¿Cuál?	6. ¿Dónde?	9. ¿Cuánto?
3. ¿Qué?	7. ¿Cómo?	10. ¿Cuántos?
4. ¿De quién?		

D. Write in Spanish:

(*a*)
1. What a man!
2. How difficult it is!
3. What they said is true.
4. What a small house!
5. Whose pen is this?
6. Which of the girls do you prefer?
7. The one who is working is Charles.
8. With whom did she go?
9. What does he write with?
10. What book is he studying?

(*b*)
1. I would go home if I didn't have a class.
2. If the professor explains the lesson I will understand it.
3. If I knew what they wanted I would give it to them.
4. If he wins he will buy candy and flowers for his sweetheart.
5. If I knew her I would speak to her.

VOCABULARY

cantar *to sing*
cerrar (ie) *to close*
declarar *to declare*
descubrir *to discover*
dispensar *to excuse, pardon*
repasar *to review*
tratar de *to try to*

el autor *author*
el capítulo *chapter*
colonial *colonial*
Cristóbal Colón *Christopher Columbus*

descubierto, -a *discovered*
la época *epoch, era*
la fecha *date*
gobernado, -a *governed*
la independencia *independence*
Los de Abajo *The Under Dogs*
un millón *a million*
moderno, -a *modern*
la novela *novel*
el Océano Pacífico *Pacific Ocean*
último, -a *last*

desde niña *since I was a little girl*
en este momento *at this moment*
hacer el papel *to play the part*
le toca a Vd. *it is your turn*

MODEL SENTENCES

1. El Nuevo Mundo fue descubierto por Cristóbal Colón.
2. Se cultiva el café en el Brasil.
3. Llamaron al muchacho a las ocho.

1. *The New World was discovered by Christopher Columbus.*
2. *Coffee is cultivated in Brazil.*
3. *The boy was called at eight o'clock.*

4. La ventana estaba abierta cuando entré.

4. *The window was open when I entered.*

5. Cien estudiantes terminaron sus estudios en mil novecientos sesenta y ocho.

5. *A hundred students finished their studies in nineteen sixty-eight.*

6. Le oí gritar. Nos vieron salir.

6. *I heard him shout. They saw us leave.*

EXPRESS IN SPANISH

1. The Pacific Ocean was discovered by Balboa. The door was opened by Mary. The books were written by Cervantes.
2. Coffee is served with the meal. Spanish is spoken in this class.
3. The girl was called at six o'clock. I was given a present.
4. The door is closed (*result of action*). The book is written in Spanish. It is well written.
5. A hundred men; the years 1776, 1510, 1941.
6. I saw him come in. They heard me shout. We heard him interrupt the professor.

Fechas importantes

Aunque hace buen tiempo hoy, Carlos y Pepe no juegan al tenis; aunque hay una película magnífica, Pedro y Pancho no piensan ir; y aunque las tiendas anuncian ventas especiales, María y Anita no van de compras. ¿Es que nadie tiene tiempo para divertirse? Es que hay
5 examen mañana y todos se han reunido en casa de Carlos para repasar los últimos capítulos del libro de español. Carlos hace el papel de profesor.

—Primero repasemos algunas fechas importantes. Vamos a ver si ustedes saben decirlas en español. Pedro, ¿cuándo se descubrió el
10 Nuevo Mundo?

—El Nuevo Mundo fue descubierto por Cristóbal Colón en el año mil cuatrocientos noventa y dos.

—¿Y el Océano Pacífico, Pancho?

—El Océano Pacífico fue descubierto por Balboa en el año mil
15 quinientos trece.

—María, ¿cuántos años duró la época colonial?

—Los países americanos fueron gobernados por España durante trescientos años. El último país que ganó la independencia fue Cuba, en el año mil ochocientos noventa y ocho.

175

20 —Ahora, Anita, le toca a Vd. decirnos cuándo se declaró la independencia de las colonias inglesas.

—Ésa es una fecha que sé desde niña. Fue en el año mil setecientos setenta y seis.

En este momento Pepe interrumpió diciendo: —Dispénseme,
25 Carlos; quisiera hablar de otra cosa. Muchas veces he querido preguntarle si todos estos libros de su padre son de autores mexicanos.

—No, Pepe, algunos son de autores españoles. Miren Vds., este libro grande es *Don Quijote*, escrito por el gran autor español Miguel Cervantes, hace más de trescientos años. Pero muchos de estos pequeños
30 libros son novelas de autores mexicanos. Mi padre los trajo de México.

—¿Ha leído Vd. algunas de esas novelas, Carlos?

—Sí, he leído cuatro o cinco. Los libros que más me gustan son *Los de abajo* y *El Indio*, que fueron escritos por autores modernos. Quisiera contarles algo sobre ellos... pero ahora debemos seguir
35 repasando.

QUESTIONS

A. Answer in complete sentences in Spanish:

1. ¿Por qué no tiene nadie tiempo para divertirse?
2. ¿Dónde se han reunido todos?
3. ¿Para qué se han reunido?
4. ¿Quién hace el papel de profesor?
5. ¿Qué van a repasar primero?
6. ¿Cuándo se descubrió el Nuevo Mundo?
7. ¿Por quién fue descubierto el Nuevo Mundo?
8. ¿Cuál fue el último país americano que ganó su independencia?
9. ¿En qué año la ganó?
10. ¿Cuál es la fecha de nuestro día de independencia?

B. Personalized questions. Answer in complete sentences in Spanish:

1. ¿Se habla español en los Estados Unidos?
2. ¿Dónde se vende un buen biftec?
3. ¿Está abierta la puerta de la sala de clase?
4. ¿Por quién fue descubierto el Océano Pacífico?
5. ¿En qué año nació Vd.?
6. ¿Cuál es la fecha de hoy?

7. ¿Cuál es la fecha del último día de clases?
8. ¿Cuál es la capital de los Estados Unidos?
9. ¿Cuántos habitantes tiene este país?
10. ¿Cuántas páginas tiene este libro?

C. Pregúntele a un amigo:

1. cuántos años tiene.
2. cuántos habitantes tiene el pueblo en que vive.
3. si se habla español en su casa.
4. cuándo se celebra el Día de Año Nuevo.
5. por quién fue escrito *Don Quijote*.

GRAMMAR

104. Passive Voice

In the *active voice* the subject performs the act expressed by the verb.

Charles closed the door.

In the *passive voice* the subject is acted upon by an agent.

The door was closed by Charles.

The passive voice is not used as frequently in Spanish as in English. As explained in Lesson 13, when the subject of a verb is a *thing* a reflexive construction is often used in Spanish instead of the passive voice.

Se habla español aquí.   *Spanish is spoken here.*
Se venden sombreros allí.   *Hats are sold there.*

If the reflexive construction were used with a person being acted upon the meaning would not always be clear. For example, **se oyó** would mean *he heard himself* rather than *he was heard.* An active verb in the third person plural is a common substitute for the English passive voice if persons are acted upon.

I was called at nine o'clock.
(*They called me at nine o'clock.*) Me llamaron a las nueve.

He was given a book.
(*They gave him a book.*) Le dieron un libro.

177

The true passive is formed by the verb **ser** with the past participle, which agrees in number and gender with the subject. The true passive is used when the agent is expressed.

These books were written by Azuela. Estos libros fueron escritos por Azuela.
The door was closed by Charles. La puerta fue cerrada por Carlos.

105. *Estar* with the Past Participle

In Spanish **estar** is used with a past participle to describe the result of an action.

La ventana está abierta. *The window is open.*

There is no action expressed here; the state of the window is being mentioned. It is the result of an action which has already taken place.

106. The Infinitive

(*a*) The infinitive may be used as a verbal noun in Spanish. As a subject it is sometimes accompanied by the definite article.

El comer es necesario. *Eating is necessary.*
Ver es creer. *Seeing is believing.*

(*b*) The infinitive is used as the object of a preposition. (Lesson 11)

antes de llegar *before arriving*
después de estudiar *after studying*

(*c*) The infinitive is used after verbs of seeing and hearing. The infinitive directly follows the main verb.

Me vio entrar. *He saw me enter.*
Oí cantar a María. *I heard Mary sing.*

(*d*) The infinitive may be used after **hacer, mandar, dejar** and **permitir** instead of a subjunctive clause.

Él me hizo repasar la lección. *He had (made) me review the lesson.*
Le mandaron abrirlo. *They ordered him to open it.*

107. Prepositions Required before an Infinitive

(*a*) Verbs of motion, and verbs of beginning, teaching and learning, require **a** before an infinitive.

Él va a levantarse.	*He is going to get up.*
Ella comenzó a tocar el piano.	*She began to play the piano.*
Me enseñaron a leer el latín.	*They taught me to read Latin.*
No aprendí a hablar español.	*I didn't learn to speak Spanish.*

(*b*) Some verbs require **de** before an infinitive. The most common are **acabar, acordarse, alegrarse, dejar** and **tratar.**

Acaban de hacerlo.	*They have just done it.*
Me alegro de verle.	*I am glad to see you.*
Dejaron de trabajar.	*They stopped working.*
Trató de convencerme.	*He tried to convince me.*

(*c*) A few verbs require **en.** Among them are **insistir** and **tardar.**

Insistieron en pagar.	*They insisted on paying.*
Tardó en llegar.	*He was a long time in arriving.*

108. Numbers over One Hundred

100 ciento, cien	700 setecientos, -as
101 ciento uno, -a	800 ochocientos, -as
125 ciento veinte y cinco	900 novecientos, -as
200 doscientos, -as	1,000 mil
300 trescientos, -as	1,110 mil ciento diez
400 cuatrocientos, -as	1,043 mil cuarenta y tres
500 quinientos, -as	1,000,000 un millón
600 seiscientos, -as	2,000,000 dos millones

(*a*) **Uno** becomes **un** before a masculine noun, and **ciento** shortens to **cien** before a noun or a larger number.

veinte y un lápices	*twenty-one pencils*
cien dólares	*a hundred dollars*
cien mil personas	*a hundred thousand people*

(b) Note that the article **un** is omitted before **cien(to)** and **mil,** and that the conjunction **y** is used in Spanish only between tens and numbers less than ten.

ciento cincuenta hombres	*one hundred and fifty men*
mil libros	*a thousand books*
doscientos cincuenta y cinco	*two hundred and fifty-five*
trescientos uno	*three hundred and one*

(c) The numerals, from two hundred to nine hundred, agree with the noun they modify. Contrary to English usage, counting by hundreds goes only through nine hundred.

> trescientas novelas   *three hundred novels*
>
> el año mil cuatrocientos noventa y dos
> *the year fourteen hundred and ninety-two*

(d) **Millón** is the only number that is a noun. It has a plural form and requires **de** before the noun to which it refers.

> un millón de dólares   *a million dollars*
> dos millones de dólares   *two million dollars*

EXERCISES

A. Change the following sentences in the active voice to the passive voice:

EXAMPLE: Mi madre preparó la sopa.
La sopa fue preparada por mi madre.

1. Mi madre preparó la sopa.
2. El señor Pérez escribió este artículo.
3. España gobernó los países latinoamericanos.
4. La señora Martínez compró ese coche.
5. López y Fuentes escribió la novela.
6. María abrió los libros.
7. Carlos cerró la puerta.
8. Los jóvenes presentaron el programa.

B. Use the following verbs with **se** in a short sentence in Spanish as a substitute for the passive voice:

> EXAMPLE: se venden
>
> Se venden artículos de plata en México.

1. se venden	4. se compró	6. se cerrará
2. se cultiva	5. se escribieron	7. se abrieron
3. se habla		

C. Give in Spanish:

1. 100 rooms; 2,000 children; three million women
2. 33; 440; 507
3. 1,172; 3,756; 1,968
4. the first day; the third chapter; the tenth page
5. $5,199; $3,200; $5,000,000

D. Insert the proper Spanish preposition:

1. Comenzaron _____ estudiar.
2. Acabo _____ comer.
3. Se alegraron _____ verlos.
4. Ella no insiste _____ hacerlo.
5. Me enseñó _____ jugar al tenis.
6. Nunca aprenderá _____ hablar bien.
7. No tardará _____ entrar.
8. Dejó _____ cantar.
9. Trataré _____ llegar temprano.
10. No iban _____ hacerlo.

E. Write in Spanish:

1. Travel is interesting.
2. I was given a hundred dollars.
3. This book was written in 1950.
4. The windows were open.
5. Our professor wants us to read three difficult books.
6. English is never spoken in that class.
7. The novel was written by Azuela.
8. I gave him $575 for the car.
9. Before coming to the class I began to review the lessons.
10. I hope that we have finished the last lesson.

APPENDIX
VOCABULARIES
INDEX

APPENDIX

109. Regular Verbs

INDICATIVE MOOD

First Conjugation	*Second Conjugation*	*Third Conjugation*
	INFINITIVE	
hablar *to speak*	**aprender** *to learn*	**vivir** *to live*
	PRESENT PARTICIPLE	
hablando *speaking*	aprendiendo *learning*	viviendo *living*
	PRESENT TENSE	
I speak, do speak,	*I learn, do learn,*	*I live, do live,*
am speaking, etc.	*am learning,* etc.	*am living,* etc.
hablo	aprendo	vivo
hablas	aprendes	vives
habla	aprende	vive
hablamos	aprendemos	vivimos
habláis	aprendéis	vivís
hablan	aprenden	viven
	IMPERFECT	
I was speaking, used to	*I was learning, used to*	*I was living, used to*
speak, spoke, etc.	*learn, learned,* etc.	*live, lived,* etc.
hablaba	aprendía	vivía
hablabas	aprendías	vivías
hablaba	aprendía	vivía
hablábamos	aprendíamos	vivíamos
hablabais	aprendíais	vivíais
hablaban	aprendían	vivían

185

I spoke, did speak, etc.	*I learned, did learn,* etc.	*I lived, did live,* etc.
hablé	aprendí	viví
hablaste	aprendiste	viviste
habló	aprendió	vivió
hablamos	aprendimos	vivimos
hablasteis	aprendisteis	vivisteis
hablaron	aprendieron	vivieron

FUTURE

I shall (will) speak, etc.	*I shall (will) learn,* etc.	*I shall (will) live,* etc.
hablaré	aprenderé	viviré
hablarás	aprenderás	vivirás
hablará	aprenderá	vivirá
hablaremos	aprenderemos	viviremos
hablaréis	aprenderéis	viviréis
hablarán	aprenderán	vivirán

CONDITIONAL

I should (would) speak, etc.	*I should (would) learn,* etc.	*I should (would) live,* etc.
hablaría	aprendería	viviría
hablarías	aprenderías	vivirías
hablaría	aprendería	viviría
hablaríamos	aprenderíamos	viviríamos
hablaríais	aprenderíais	viviríais
hablarían	aprenderían	vivirían

THE PERFECT TENSES

PAST PARTICIPLES

hablado *spoken*	aprendido *learned*	vivido *lived*

PRESENT PERFECT

I have spoken, etc.	*I have learned,* etc.	*I have lived,* etc.
he hablado	he aprendido	he vivido
has hablado	has aprendido	has vivido
ha hablado	ha aprendido	ha vivido
hemos hablado	hemos aprendido	hemos vivido
habéis hablado	habéis aprendido	habéis vivido
han hablado	han aprendido	han vivido

PLUPERFECT

I had spoken, etc.	*I had learned*, etc.	*I had lived*, etc.
había habías había } hablado habíamos habíais habían	aprendido	vivido

FUTURE PERFECT

I shall (will) have spoken, etc.	*I shall (will) have learned*, etc.	*I shall (will) have lived*, etc.
habré habrás habrá } hablado habremos habréis habrán	aprendido	vivido

CONDITIONAL PERFECT

I should (would) have spoken, etc.	*I should (would) have learned*, etc.	*I should (would) have lived*, etc.
habría habrías habría } hablado habríamos habríais habrían	aprendido	vivido

SUBJUNCTIVE MOOD

PRESENT

(*That*) *I may speak, let me speak*, etc.	(*That*) *I may learn, let me learn*, etc.	(*That*) *I may live, let me live*, etc.
(que) hable	(que) aprenda	(que) viva
(que) hables	(que) aprendas	(que) vivas
(que) hable	(que) aprenda	(que) viva

187

(que) hablemos	(que) aprendamos	(que) vivamos
(que) habléis	(que) aprendáis	(que) viváis
(que) hablen	(que) aprendan	(que) vivan

IMPERFECT (Past) **-ra** FORM

(That) I might or should speak, etc.	*(That) I might or should learn*, etc.	*(That) I might or should live*, etc.
(que) hablara	(que) aprendiera	(que) viviera
(que) hablaras	(que) aprendieras	(que) vivieras
(que) hablara	(que) aprendiera	(que) viviera
(que) habláramos	(que) aprendiéramos	(que) viviéramos
(que) hablarais	(que) aprendierais	(que) vivierais
(que) hablaran	(que) aprendieran	(que) vivieran

IMPERFECT (Past) **-se** FORM

(que) hablase	(que) aprendiese	(que) viviese
(que) hablases	(que) aprendieses	(que) vivieses
(que) hablase	(que) aprendiese	(que) viviese
(que) hablásemos	(que) aprendiésemos	(que) viviésemos
(que) hablaseis	(que) aprendieseis	(que) vivieseis
(que) hablasen	(que) aprendiesen	(que) viviesen

PRESENT PERFECT

haya
hayas
haya
hayamos   }hablado   aprendido   vivido
hayáis
hayan

PLUPERFECT (**-ra** form)

hubiera
hubieras
hubiera
hubiéramos   }hablado   aprendido   vivido
hubierais
hubieran

APPENDIX

PLUPERFECT (-se form)

hubiese
hubieses
hubiese
}hablado   aprendido   vivido
hubiésemos
hubieseis
hubiesen

110. Commands and the Imperative Mood

The true imperative mood is used only in familiar affirmative commands.

| habla (tú) | hablad (vosotros) | *speak* |
| aprende (tú) | aprended (vosotros) | *learn* |

This singular form is like the third person singular form of the present indicative in all regular verbs and in some irregular ones.

The plural form of the imperative is regular in all verbs. It is formed by dropping the **-r** of the infinitive ending and adding **-d.**

To give familiar commands in the negative and to express all formal commands, both affirmative and negative, the present subjunctive is used. (See Section 83.)

Following is a table of the command forms of regular verbs, of two irregular verbs (**dar** and **decir**) and of a reflexive verb (**levantarse**).

Commands and Imperatives

1. hablar

		SINGULAR	PLURAL	
Familiar	Positive	habla tú	hablad vosotros	*speak*
	Negative	no hables tú	no habléis vosotros	*do not speak*
Polite or	Positive	hable usted	hablen ustedes	*speak*
Formal	Negative	no hable usted	no hablen ustedes	*do not speak*

2. aprender

Familiar	Positive	aprende tú	aprended vosotros	*learn*
	Negative	no aprendas tú	no aprendáis vosotros	*do not learn*
Polite or	Positive	aprenda usted	aprendan ustedes	*learn*
Formal	Negative	no aprenda usted	no aprendan ustedes	*do not learn*

3. escribir

Familiar	Positive	escribe tú	escribid vosotros	*write*
	Negative	no escribas tú	no escribáis vosotros	*do not write*
Polite or	Positive	escriba usted	escriban ustedes	*write*
Formal	Negative	no escriba usted	no escriban ustedes	*do not write*

4. dar

Familiar	Positive	da tú	dad vosotros	*give*
	Negative	no des tú	no deis vosotros	*do not give*
Polite or	Positive	dé usted	den ustedes	*give*
Formal	Negative	no dé usted	no den ustedes	*do not give*

5. decir

Familiar	Positive	di tú	decid vosotros	*tell*
	Negative	no digas tú	no digáis vosotros	*do not tell*
Polite or	Positive	diga usted	digan ustedes	*tell*
Formal	Negative	no diga usted	no digan ustedes	*do not tell*

6. levantarse

Familiar	Positive	levántate tú	levantaos vosotros	*get up*
	Negative	no te levantes tú	no os levantéis vosotros	*do not get up*
Polite or	Positive	levántese usted	levántense ustedes	*get up*
Formal	Negative	no se levante usted	no se levanten ustedes	*do not get up*

111. Verbs with Spelling Changes

See Sections 87 and 88 for an explanation of spelling changes. Verbs of this type used in this text are:

c > qu: acercarse (a), buscar, dedicar, explicar, practicar, sacar, tocar

g > gu: entregar, jugar (*ue*), llegar, pagar, rogar (*ue*)

z > c: comenzar (*ie*), empezar (*ie*)

c > zc: aparecer, conocer, ofrecer, parecer

g > j: coger, dirigir, escoger, recoger

gu > g: conseguir (*i, i*), distinguir, seguir (*i, i*)

APPENDIX

112. Cardinal Numbers

1. un(o), una	16. diez y seis	90. noventa
2. dos	17. diez y siete	100. ciento, cien
3. tres	18. diez y ocho	101. ciento un(o)
4. cuatro	19. diez y nueve	200. doscientos, -as
5. cinco	20. veinte	300. trescientos, -as
6. seis	21. veinte y un(o)	400. cuatrocientos, -as
7. siete	22. veinte y dos	500. quinientos, -as
8. ocho	30. treinta	600. seiscientos, -as
9. nueve	31. treinta y un(o)	700. setecientos, -as
10. diez	32. treinta y dos	800. ochocientos, -as
11. once	40. cuarenta	900. novecientos, -as
12. doce	50. cincuenta	1,000. mil
13. trece	60. sesenta	2,000. dos mil
14. catorce	70. setenta	1,000,000. un millón (de)
15. quince	80. ochenta	2,000,000. dos millones (de)

113. Summary of the Uses of the Subjunctive

1. In all formal commands, and in familiar commands when negative.

Siéntese aquí. *Sit down here.*
Aprenda la lección. *Learn the lesson.*

No lo comas. *Don't eat it.*
No me lo digas. *Don't tell me.*

2. In indirect commands.

Que lo haga él. *Let him do it.*
Que lo compre Anita. *Have Anne buy it.*
No nos levantemos. *Let's not get up.*

3. In a dependent noun clause after certain verbs.

A. After verbs of volition with a change of subject.

Quiero que Carlos vaya conmigo.
I want Charles to go with me.

Le pedí a mi padre que me mandara dinero.
I asked my father to send me some money.

B. After verbs of emotion when there is a definite subject in the subordinate (dependent) clause.

Siento que él esté enfermo. *I am sorry that he is sick.*
María se alegraba de que viniésemos. *Mary was glad that we were coming.*

C. After verbs of doubt or denial used affirmatively, and usually after verbs of thinking or believing used in the negative.

Dudo que ustedes estudien.	*I doubt that you are studying.*
No creen que ella sea rica.	*They do not believe that she is rich.*

D. After an impersonal expression, if a subject is mentioned.

Es necesario que Vd. lo haga.	*It is necessary for you to do it.*
Era necesario que Vd. lo hiciera.	*It was necessary for you to do it.*

4. In a relative (adjective) clause modifying a negative, non-existent, or indefinite antecedent.

No hay nadie que lo conozca.
There is no one who knows him.

Busco un lugar donde no haya mucho tráfico.
I am looking for a place where there is not much traffic.

5. In adverbial clauses.

A. The subjunctive is always used after the following conjunctions:

antes (de) que	*before*	a menos que	*unless*
como si	*as if*	para que	*in order that, so that*
con tal que	*provided that*	sin que	*without*

Lo haré antes de que Vd. llegue.	*I shall do it before you arrive.*
Salieron sin que yo lo supiera.	*They left without my knowing it.*

B. After conjunctions of purpose, concession, proviso, etc., if the action is to take place in the future. Some conjunctions of this type are:

aunque	*although*	donde	*where(ever)*
como	*how(ever)*	de modo que	*so that, in such a way that*
a fin de que	*so that*		

Aunque sea caro, lo compraré.
Although it may be expensive, I shall buy it.

Hablarán despacio de modo que yo pueda entender.
They will speak slowly so that I can understand.

C. In time clauses which refer to a future time. Common conjunctions which introduce clauses of time are:

cuando *when*   tan pronto como *as soon as*
hasta que *until*   mientras *while*
en cuanto *as soon as*   después (de) que *after*

> Anita estudiará hasta que termine.
> *Anne will study until she finishes.*
>
> Ella dijo que estudiaría hasta que terminara.
> *She said she would study until she finished.*

6. In the "if clause" of a condition which is doubtful or contrary to fact. The other clause in English is always a *should* or *would* clause.

> Si yo tuviera bastante dinero yo compraría un aparato de televisión.
> *If I had enough money I would buy a television set.*
>
> Si él hubiera estado aquí yo le habría visto.
> *If he had been here I would have seen him.*

SPANISH–ENGLISH VOCABULARY

a   to, at
el abanico   fan
abierto (*past p. of* **abrir**)   open, opened
abril   April
abrir   to open
la abuela   grandmother
el abuelo   grandfather
la abundancia   abundance
acabar   to finish, end; **acabar de** + *inf.*   to have just + *past p.*
el acento   accent
aceptar   to accept
acercarse   to approach
acompañar   to accompany
acordarse (ue) (de)   to remember
acostarse (ue)   to go to bed
además   besides, moreover
adiós   good-bye
el adjetivo   adjective
el administrador de correos   postmaster
agosto   August
agradable   pleasant, agreeable
el agua (*f.*)   water
ahora   now
al (**a** + **el**)   to the; **al** + *inf.*   upon (on) + *pres. p.*; **al salir**   upon leaving
alegrarse (de)   to be glad
alegre   happy, gay
alegremente   happily, gayly
algo   something, anything
alguien   some one, somebody
algún (*shortening of* **alguno** *before a masc. sing. noun*)
alguno, -a   some, any; *pl.,* some, several
alto, -a   high, tall

la alumna   student (*f.*)
el alumno   student (*m.*)
allí   there
amable   pleasant, kind
amar   to love
amarillo, -a   yellow
América   America
la América Latina   Latin America
americano, -a   American
la amiga   friend (*f.*)
el amigo   friend (*m.*)
el animal   animal
Anita   Anne
anoche   last night
antes de (que)   before
anunciar   to announce, advertise
añadir   to add
el año   year; **tener diez años**   to be ten years old; **¿Cuántos años tiene?**   How old is he?; **el año pasado**   last year
aparecer   to appear
el apartado   mailbox
el apellido   surname, family name
el apetito   appetite; **tener apetito**   to be hungry
aprender   to learn
aprovechar(se)   to profit by, take advantage of
apurarse   to hurry
aquel, aquella *adj.*   that; **aquellos, aquellas**   those; **aquél, aquélla** *pron.*   that (one); **aquéllos, aquéllas**   those
aquí   here
el árbol   tree
arriba   upstairs, up

el **artículo** article
así so, thus
el **asiento** seat
asistir (a) to attend
la **atención** attention
aunque although, even though
el **autobús** bus
el **autor** author
el **avión** plane
¡ay! exclamation of surprise
ayer yesterday
ayudar (a) to help, assist
azul blue

bailar to dance
el **baile** dance
bajar to get off, to go (come) down
bajo, -a low, short
el **banco** bank
la **banda** band
el **baño** bath; **tomar baños de mar** to go swimming
barato, -a cheap
el **barco** boat
el **básquetbol** basketball
bastante *adj.* enough, sufficient; *adv.* quite, rather
bastar to be enough
el **béisbol** baseball
la **belleza** beauty
bello, -a beautiful
la **biblioteca** library
bien well
la **bienvenida** welcome; **dar la bienvenida** to welcome
el **biftec** beefsteak
el **billete** bill, ticket; **billete de ida y vuelta** round-trip ticket
blanco, -a white
la **blusa** blouse
la **bondad** kindness; **tenga la bondad de +** *inf.* please
bondadoso, -a kind
bonito, -a pretty
bueno, -a good, well
buen (*shortening of* **bueno** *before a masc. sing. noun*)
buscar to look for; **ir a buscar** go to get

el **caballo** horse
cada (*invariable*) each
el **café** coffee; café
la **cafetería** cafeteria
el **calor** heat; **hacer calor** to be warm (*weather*); **tener calor** to be warm (*persons*)
la **calle** street
la **cama** bed
la **cámara** camera
caminar to walk, go
el **camino** road
la **camisa** shirt
el **campeonato** championship
el **campo** country (*not town*)
la **cancha** court (*tennis*)
cansado, -a tired
cantar to sing
la **capital** capital (*city*)
el **Capitolio** Capitol
el **capítulo** chapter
Carlos Charles
la **carne** meat
la **carnicería** butcher shop
caro, -a expensive, dear
la **carrera** profession
la **carretera** highway
la **carta** letter
la **casa** house, home; **a casa** home; **en casa** at home
casarse con to marry, get married
casi almost
el **castillo** castle
catorce fourteen
la **causa** cause
la **celebración** celebration
celebrar to celebrate; **celebrarse** to be celebrated
el **centavo** cent
el **centro** downtown district, center
cerca de near
el **cereal** cereal
cerrar (ie) to close
certificado, -a registered
ciento (cien) one hundred
cierto, -a certain
el **cigarrillo** cigarette
cinco five
cincuenta fifty
el **cine** movies

la ciudad city
claro, -a evident, clear, light (*color*)
la clase class; kind
el clavel carnation
la cocina kitchen
el coche car
colombiano, -a Colombian
Colón Columbus
colonial colonial
el color color
el comedor dining room
comenzar (ie) to begin
comer to eat, have dinner
cometer to commit
la comida dinner, meal
como as, like; **como si** as if
¿cómo? how?; **¿Cómo está usted?** How
 are you?
la comparación comparison
completo, -a complete, full
la compra purchase; **ir de compras** to go
 shopping
comprar to buy
comprender to understand
con with
el concierto concert
confundir to confuse
conmigo with me
conocer to know, be acquainted with
conseguir (i, i) to get, obtain
consigo with himself, herself, yourself,
 themselves
contar (ue) to tell, count
contento, -a happy, satisfied
contestar (a) to answer
contigo with you (*fam.*)
el contraste contrast
la conversación conversation
correctamente correctly
el correo post office
cortés courteous, polite
corto, -a short
la cosa thing
costar (ue) to cost
creer to believe, think; **¡ya lo creo!** of
 course!; **creo que no** I think not; **creo**
 que sí I think so
creyendo believing, thinking
el cuaderno notebook
cual: el cual, la cual, los cuales, las cuales,

rel. pron. that which, who; **¿cuál?**
 which one? what?
cualquier(a) any, any one
cuando when; **¿cuándo?** when?
cuanto: en cuanto as soon as; **¿cuánto?**
 how much? **¿cuánto vale?** what is the
 price?
¿cuántos, -as? how many?
cuarenta forty
el cuarto quarter; room; fourth
cuatro four
cuatrocientos, -as four hundred
Cuba Cuba
cubano, -a Cuban
el cuento story
Cuernavaca an important town south of
 Mexico City
la cuestión question
el cuidado anxiety, worry; **no tenga cuidado**
 don't worry
cultivar to cultivate, raise
el cumpleaños birthday

charlar to talk, chat
el cheque check
chico, -a small
el chico boy; fellow (*colloquial*)

dar to give; **dar un paseo** to take a walk
 or ride
de of, from; (*after a superlative*) in;
 (*before a number*) than
deber ought, must
decidir, decidirse to decide
décimo, -a tenth
decir to say, tell; **decir que sí (no)** to say
 yes (no); **quiere decir** means
la declaración declaration
declarar to declare
dedicar to devote
dejar (*trans.*) to leave; let; allow; **dejar**
 de + inf. to stop, cease
del = de + el of (*from*) the
delante de in front of
dentro de within, inside of
la dependiente clerk
el deporte sport

la **derecha** right hand, right; **a la derecha** on the right

desayunarse to eat breakfast

el **desayuno** breakfast; **para el desayuno** for breakfast; **tomar el desayuno** to eat breakfast

descansar to rest

descubierto, -a discovered

descubrir to discover

desde from, since; **desde niña** since I was a little girl

desear to want, desire

el **deseo** desire; **tener deseos de** to be eager to

desocupado, -a vacant, unoccupied

despacio slowly

despedirse (i, i) (de) to say good-bye (to)

el **despertador** alarm clock

despertarse (ie) to wake up

despidiéndose saying good-bye

después afterwards: **después de (que)** after

detenerse to stop

detrás de behind

el **día** day; **buenos días** good morning; **todos los días** every day

el **diccionario** dictionary

diciembre December

diciendo saying, telling

dicho said, told

diez ten; **diez y seis (siete, etc.)** sixteen (seventeen, etc.)

difícil difficult, hard

la **dificultad** difficulty

el **dinero** money

Dios God; **¡por Dios!** for Heaven's sake!

discutir to discuss

dispensar to excuse

la **diversión** amusement

divertido, -a amusing

divertirse (ie, i) to have a good time

divirtiéndose having a good time

dobles doubles (*tennis*)

doce twelve

la **docena** dozen

el **dólar** dollar

el **domingo** (*on*) Sunday; **los domingos** (*on*) Sundays

donde where; **¿dónde?** where?

dormir (ue, u) to sleep; **dormirse (ue, u)** to go to sleep

el **dormitorio** dormitory

dos two

doscientos, -as two hundred

la **duda** doubt

dudar to doubt

los **dulces** candy

durante during

durar to last

durmiendo sleeping

e and (*before* **i** *or* **hi**)

el **edificio** building

el **ejercicio** exercise

él he; (*after prep.*) him, it

el (*def. art.*) the; **el de** the one of, that of; **el que** the one who, he who

ella she; (*after prep.*) her, it

ellas they (*f.*); (*after prep.*) them

ello (*neuter pron.*) it

ellos they (*m.*); (*after prep.*) them

emocionante exciting

empezar (ie) to begin

el **empleado** clerk, employee

en in, into; on; at

encantar to charm, fascinate

encontrar (ue) to find; **encontrarse con** to meet, come across

enero January

enfermo, -a sick

enfrente de in front of

engañar to deceive

enseñar to teach, show

entender (ie) to understand

entonces then

entrar (en) to enter, come in

entre among, between

entregar to hand over

la **época** epoch, era

el **equipaje** baggage

el **equipo** team

el **error** mistake, error

escoger to select

escribir to write

escrito written

escuchar to listen (*to*)

la **escuela** school; **a la escuela** to school; **en la escuela** at school; **la escuela superior** high school

ese, esa *dem. adj.* that; **esos, esas** those

ése, ésa *dem. pron.* that (*one*); **ésos, ésas** those

eso that; **eso no** not that; **por eso** for that reason; **a eso de** about (*that time*)

España Spain

español (-ola) *adj.* Spanish

el español Spanish (*language*); Spaniard

especial special

especialmente especially

el espectáculo spectacle, show

el espejo mirror

esperar to expect; wait for; hope; **espero que no (sí)** I hope not (so)

la esposa wife

el esposo husband

la estación season; station

el estadio stadium

los Estados Unidos United States

estar to be; **estar bien** to be well, be all right

este, esta *dem. adj.* this; **estos, estas** those

éste, ésta *dem. pron.* this (*one*); **éstos, éstas** these

el estilo style

esto this

el estudiante student (*m.*)

la estudiante student (*f.*)

estudiar to study

el estudio study

el ex-alumno alumnus

el examen examination

excelente excellent

exclamar to exclaim

la excursión excursion; **hacer una excursión al campo** to go on a picnic

la experiencia experience

la explicación explanation

explicar explain

extranjero, -a foreign

fácil easy

fácilmente easily

la facultad school, faculty

la falta lack

faltar to lack

la familia family

famoso, -a famous

el favor favor, kindness; **haga el favor de +** *inf.* please

favorito, -a favorite

febrero February

la fecha date

feliz (*pl.* **felices**) happy

la fiesta celebration, party; **día de fiesta** holiday

figurarse to imagine

el fin end; **al fin** finally

la finca farm

la flor flower

el francés French (*language*)

francés (-esa) *adj.* French

Francia France

la frase sentence

frente: en frente de in front of

el frío cold; **hacer frío** to be cold (*weather*) **tener frío** to be cold (*persons*)

la fruta fruit

la función performance

el fútbol football

el futuro future

la gana desire, inclination; **tener ganas de** to feel like

ganar to win

gastar to spend

el gasto expense

el gato cat

el gaucho South American cowboy

el general general

gobernado, -a governed

gracias thank you, thanks

graduarse to be graduated

la gramática grammar

gran great (*shortening of* **grande** *before sing. noun*)

grande large, big

gritar to shout, cry out

el grupo group

guapo, -a handsome, fine-looking

gustar to be pleasing, like

el gusto pleasure; **tengo mucho gusto en conocerle** I am glad to meet you; **con mucho gusto** gladly

haber to have (*as an auxiliary*); **hay** there is, are; **había** there was, were; **habrá**

there will be; **hay luna** the moon is shining
el habitante inhabitant
hablar to speak
hacer to do, make; to be (*weather*); **hacer una pregunta** to ask a question; **hacer un papel** to play a part; **hace un año** a year ago
hacia toward
hágame el favor de + *inf.* please
el hambre (*f.*) hunger; **tener hambre** to be hungry
hasta until, up to; **hasta que** until; **hasta luego** see you later; **hasta mañana** see you tomorrow
hay there is, there are; **hay luna** the moon is shining; **hay sol** it is sunny
hecho done, made (*past p. of* **hacer**)
helado, -a iced
el helado ice cream
la hermana sister
el hermano brother; *pl.* brothers and sisters
hermoso, -a beautiful, handsome
la heroína heroine
la hija daughter
el hijo son; **los hijos** sons and daughters; children
la historia history
histórico, -a historical
el hombre man
la hora hour, time (*of day*); **¿qué hora es?** what time is it?; **es hora de comer** it is time to eat
el hotel hotel
hoy today; **hoy mismo** this very day
el huésped guest
el huevo egg
humano, -a human

ida: see **billete**
ido gone
la iglesia church; **a la iglesia** to church
importar to be important, matter; **no importa** it doesn't matter
la impresión impression
inconveniente inconvenient
la independencia independence
el indio, -a Indian
inesperado, -a unexpected

los informes information
inglés (-esa) *adj.* English
el inglés English (*language*)
inteligente intelligent
el interés interest
interesante interesting
interesar to interest
interrumpir to interrupt
el invierno winter
la invitación invitation
invitar (a) to invite
ir to go; **irse** to go away; **ir a** + *inf.* to be going to; **vamos** let's go; **ir de compras** to go shopping
Isabel Elizabeth
la isla island
la izquierda left hand, left; **a la izquierda** on the left

jamás never, ever
José Joseph
joven young
el joven young man
la joven young woman
los jóvenes young people
la joya jewel
Juan John
el juego game
el jueves (*on*) Thursday; **los jueves** (*on*) Thursdays
el jugador player
jugar (ue) (a) to play (*a game*); **jugar al tenis** to play tennis
el jugo juice
julio July
Julio Julius
junio June
juntos, -as together

la, las the; **la que (cual)** she who, the one that
la *obj. pron.* her, it (*f.*), you (*f.*)
el lado side; **al lado de** beside
el lápiz (*pl.* **lápices**) pencil
largo, -a long
la lástima pity; **es lástima** it is a pity, **¡qué lástima!** what a pity!
latino, -a Latin

latinoamericano, -a Latin American
le you, him; to you, to him, to her
la lección lesson
la leche milk
la lectura reading
leer to read
las legumbres vegetables
lejos far, distant; **lejos de** far from; **de lejos** from a distance
la lengua language, tongue
les you, them; to you, to them
levantar to raise; **levantarse** to get up
la ley law
leyendo reading
la libertad liberty
libre free
el librito pamphlet, program
el libro book
limpiar to clean
limpio, -a clean
listo, -a ready
lo it (*m.*), him, you
lo the; **lo que** that which; **lo mismo** the same
los the (*pl. def. art.*); them, you (*obj. pron.*)
luego later, afterward, then
el lugar place
la luna moon; **hay luna** the moon is shining
el lunes (*on*) Monday; **los lunes** (*on*) Mondays
la luz (*pl.* **luces**) light

llamar to call; **llamarse** to be called, be named
llegar to arrive
lleno, -a (de) full (of)
llevar to take, carry; wear
llover to rain

la madre mother
magnífico, -a magnificent
el maíz corn
mal badly
mal (*shortening of* **malo** *before a masc. sing. noun*)

la maleta suitcase; **hacer la maleta** to pack the suitcase
malo, -a bad; sick; poor
mandar to command, order; send
la manera manner
la mano hand; **a mano** by hand
la manzana apple
mañana tomorrow; **hasta mañana** see you tomorrow, until tomorrow
la mañana morning; **a la mañana siguiente** the next morning; **de la mañana** in the morning; **por la mañana** in the morning
la máquina machine
la mar sea
María Mary
marino, -a navy (*color*)
el martes (*on*) Tuesday; **los martes** (*on*) Tuesdays
marzo March
más more, most
mayo May
mayor greater, older; greatest, oldest
me me, to me, myself
el médico doctor
medio, -a half
el mediodía noon
mejor better, best; **lo mejor** the best
menor smaller, younger, smallest, youngest
menos less, least, minus; except; **a menos que** unless; **al menos** except
el mercado market
el mes month
la mesa table
mexicano, -a Mexican
México Mexico
mí me, myself
mi, mis my
el miedo fear; **tener miedo** to be afraid
el miembro member
mientras while
el miércoles (*on*) Wednesday; **los miércoles** (*on*) Wednesdays
mil thousand
el millón million
el millonario millionaire
mío (-a, -os, -as) my, of mine
mirar to look (*at*)
mismo, -a same; self; very; **lo mismo** the same (thing)
moderno, -a modern

el modo manner; de modo que so that
molestar to trouble
el momento moment
la montaña mountain
moreno, -a dark, brunette
morir (ue, u) to die
la muchacha girl
el muchacho boy
muchísimo very much
mucho, -a much; *pl.* many; *adv.* a great
  deal
el mundo world; todo el mundo everybody
la música music
muy very

nacer to be born
nada nothing, not anything
nadie no one, nobody; not anyone
la naranja orange
naturalmente naturally
la Navidad Christmas, Nativity
necesario, -a necessary
necesitar to need
el negocio business
negro, -a black
nervioso nervous; ponerse nervioso to become nervous
ni nor; ni... ni neither ... nor
el nilón nylon
ningún (*shortening of* ninguno *before masc.*
  sing. noun)
ninguno, -a no, none, no one, not any
la niña girl, child
el niño child, boy; *pl.* children
no no, not; decir que no to say no
la noche night; buenas noches good evening, good night; esta noche tonight;
  por la noche at night; todas las noches
  every night
el nombre name
norteamericano, -a North American
nos us, to us; ourselves
nosotros, -as we; us
notar to note
las noticias news
novecientos, -as nine hundred
la novela novel
noveno, -a ninth

noventa ninety
la novia sweetheart
noviembre November
nuestro, -a our, of ours; el nuestro ours
nueve nine
nuevo, -a new
el número number
nunca never; not ever

o or; o... o either ... or
la obligación debt, obligation
el Océano Pacífico Pacific Ocean
octavo, -a eighth
octubre October
ocupado, -a busy
ochenta eighty
ocho eight
ochocientos, -as eight hundred
la oficina office
ofrecer to offer
oir to hear
el ojo eye
olvidarse (de) to forget
once eleven
la oportunidad opportunity
ordeñar to milk
la orquesta orchestra
os you (*fam.*), to you; yourselves
el otoño autumn
otro, -a another; *pl.* other
oyendo hearing

el padre father; *pl.* parents
pagar to pay
la página page
el país country
la palabra word
Pancho Frank
el papel paper; hacer un papel to play a
  part
el paquete package
el par pair
para for, in order to; para que in order
  that; ¿para qué? why?
parecer to seem
parecido, -a similar
la pareja couple
el parque park

la **parte** part; **por todas partes** everywhere
el **partido** game, match
pasado, -a past; last; el **verano pasado** last summer
el **pasaporte** passport
pasar to pass, spend (*time*); happen; **pase Vd.** come in
el **paseo** walk, ride; **dar un paseo** to take a walk, ride
el **patio** yard
pedir (i, i) to ask for, request
Pedro Peter
la **película** film
el **pelo** hair
pensar (ie) to think; (+ *inf.*) to intend, to plan; **pensar en** to think about
peor worse, worst
Pepe Joe
pequeño, -a small, little
la **pera** pear
perder (ie) to lose, miss; waste
el **perfume** perfume
permitir to permit
pero but
la **persona** person
el **perro** dog
el **peso** Mexican dollar
pidiendo asking for
el **pie** foot
la **pizarra** blackboard
la **plata** silver
el **plato** plate, dish
la **playa** beach
la **pluma** pen
pobre poor
poco little; *pl.* few
poder to be able (*can*)
el **pollo** chicken
poner to put, to place; **ponerse** to put on, become; **poner la mesa** to set the table
por for, by, through; for the sake of; along; because of; **¿por qué?** why?; **por lo menos** at least; **por supuesto** of course
porque because, for
posible possible
practicar to practice
práctico, -a practical
el **precio** price

preferir (ie, i) to prefer
la **pregunta** question; **hacer una pregunta** to ask a question
preguntar to ask (*a question*)
preparar to prepare
presenciar to see, be present at
presentar introduce, present
la **primavera** spring
primer (*shortening of* **primero** *before a masc. sing. noun*)
primero, -a first
el **primo, la prima** cousin
la **prisa** haste; **tener prisa** to be in a hurry
probable probable
el **profesor, la profesora** teacher, professor
el **programa** program
prometer to promise
pronto soon, quickly; **de pronto** suddenly
pronunciar to pronounce
pudiendo being able
el **pueblo** town, nation, country
la **puerta** door
pues since; well
puesto put, placed (*p. p. of* **poner**)
punto point; **en punto** exactly

que that, who, which; whom; el **que** who, which, the one that
que than (*after a comparison*)
¿qué? what?, which?; **¡qué!** how!
quedar to remain, be left; **quedarle bien** to be becoming; **quedarse** to stay
quejarse to complain
querer to wish, want; **no querer** to refuse; **querer a** + *a pers. obj.* to love
quien who, whom, he who; **¿quién?** who?; **¿a quién?** to whom?, whom?; **¿de quién?** whose?
quince fifteen; **quince días** two weeks
quinientos, -as five hundred
quinto, -a fifth
quisiera I (he) should (would) like

rápidamente rapidly
rápido, -a rapid
la **raqueta** tennis racket
la **razón** reason; **tener razón** to be right

recibir to receive
recitar to recite
recordar (ue) to remember
el regalo present, gift
la regla rule
reírse to laugh
repasar to review
repetir (i, i) to repeat
responder to respond
el restaurante restaurant
reunirse to meet, get together
el rey king
los Reyes Magos Wise Men (Kings)
rico, -a rich
la risa laughter
rogar (ue) to beg
rojo, -a red
romántico, -a romantic
la ropa clothes
la rosa rose
la roseta de maíz popcorn
rubio, -a blonde, fair

el sábado (*on*) Saturday; **los sábados** (*on*) Saturdays
saber to know a fact, know how; find out, learn
sacar to take out
el saco sack, bag
la sala large room; living room; **sala de clase** classroom; **sala de lectura** reading room
salir (de) to leave, to go out
satisfecho, -a satisfied
se for **le** or **les** to him, to her, to you, to it, to them
se himself, herself, yourself, themselves
se one, people, they, you (*impersonal*)
la sed thirst; **tener sed** to be thirsty
seguida: en seguida at once
seguir (i, i) to follow, continue
según according to
segundo, -a second
seguro, -a sure; **estar seguro de** to be sure of
seis six
seiscientos, -as six hundred
la semana week
sentado, -a seated, sitting

sentarse (ie) to sit down
sentir (ie, i) to be sorry, regret; **sentirse** to feel (*sad, happy*)
el señor Mr., sir, gentleman; **los señores** Mr. and Mrs.; gentlemen
la señora Mrs., lady
la señorita Miss, young lady
septiembre September
séptimo, -a seventh
ser to be
servir (i, i) to serve; **¿en qué puedo servirle?** what can I do for you?
sesenta sixty
setecientos, -as seven hundred
setenta seventy
severo, -a strict, hard
sexto, -a sixth
sí yes; **creer que sí** to believe so
sí himself, herself, yourself, themselves, yourselves
si if, whether
siempre always
siete seven
siguiendo following, continuing
siguiente following, next; **al día siguiente** the next day
la silla chair
simpático, -a attractive, charming
sin without; **sin que** without
sino but
sintiendo regretting, feeling
el sitio place, site
sobre above, over, on; about
el sol sun; **hace (hay) sol** it is sunny; **tomar el sol** to enjoy the sunshine
solamente only
solo, -a alone
sólo only
la sombrerería millinery store
el sombrero hat
sonar (ue) to ring, sound
la sonrisa smile
la sopa soup
sorprenderse to be surprised
la sorpresa surprise
Sr. Mr., sir
Sra. Mrs., lady
Sres. Mr. and Mrs.; gentlemen
su, sus his, her, its, your, their
el sueño sleep; **tener sueño** to be sleepy

la suerte luck; **tener suerte** to be lucky
sufrir to suffer; **sufrir un examen** to take an examination
superior: la escuela superior high school
supuesto: por supuesto of course
el surtido stock
suyo, -a his, of his, her, of hers, your, their; **el suyo** his, hers, yours, theirs

tal such; such a; **¿qué tal?** how goes it? **con tal que** provided
también also, too
tampoco neither; not . . . either
tan so, as
tanto, -a as (so) much; *pl.* as (so) many **tanto... como** as much . . . as
tarde late; **más tarde** later
la tarde afternoon; **buenas tardes** good afternoon; **de la tarde, por la tarde** in the afternoon; **todas las tardes** every afternoon
la tarjeta card; **la tarjeta de turista** tourist card
el taxi taxi
te you, to you, yourself
el té tea
el teatro theater
Tejas Texas
la tela material, cloth
el teléfono telephone; **llamar por teléfono** to phone, call up
la televisión television
temer to be afraid
la temporada season
temprano early
tener to have; **tener que** + *inf.* to have to + *verb*
el tenis tennis
tercer (*shortening of* **tercero** *before masc. sing. noun*)
tercero, -a third
terminar to end, finish
ti you, yourself
el tiempo time, weather; **a tiempo** on time; **¿cuánto tiempo?** how long? **hace buen (mal) tiempo** it is good (bad) weather; **hace frío**, etc. it is cold, etc.
la tienda shop, store; **tienda de ropa** clothing store

la tía aunt
la tierra land, country
típico, -a typical
la toalla towel
tocar to play (*a musical instrument*); **tocarle a uno** to be one's turn
el tocino bacon
todavía yet, still
todo, -a all, every; everything; **todo el mundo** everybody; **todos los días** every day
tomar to take; **tomar el sol** to enjoy the sunshine
el tomate tomato
tonto, -a foolish
las tostadas toast
trabajar to work
el trabajo work
traer to bring
el traje suit; **traje de baño** bathing suit
tratar de to try to; treat
trayendo bringing
trece thirteen
treinta thirty
el tren train
tres three
trescientos, -as three hundred
triste sad
tu, tus your (*fam.*)
tú you (*fam.*)
tuyo, -a your, of yours (*fam.*)

u or (*used before* **o** *or* **ho**)
último, -a last
un, una a, an
la universidad university
uno, -a one; **unos, -as** some, a few
usar to use
usted (Vd.), ustedes (Vds.) you
la uva grape

la vaca cow
las vacaciones vacation
valer to be worth; **¿cuánto vale?** what is the price?
el valor value
vamos let's go
vamos a + *inf.* let's + *verb*

varios, -as several
el vaso glass
Vd., Vds. you
veces times, *pl. of* vez
veinte twenty
la vendedora seller, vendor (*f.*)
vender to sell
la venida arrival, coming
venir to come; **venir bien con** to look well with
la venta sale; **de venta** for sale
la ventana window
ver to see
el verano summer; **el verano que viene** next summer
veras: de veras really
el verbo verb
la verdad truth; **es verdad** it is true; **¿no es verdad?** isn't it, aren't they, don't you?
verdaderamente truly, really
el vestido dress
vestirse (i, i) to dress
el veterano veteran
la vez (*pl.* veces) time (*in a series*); **a la vez** at the same time; **a veces** at times; **algunas veces** some times; **en vez de** instead of; **muchas veces** often; **otra vez** again; **tal vez** perhaps; **varias veces** several times
viajar to travel

el viaje trip; **hacer un viaje** to take a trip
el viajero traveler
la vida life
viejo, -a old
el viento wind; **hace viento** it is windy
el viernes (*on*) Friday; **los viernes** (*on*) Fridays
viniendo coming
la visita visit; **de visita** on a visit
visitar to visit
visto seen
vivir to live
el vocabulario vocabulary
volver (ue) to return
vosotros you, yourselves
la voz (*pl.* voces) voice
la vuelta return; **billete de ida y vuelta** round-trip ticket
vuelto returned (*p.p. of* volver)
vuestro, -a your, of yours

y and
ya now, already; presently
yendo going
yo I

la zapatería shoe store
el zapato shoe

ENGLISH–SPANISH VOCABULARY

a, an un, una
able: be able poder
about de, sobre; (*time*) a eso de
above sobre
abundance la abundancia
accent el acento
accept aceptar
accompany acompañar
acquainted: be acquainted with conocer
add añadir
adjective el adjetivo
advantage: take advantage of aprovechar
advertise anunciar
after después de; después que
afternoon la tarde; **good afternoon** buenas tardes; **in the afternoon** de la tarde, por la tarde; **every afternoon** todas las tardes
afterwards después; más tarde, luego
again otra vez
ago: twenty-five years ago hace veinte y cinco años
alarm clock el despertador
all todo, -a
allow dejar, permitir
almost casi
alone solo, -a
along por
already ya
also también
although aunque
alumnus el ex-alumno
always siempre
America la América; Norteamérica
American americano, -a; norteamericano, -a

among entre
amusement la diversión
amusing divertido, -a
and y; (*before* i *or* hi) e
animal el animal
Anne Anita
announce anunciar
another otro, -a
answer contestar (a)
any cualquier(a); (*after a negative*) ninguno, -a (ningún)
anyone alguien; (*after negative*) nadie
anything algo; **not anything** nada
anxiety el cuidado
anxious: be anxious to tener ganas de; tener deseos de
appear aparecer
appetite el apetito
apple la manzana
approach acercarse (a)
April abril
around por; **around here** por aquí
arrive (at *or* **in)** llegar (a)
article el artículo
as como, tan; **as...as** tan... como; **as if** como si; **as much (many)** tanto(s); **as much (many)...as** tanto(s)... como; **as soon as** tan pronto como, en cuanto
ask for pedir (i, i)
ask (*a question*) preguntar
at a, en; **at home** en casa; **at the same time** a la vez; **at once** en seguida
attend asistir (a)
attractive simpático, -a
August agosto

207

aunt la tía
author el autor
automobile el coche, el automóvil
autumn el otoño

back: on the way back de regreso
bacon el tocino
bad malo, -a; mal
badly mal
bag el saco
baggage el equipaje
band la banda
bank el banco
baseball el béisbol
basketball el básquetbol
bath el baño
bathing suit traje de baño
be estar; ser; **be able** poder; **be becoming** quedarle bien; **be good (bad) weather** hacer buen (mal) tiempo; **be hungry (right, sleepy, thirsty, warm, cold)** tener hambre (razón, sueño, sed, calor, frío); **be left** quedar a; **be sorry** sentir (ie, i)
beach la playa
beautiful bello, -a; hermoso, -a
beauty la belleza
because porque; **because of** por
become ponerse
bed la cama; **go to bed** acostarse (ue)
beefsteak el biftec
before antes de (que)
beg rogar (ue)
begin comenzar (ie), empezar (ie)
behind detrás (de)
believe creer; **believe so (not)** creer que sí (no)
besides además
best mejor; **the best** lo mejor
better mejor
between entre
big grande
bill (*money*) el billete
birthday el cumpleaños
black negro, -a
blackboard la pizarra
blond(e) rubio, -a
blouse la blusa
blue azul; **navy blue** azul marino
boat el barco

book el libro
born: be born nacer
boulevard el paseo
boy el muchacho; **little boy** el niño
breakfast el desayuno; **for breakfast** para el desayuno; **eat breakfast** tomar el desayuno, desayunarse
briefly brevemente
bring traer
brother el hermano
brothers (and sisters) los hermanos
brunette moreno, -a
building el edificio
bunch (*flowers*) el ramo
bus el autobús
business el negocio
busy ocupado, -a
but pero; sino
butcher shop la carnicería
buy comprar
by por; (*time*) para

café el café
cafeteria la cafetería
call llamar; **be called** llamarse
candy los dulces
capital (*city*) la capital
capitol el capitolio
car el coche, el automóvil
card la tarjeta
carnation el clavel
carry llevar
castle el castillo
cat el gato
cause la causa
cease dejar de + *inf.*
celebrate celebrar; **be celebrated** celebrarse
celebration la celebración, la fiesta
cent el centavo
center el centro
cereal el cereal
certain cierto, -a
chair la silla
championship el campeonato
chapter el capítulo
Charles Carlos
charm encantar
charming simpático, -a
chat charlar

cheap barato, -a, bajo, -a
cheat engañar
check el cheque
chicken el pollo
child niño, niña; **children** los niños; los hijos
Christmas la Navidad
church la iglesia; **go to church** ir a la iglesia
cigarette el cigarillo
city la ciudad
class la clase
classroom la sala de clase
clean limpio, -a; limpiar
clear claro, -a
clerk el (la) dependiente; el (la) empleado (-a)
clock (*alarm*) el despertador
close cerrar (ie); **close to** cerca de
cloth la tela
clothes la ropa; los vestidos
coffee el café
cold el frío; **be cold** (*weather*) hacer frío; (*of persons and animals*) tener frío
Colombian colombiano, -a
colonial colonial
color el color
Columbus Colón
come venir; **come in** entrar (en); pasar
command mandar
commit cometer
comparison la comparación
complain quejarse
complete completo, -a
concert el concierto
confuse confundir
continue seguir (i, i), continuar
contrast el contraste
conversation la conversación
corn el maíz; **popcorn** roseta de maíz
correctly correctamente
cost costar (ue)
could (*from* poder), podía, etc.
count contar (ue)
country (*nation*) el país; (*not city*) el campo
couple la pareja
course (*of study*) el curso; **of course** por supuesto; ¡ya lo creo!
court (*tennis*) la cancha

courtyard el patio
cousin el primo, la prima
cow la vaca
cream: ice cream el helado
Cuba Cuba
Cuban cubano, -a
cultivate cultivar
custom la costumbre

dance el baile; bailar
dark moreno, -a; negro, -a
date la fecha
daughter la hija
day el día; **all day** todo el día; **every day** todos los días; **on the next day** al día siguiente
deal: a great deal mucho
dear querido, -a; caro, -a
debt la obligación
deceive engañar
December diciembre
decide decidir, decidirse a
declaration la declaración
declare declarar
desire el deseo, la gana; desear, querer
devote dedicar
dictionary el diccionario
die morir (ue, u)
different distinto, -a
difficult difícil
difficulty la dificultad
dining room el comedor
dinner la comida
discover descubrir (*past p.* descubierto)
discuss discutir
dish el plato
distant lejos
do hacer
doctor el médico
dog el perro; **little dog** el perrito
dollar el dólar; **Mexican dollar** el peso
door la puerta
dormitory el dormitorio
doubles (*tennis*) dobles
doubt la duda; dudar
down: go down bajar
downtown district el centro
dozen la docena
dress vestirse (i, i); el vestido

drink tomar
during durante

each cada (*invariable*)
eager: to be eager tener deseos de
early temprano
easily fácilmente
easy fácil
eat comer; **eat dinner** comer; **eat breakfast** desayunarse, tomar el desayuno
egg el huevo
eight ocho; **eight hundred** ochocientos, -as
eighteen diez y ocho
eighth octavo, -a
eighty ochenta
either ni... tampoco; **either ... or** o... o
eleven once
Elizabeth Isabel
else: anything else otra cosa
employee el empleado, la empleada
end el fin; terminar, acabar
English (*language*) el inglés; (*adj.*) inglés, inglesa
enough bastante; **be enough** bastar
enter entrar (en)
entire entero, -a
epoch la época
era la época
error el error
especially especialmente
even: even though aunque
evening la noche; **good evening** buenas noches
ever jamás
every todo, -a; **everybody** todo el mundo, todos; **every day** todos los días; **everything** todo; **everywhere** por todas partes
evident claro, -a
exactly (*time*) en punto
examination el examen (*pl.* los exámenes)
excellent excelente
except menos
exciting emocionante
exclaim exclamar
excursion la excursión
excuse dispensar
exercise el ejercicio
expect esperar; pensar (ie)
expense el gasto

expensive caro, -a
experience la experiencia
explain explicar
explanation la explicación
extremely muy; -ísimo, -a
eye el ojo

fact: the fact is es que
fair rubio, -a
fall el otoño
family la familia
famous famoso, -a
fan el abanico
far lejos; **far from** lejos de
farm la finca
fascinate encantar
father el padre
favor el favor
favorite favorito, -a
fear el miedo; temer, tener miedo
February febrero
feel sentir (ie, i); **feel (well, happy)** sentirse (ie, i) (bien, alegre); **feel like** tener ganas de + *inf.*
few pocos, -as; **a few** algunos, unos
fifteen quince
fifth quinto, -a
fifty cincuenta
film la película
finally al fin
find encontrar (ue)
fine bueno, -a; **fine-looking** guapo, -a
finish acabar, terminar
first primero (primer), -a
five cinco
five hundred quinientos, -as
flower la flor
follow seguir (i, i)
following siguiente; **the following day** al día siguiente
foolish tonto, -a
foot el pie
football el fútbol
for para; por; pues
foreign extranjero, -a
forget olvidarse (de)
forty cuarenta
four cuatro
four hundred cuatrocientos, -as

fourteen catorce
fourth cuarto, -a
France Francia
Frank Pancho
free libre
French (*language*) el francés; (*adj.*) francés, francesa
Friday el viernes; **on Friday** el viernes; **on Fridays** los viernes
friend el amigo, la amiga
from de, desde
front: in front of en frente de; delante de
fruit la fruta
full lleno, -a; completo, -a
fun la diversión
future el futuro

game el partido, el juego
general el general
gentleman el señor; **gentlemen** los señores
get buscar; conseguir (i, i); ir a buscar; **get married** casarse (con); **get up** levantarse; **get together** reunirse
gift el regalo
girl la muchacha; la niña
give dar
glad: be glad alegrarse (de), tener gusto en; **I am glad to meet you** tengo mucho gusto en conocerle
gladly con mucho gusto
glass el vaso
go ir, caminar; **go away** irse; **go down** bajar; **go on** seguir (i, i); **go out** salir; **go to bed** acostarse (ue); **go shopping** ir de compras; **let's go** vamos
God Dios
gone ido
good bueno (buen), -a
good-bye adiós; **to say good-bye** despedirse (i, i) (de)
governed gobernado, -a
graduated (be) graduarse
grammar la gramática
grandfather el abuelo
grandmother la abuela
grandparents los abuelos
grape la uva
great grande (gran); **a great deal** mucho
greater mayor

greatest el mayor
group el grupo
guest el huésped

hair el pelo
half medio, -a; **half an hour** media hora
hand la mano; **hand over** entregar
handsome guapo, -a; hermoso, -a
happen pasar
happily alegremente
happy alegre, contento, -a
hard difícil; mucho; severo, -a; **(work) hard** (trabajar) mucho
hat el sombrero; **hat shop** sombrerería
have tener; haber (*auxiliary*); **have to** tener que + *inf.*; **have just** acabar de + *inf.*; **have a good time** divertirse (ie, i); **have left** quedar a; **have** (*indirect command*) que + *3rd person of pres. subj.*
he él; **he who** el que, quien
hear oir
heat el calor
heaven: for Heaven's sake ¡ por Dios!
hello hola
help ayudar (a)
her su, sus; de ella (*poss. pron.*)
her la (*dir. obj.*); le (*ind. obj.*); ella (*after prep.*)
here aquí; **around here** por aquí
heroine la heroína
hers el suyo, la suya, etc.; **of hers** suyo, -a; de ella
herself se; sí (*after prep.*)
high alto, -a
high school la escuela superior
highway la carretera; el camino
him le, lo (*obj. pron.*); él (*after prep.*)
himself se; sí (*after prep.*)
his su, sus; de él; el suyo, la suya, etc.; el (la) de el, etc.; **of his** suyo, -a; de él
historical histórico
holiday día de fiesta; vacaciones
home la casa; **at home** en casa; **go home** ir a casa
hope esperar; **to hope not (so)** esperar que no (sí)
horse el caballo
hot: to be hot (weather) hacer calor; **(of persons and animals)** tener calor

hotel el hotel
hour la hora
house la casa
how? ¿cómo? ¿qué tal?; **how pretty!**
¡ qué bonita!; **how are you?** ¿cómo está
usted?; **how long?** ¿cuánto tiempo?;
how much (many)? ¿cuánto(s)?
human humano, -a
hundred ciento (cien)
hunger el hambre
hungry: be hungry tener hambre
hurry apurarse; **to be in a hurry** tener
prisa

I yo
ice cream el helado
iced helado, -a
if si
ill enfermo, -a
imagine figurarse
immediately en seguida
important importante; **be important** importar
impossible imposible
impression impresión
in en; (*after a superlative*) de; **in the morning (afternoon)** por la mañana (tarde);
(at two) in the afternoon (a las dos) de
la tarde
inclination la gana
independence la independencia
Indian indio, -a
information los informes
inhabitant el habitante
inside (of) dentro de
instead of en vez de
intelligent inteligente
intend pensar (ie) + *inf.*
interest el interés; interesar
interesting interesante
interrupt interrumpir
into en
introduce presentar
invitation la invitación
invite invitar (a + *inf.*)
island la isla
it (*dir. obj.*) lo, la; (*not expressed as subject*); (*after prep.*) él, ella
its su, sus

January enero
jet avión a reacción
jewel la joya
Joe Pepe
John Juan
Joseph José
juice el jugo
Julius Julio
July julio
June junio
just: to have just acabar de + *inf.*

keep on seguir (i, i)
kind la clase; bondadoso, -a
kindness el favor; la bondad
king el rey
kitchen la cocina
know (*fact*) saber; **(be acquainted with)**
conocer; **(know how)** saber
kodak la cámara fotográfica

lack la falta; faltar; **he lacks money** le
falta dinero
lady la señora; **young lady** la señorita
land la tierra
language la lengua
large grande
last (*in a series*) último, -a; durar; **last
year** el año pasado
late tarde
later más tarde; luego; **see you later**
hasta luego
Latin latino, -a
Latin America la América Latina
Latin American latinoamericano, -a
laugh reírse (i, i)
laughter la risa
law la ley; **Law School** la Facultad de
Leyes
learn aprender (a)
least el menos; **at least** al menos; por lo
menos
leave salir (de); dejar (*trans.*)
left: on the left hand a la izquierda; **to have
left** quedarle
less menos
lesson la lección
let dejar; permitir

let's vamos a + *inf.*
letter la carta
liberty la libertad
library la biblioteca
life la vida
lift levantar
light la luz (*pl.*) luces; (*color*) claro, -a
like gustar; (*a person*) querer a; como;
  to feel like tener ganas de; **I should like**
  (**he would like**) quisiera
listen to escuchar
little (*small*) pequeño, -a; **a little** (un)
  poco
live vivir
living room la sala
long largo, -a; **how long?** ¿cuánto tiempo?
look (at) mirar
look (for) buscar
lose perder (ie)
love querer (a); amar
lovely bello, -a
low bajo, -a
luck la suerte; **be lucky** tener suerte

machine la máquina
magnificent magnífico, -a
mail box el apartado (de correos)
make hacer
man el hombre
manner la manera; el modo
many muchos, -as; **as (so) many . . . as**
  tantos, -as... como
March marzo
market el mercado
marry casarse (con)
Mary María
match (*game*) el partido
material la tela
matter importar; **it doesn't matter** no
  importa
May mayo
me (*dir. and ind. obj. pron.*) me; (*after
  prep.*) mí
meal la comida
meat la carne
meet (**make acquaintance of**) conocer; (**run
  into**) encontrarse (con)
member el miembro
memorandum book librito

Mexican mexicano, -a
Mexico México
milk la leche; ordeñar
millinery store la sombrerería
million un millón (de)
millionaire el millonario
mine (*adj.*) mío, -a; (*pron.*) el mío; **of mine**
  mío, -a
minus menos
mirror el espejo
Miss la señorita
miss perder (ie)
mistake el error
modern moderno, -a
moment el momento
Monday el lunes; **on Monday** el lunes
money el dinero
month el mes
moon la luna; **in the moonlight** a la luz de
  la luna
more más; **more than** más que; (*followed
  by a number*) más de
morning la mañana; **in the morning** por
  la mañana; de la mañana
most más
mother la madre
mountain la montaña
movies el cine
Mr. el señor, Sr.; **Mr. and Mrs.** los
  señores
Mrs. la señora, Sra.
much mucho, -a; **very much** muchísimo,
  -a; **as (so) much . . . as** tanto, -a... como;
  how much? ¿cuánto, -a?
music la música
must deber + *inf.*; tener que + *inf.*
my mi; mío, -a
myself me; (*after prep.*) mí

name el nombre; **be named** llamarse;
  his name is él se llama; **family name** el
  apellido
naturally naturalmente
navy (*color*) marino, -a
near cerca de
nearly casi
necessary necesario, -a
need necesitar
neither tampoco; **neither . . . nor** ni... ni

nervous nervioso, -a
never nunca; jamás
new nuevo, -a
news las noticias
next siguiente; **the next day** al día siguiente; **next summer** el verano que viene
night la noche; **at night** por la noche; **last night** anoche; **tonight** esta noche
nine nueve
nine hundred novecientos, -as
nineteen diez y nueve
ninety noventa
ninth noveno, -a
no (*adj.*) ninguno, -a; (*adv.*) no
noise el ruido
none ninguno, -a; ningún
noon el mediodía; **at noon** al mediodía
nor: neither . . . nor ni... ni
not no
note notar
notebook el cuaderno
nothing nada
notice las noticias
novel la novela
November noviembre
now ahora; ya; **right now** ahora mismo
number el número
nylon el nilón

obtain conseguir (i, i)
ocean el océano; **Pacific Ocean** el Océano Pacífico
o'clock: it is one o'clock es la una; **it is two o'clock** son las dos
October octubre
of de
off: to get off bajar
offer ofrecer
office la oficina
often muchas veces
oh! ¡ah!; ¡ay!
old viejo, -a; **be ten years old** tener diez años
older, oldest mayor
on en; sobre; **on entering** al entrar
once una vez; **at once** en seguida
one uno, -a; se; **the one who** el que
only sólo, solamente
open abrir; abierto, -a

opportunity la oportunidad
or o; (*before* o) u; **either . . . or** o... o
orange la naranja
orchestra la orquesta
order mandar; pedir (i, i); **in order that** para que; **in order to** para
other otro, -a
ought deber + *inf.*
our (of ours) nuestro, -a
ours el nuestro
ourselves nos
over sobre

Pacific Pacífico
pack: to pack a suitcase hacer una maleta
package el paquete
page la página
pair el par
pamphlet el librito
paper el papel
pardon perdonar; dispensar
parents los padres
park el parque
part la parte; **to play the part** hacer el papel
party la fiesta
pass pasar; (*a course of study*) salir bien
passport el pasaporte
past pasado, -a
pay pagar; **pay a visit** hacer una visita
pear la pera
pen la pluma
pencil el lápiz, (*pl.*) lápices
people la gente; el pueblo; se
performance la función
perfume el perfume
perhaps tal vez
permit permitir, dejar
person la persona
phone teléfono; llamar por teléfono
physician el médico
picnic la excursión al campo
picture-show el cine
pity la lástima; **it is a pity** es lástima; **what a pity!** ¡qué lástima!
place el sitio; poner
plan pensar (ie) + *inf.*
plane el avión; **by plane** en (por) avión
plate el plato

play jugar (ue); **to play ball** jugar al béisbol; (*musical instrument*) tocar; **play the part** hacer el papel

player el jugador

pleasant agradable, amable

please haga el favor de + *inf.*; tenga la bondad de + *inf.*

pleasure el gusto

poor pobre; malo, -a

popcorn la roseta de maíz

possible posible

postmaster el administrador de correos

post office el correo; **post office box** el apartado

practical práctico, -a

practice practicar

prefer preferir (ie, i)

prepare preparar

present el regalo; el presente; presentar; **be present** presenciar

pretty bonito, -a; lindo, -a

price el precio; **what is the price?** ¿cuánto vale?

probable probable

profession la carrera

professor el profesor, la profesora

profit aprovechar

program el programa

promise prometer

pronounce pronunciar

provided con tal que

pupil el alumno, la alumna

purchase la compra; comprar

put poner; **put on** ponerse

quarter el cuarto

question la pregunta; la cuestión; **to ask a question** preguntar, hacer una pregunta

quickly pronto

quite bastante

racket (*tennis*) la raqueta

rain llover (ue)

raise levantar; (*plants*) cultivar

rapidly rápidamente

rather bastante

read leer

reading la lectura

ready listo, -a

really de veras; verdaderamente

reason la razón

receive recibir

recite recitar

red rojo, -a

refuse no querer

registered certificado, -a

regret sentir (ie, i)

remain quedar; quedarse

remember acordarse (ue) (de)

repeat repetir (i, i)

reply responder

request pedir (i, i)

resemble parecerse

rest descansar

restaurant el restaurante

return el regreso; la vuelta; volver (ue)

review repasar

rich rico, -a

ride: to take a ride dar un paseo en coche

right: on the right hand a la derecha; **be right** tener razón; **all right** está bien

ring sonar (ue)

road el camino

romantic romántico, -a

room el cuarto; (*large*) la sala; **classroom** sala de clase; **reading room** sala de lectura

rose la rosa

round trip: round trip ticket billete de ida y vuelta

rule la regla

sack el saco

sad triste

sale la venta; **for sale** de venta

saleswoman la vendedora

same mismo, -a; **the same** lo mismo

satisfied satisfecho, -a; contento, -a

Saturday el sábado; **on Saturday** el sábado

say decir; **say good-bye** despedirse (i, i) (de); **say yes (no)** decir que sí (no); **that is to say** es decir

school la escuela; la facultad; **to school** a la escuela; **at school** en la escuela; **high school** escuela superior

sea el (la) mar

season la estación; la temporada

215

seat   el asiento
seated (sitting)   sentado, -a
second   segundo, -a
see   ver; presenciar; let's see   vamos a ver
seem   parecer
select   escoger
self   mismo, -a
sell   vender
seller (f.)   la vendedora
send   mandar
sentence   la frase
September   septiembre
serve   servir (i, i)
set (table)   poner
seven   siete
seven hundred   setecientos, -as
seventeen   diez y siete
seventh   séptimo, -a
seventy   setenta
several   varios, -as
she   ella; she who   la que
shine: the sun is shining   hace (hay) sol
shirt   la camisa
shoe   el zapato
shop   la tienda
shopping: to go shopping   ir de tiendas
short   bajo, -a; corto, -a
shout   gritar
show   mostrar (ue); enseñar
shut   cerrar (ie)
sick   enfermo, -a; malo, -a
side   el lado; beside   al lado de
silver   la plata
similar   parecido, -a
since   desde; pues; since I was a little girl   desde niña
sing   cantar
sir   el señor
sister   la hermana
sit down   sentarse (ie)
site   el sitio
six   seis
six hundred   seiscientos, -as
sixteen   diez y seis
sixth   sexto, -a
sixty   sesenta
sleep   dormir (ue); go to sleep   dormirse
slowly   despacio
small   pequeño, -a; chico, -a

smaller, smallest   menor
smile   la sonrisa
so   así; (with adj. or adv.) tan; so that   de modo que; para que; I think so   creo que sí
some   alguno, -a; algún; algunos, -as; unos, -as
someone   alguien
something   algo
sometimes   algunas veces, a veces
son   el hijo
soon   pronto; as soon as   en cuanto
sorry: be sorry   sentir (i, i); I am sorry   lo siento
sound   sonar (ue)
soup   la sopa
south   el sur
South America   la América del Sur
Spain   España
Spaniard   el español; la española
Spanish (language)   el español; (adj.) español (-ola)
speak   hablar
special   especial
spectacle   el espectáculo
spend (money)   gastar; (time) pasar
sport   el deporte
spring   la primavera
stadium   el estadio
stand up   levantarse
station   la estación
stay   quedarse
steak   el biftec
still   todavía
stock   el surtido
stop   detenerse; dejar de + inf.
store   la tienda; clothing store   tienda de ropa; shoe store   la zapatería
story   el cuento
street   la calle
strict   severo, -a
student   el alumno; la alumna; el (la) estudiante
study   el estudio; estudiar
style   el estilo
such (a)   tal
suddenly   de pronto
suffer   sufrir
sufficient   bastante
suit   el traje; bathing suit   traje de baño

suitcase la maleta; **to pack a suitcase** hacer una maleta

summer el verano; **last summer** el verano pasado; **next summer** el verano que viene

sun el sol; **it is sunny** hace (hay) sol; **to enjoy the sunshine** tomar el sol

Sunday el domingo; **on Sunday** el domingo

sure seguro; **be sure of** estar seguro de

surname el apellido

surprise la sorpresa; **be surprised** sorprenderse

sweetheart la novia

swimming: go swimming tomar baños de mar

table la mesa

take tomar; (*carry*) llevar; **take a walk** dar un paseo; **take advantage of** aprovechar(se); **take leave of** despedirse (i, i) (de); **take out** sacar; **take a trip** hacer un viaje; **take care of** cuidar; **take an examination** sufrir un examen

talk hablar; charlar

tall alto, -a

taxi el taxi

tea el té

teach enseñar

teacher el profesor, la profesora

team el equipo

telephone el teléfono; **to telephone** llamar por teléfono

television la televisión

tell decir; contar (ue)

ten diez

tennis el tenis; **tennis court** la cancha

tenth décimo, -a

Texas Tejas

than (*after a comparison*) que; (*before a number*) de

thank you gracias

that (*dem. adj.*) ese, esa; aquel, aquella; (*pron.*) eso, aquello; **that one** ése, ésa; aquél, aquélla; (*rel. pron.*) que; (*conj.*) que; **so that** para que, de modo que

the el (la, los, las); lo

theater el teatro

their su; **theirs** suyo, el suyo

them (*dir. obj.*) los, las, les; (*ind. obj.*) les, se; (*obj. of prep.*) ellos, -as

themselves se; (*after prep.*) sí

then entonces; luego

there allí; **there is, are** hay; **there was, were** había

therefore por eso

these (*dem. adj.*) estos, estas; (*pron.*) éstos, éstas

they ellos, ellas

thing la cosa

think pensar (ie); creer; **think about** pensar en; **I think so** creo que sí

third tercero, -a; tercer

thirst la sed; **be thirsty** tener sed

thirteen trece

thirty treinta

this (*dem. adj.*) este, esta; (*pron.*) esto; **this one** éste, ésta

those (*dem. adj.*) esos, esas; aquellos, aquellas; (*pron.*) ésos, ésas; aquéllos, aquéllas

thousand mil

three tres

three hundred trescientos, -as

through por

Thursday el jueves; **on Thursday** el jueves

thus así

ticket el billete; **round-trip ticket** billete de ida y vuelta

time (*of day*) la hora; (*in general*) tiempo; (*in a series*) vez; **at the same time** a la vez; **at times** a veces; **for a long time** mucho tiempo; **have a good time** divertirse (ie, i); **on time** a tiempo; **it is time to eat** es hora de comer; **what time is it?** ¿qué hora es?

tired cansado, -a

to a; para; **to the** al; **in order to** para

toast las tostadas

today hoy; **this very day** hoy mismo

together juntos, -as; **to get together** reunirse

tomato el tomate

tomorrow mañana

tonight esta noche

too también

tourist card tarjeta de turista

toward hacia

towel la toalla

town el pueblo

train el tren

travel viajar
traveler el viajero
treat tratar
tree el árbol
trip el viaje; **take a trip** hacer un viaje
trouble molestar
true: it is true es verdad
truly verdaderamente
truth la verdad
try to tratar de
Tuesday el martes; **on Tuesday** el martes
turn: be one's turn tocarle a uno
Twelfth Night el Día de los Reyes Magos
twelve doce
twenty veinte
two dos
two hundred doscientos, -as
typical típico, -a

understand entender (ie); comprender
unexpected inesperado, -a
United States los Estados Unidos
university la universidad
unless a menos que
unoccupied libre
until (*conj.*) hasta que; (*prep.*) hasta; **until tomorrow** hasta mañana
up arriba
upon sobre; **upon** + *pres. part.* al + *inf.*
upstairs arriba
us (*obj. of verb*) nos; (*after prep.*) nosotros
use usar, emplear
used to *expressed by imperfect tense*

vacant desocupado, -a
vacation las vacaciones
value el valor
vegetables las legumbres
vendor (*f.*) la vendedora
verb el verbo
very muy; mucho; **very much** muchísimo
veteran el veterano
visit la visita; visitar
vocabulary el vocabulario
voice la voz, (*pl.*) voces

wait (for) esperar
wake up despertarse (ie)

walk el paseo; caminar; **take a walk** dar un paseo
want querer; desear; tener ganas de
warm: be warm (*persons*) tener calor; (*weather*) hacer calor
water el agua (*f.*)
way el camino
we nosotros, -as
wear llevar
weather el tiempo; **how is the weather?** ¿qué tiempo hace? **it is good (bad) weather** hace buen (mal) tiempo
Wednesday el miércoles; **on Wednesday** el miércoles
week la semana; **two weeks** quince días
weekend el fin de semana
welcome la bienvenida; dar la bienvenida
well (*adj.*) bueno, -a; (*adv.*) bien
what? ¿qué?; ¿cómo?; ¿cuál?
what (*that which*) lo que
when cuando; ¿cuándo?
where donde; ¿dónde?
whether si
which? ¿cuál?, (*pl.*) ¿cuáles?
which (*rel.*) que, el cual, el que
while mientras (que)
white blanco, -a
White Blanco (surname)
who? ¿quién?
who (*rel.*) que, quien, el que
whole entero, -a
whom? ¿a quién?
whom (*rel.*) que, a quien
whose? ¿de quién? ¿de quiénes?
why? ¿por qué?
wife la esposa
will querer; *sign of future*
win ganar
wind el viento; **it is windy** hace viento
window la ventana
winter el invierno
Wise Men (Kings) los Reyes Magos
wish querer; desear
with con; **with me** conmigo
within dentro de
without sin; sin que
word la palabra
work el trabajo; trabajar
world el mundo

worry el cuidado; **don't worry** no tenga cuidado
worse, worst peor
worth: be worth valer
would *sign of the conditional*; **I would like** quisiera
write escribir

yard el patio
year el año; **last year** el año pasado
yellow amarillo, -a
yes sí

yesterday ayer
yet todavía
you (*subj. pron. and obj. of prep.*) usted, ustedes; (*dir. obj.*) le, lo, la; les, los, las; (*ind. obj.*) le, les
young joven; **young lady** la joven, la señorita; **young man** el joven; **young people** los jóvenes
younger, youngest menor
your su, sus (de usted, de ustedes)
yours suyo, -a; el suyo
yourself se; (*after prep.*) sí

INDEX

221

INFINITIVE	PARTICIPLES: PRESENT PAST	PRESENT INDICATIVE	IMPERFECT INDICATIVE	PRETERITE INDICATIVE	FUTURE INDICATIVE	CONDITIONAL	PRESENT SUBJUNCTIVE	IMPERFECT SUBJUNCTIVE	IMPERFECT SUBJUNCTIVE	IMPERATIVE
ser *to be*	siendo sido	soy eres es somos sois son	era eras era éramos erais eran	fui fuiste fue fuimos fuisteis fueron	seré serás será seremos seréis serán	sería serías sería seríamos seríais serían	sea seas sea seamos seáis sean	fuese fueses fuese fuésemos fueseis fuesen	fuera fueras fuera fuéramos fuerais fueran	**sé** sed
tener *to have*	teniendo tenido	tengo tienes tiene tenemos tenéis tienen	tenía tenías tenía teníamos teníais tenían	tuve tuviste tuvo tuvimos tuvisteis tuvieron	tendré tendrás tendrá tendremos tendréis tendrán	tendría tendrías tendría tendríamos tendríais tendrían	tenga tengas tenga tengamos tengáis tengan	tuviese tuvieses tuviese tuviésemos tuvieseis tuviesen	tuviera tuvieras tuviera tuviéramos tuvierais tuvieran	**ten** tened
traer *to bring*	trayendo traído	traigo traes trae traemos traéis traen	traía traías traía traíamos traíais traían	traje trajiste trajo trajimos trajisteis trajeron	traeré traerás traerá traeremos traeréis traerán	traería traerías traería traeríamos traeríais traerían	traiga traigas traiga traigamos traigáis traigan	trajese trajeses trajese trajésemos trajeseis trajesen	trajera trajeras trajera trajéramos trajerais trajeran	trae traed
valer *to be worth*	valiendo valido	valgo vales vale valemos valéis valen	valía valías valía valíamos valíais valían	valí valiste valió valimos valisteis valieron	valdré valdrás valdrá valdremos valdréis valdrán	**valdría** **valdrías** **valdría** **valdríamos** **valdrían**	valga valgas valga valgamos valgáis valgan	valiese valieses valiese valiésemos valieseis valiesen	valiera valieras valiera valiéramos valierais valieran	**val (vale)** valed
venir *to come*	viniendo venido	vengo vienes viene venimos venís vienen	venía venías venía veníamos veníais venían	vine viniste vino vinimos vinisteis vinieron	vendré vendrás vendrá vendremos vendréis vendrán	vendría vendrías vendría vendríamos vendríais vendrían	venga vengas venga vengamos vengáis vengan	viniese vinieses viniese viniésemos vinieseis viniesen	viniera vinieras viniera viniéramos vinierais vinieran	**ven** venid
ver *to see*	viendo **visto**	veo ves ve vemos veis	veía veías veía veíamos veíais	vi viste vio vimos visteis	veré verás verá veremos veréis	vería verías vería veríamos veríais	vea veas vea veamos veáis	viese vieses viese viésemos vieseis	viera vieras viera viéramos vierais	ve ved